Legal Reforms and Deprivation of Liberty in Contemporary China

This volume investigates detention powers in today's China and offers an in-depth analysis of the debates surrounding attempts at reform. Focusing not only on law and regulation but also on key events that have precipitated calls for change, the studies in this book assess the complexities inherent in the process of reform of institutions of detention in an authoritarian state.

The collection examines legal and institutional reforms to institutions of detention and imprisonment since the 1990s and is divided into three parts. It begins with the specific issues of criminal and administrative forms of deprivation of liberty and the relationship between reforms and criminal justice policy agendas. It then moves on to the academic and theoretical debates on the subject of imprisonment and detention. The study concludes by assessing the meaning of institutional reforms in the context of the changing state–society relationship in contemporary China.

This book will be of interest to criminologists and scholars of Chinese law, politics and society, human rights and comparative law.

Elisa Nesossi is an Australian Research Council Research Fellow at the Australian Centre on China in the World, Australian National University. Her research interests include Chinese law and institutions, comparative criminal justice and human rights law.

Sarah Biddulph is an Australian Research Council Future Fellow and Professor of Law at the Melbourne Law School. Her research focuses on the Chinese legal system, with a particular focus on contemporary administrative, criminal procedure and labour law and the law regulating social and economic rights.

Flora Sapio is an associate at the Australian Centre on China in the World at the Australian National University. She has published on Chinese criminal law, criminal justice, legal philosophy in China and the Chinese Communist Party regulatory system.

Susan Trevaskes is a professor and member of the Griffith Criminology Institute at Griffith University and an Adjunct Director of the Centre on China in the World at the Australian National University. Her main research interests include the death penalty, policing, drug crime, public shaming events and justice system reform in China.

The Rule of Law in China and Comparative Perspectives
Series Editors:
Yuwen Li, Erasmus University Rotterdam, The Netherlands and Fu Hualing, University of Hong Kong, Hong Kong

There is no doctrine more effective than the rule of law in portraying the complex transformation of Chinese society from the rule of men towards the rule of law – a process inaugurated in post-Mao China which is continuing to advance legal reforms to the present day. In other parts of the world, striving for the rule of law is also evident: countries in transition face a similar mission, while the developed democratic countries are forced to tackle new challenges in retaining the high benchmark of the rule of law that has been established.

Research on the legal system in China and comparisons with other countries in the framework of the rule of law covers broad topics of public and private law, substantive law and procedural law, citizens' rights and law enforcement by courts. Based on this broad understanding of the rule of law, the series presents international scholarly work on modern Chinese law including: comparative perspectives, interdisciplinary, and empirical studies.

Other titles in this series:

The Judicial System and Reform in Post-Mao China
Yuwen Li

Administrative Litigation Systems in Greater China and Europe
Edited by Yuwen Li

Conservation and Recreation in Protected Areas
Yun Ma

Legal Reforms and Deprivation of Liberty in Contemporary China

Edited by Elisa Nesossi, Sarah Biddulph, Flora Sapio and Susan Trevaskes

LONDON AND NEW YORK

First published 2016
by Routledge
2 Park Square, Milton Park, Abingdon, Oxon OX14 4RN

and by Routledge
711 Third Avenue, New York, NY 10017

First issued in paperback 2018

Routledge is an imprint of the Taylor & Francis Group, an informa business

© 2016 selection and editorial matter, Elisa Nesossi, Sarah Biddulph, Flora Sapio and Susan Trevaskes; individual chapters, the contributors

The right of Elisa Nesossi, Sarah Biddulph, Flora Sapio and Susan Trevaskes to be identified as the authors of the editorial material, and of the authors for their individual chapters, has been asserted in accordance with sections 77 and 78 of the Copyright, Designs and Patents Act 1988.

All rights reserved. No part of this book may be reprinted or reproduced or utilised in any form or by any electronic, mechanical, or other means, now known or hereafter invented, including photocopying and recording, or in any information storage or retrieval system, without permission in writing from the publishers.

Trademark notice: Product or corporate names may be trademarks or registered trademarks, and are used only for identification and explanation without intent to infringe.

British Library Cataloguing in Publication Data
A catalogue record for this book is available from the British Library

Library of Congress Cataloging in Publication Data
Names: Nesossi, Elisa, editor. | Biddulph, Sarah, editor. | Sapio, Flora, editor. | Trevaskes, Susan, 1964- editor.
Title: Legal reforms and deprivation of liberty in contemporary China / edited by Elisa Nesossi, Sarah Biddulph, Flora Sapio and Susan Trevaskes.
Series: The rule of law in China and comparative perspectives | Includes bibliographical references and index.
Subjects: LCSH: Detention of persons—China. | Correctional law—China.
Classification: LCC KNQ4657 .L44 2016 (print) | LCC KNQ4657 (ebook) | DDC 345.51/0527—dc23
LC record available at http://lccn.loc.gov/2015045522

ISBN 13: 978-1-138-60612-8 (pbk)
ISBN 13: 978-1-4724-7939-6 (hbk)

Typeset in Times New Roman
by Swales & Willis Ltd, Exeter, Devon, UK

Contents

Notes on contributors	vii
Preface	ix

1 Deprivation of liberty under scrutiny   1
ELISA NESOSSI, SARAH BIDDULPH, FLORA SAPIO AND
SUSAN TREVASKES

PART I
Administrative detention   21

2 What to make of the abolition of re-education through labour?   23
SARAH BIDDULPH

3 China's socialisation of administrative offenders in the community: an unrealistic agenda?   43
ENSHEN LI

4 Deprivation of liberty against one's will in mental health institutions in contemporary China   62
ZHIYUAN GUO

PART II
Criminal justice reforms and deprivation of liberty   77

5 Residential surveillance: evolution of a Janus-faced measure   79
JOSHUA ROSENZWEIG

6 China's pre-trial detention centres: challenges and opportunities for reform   95
LEI CHENG AND ELISA NESOSSI

7 Addressing the 'hide and seek' scandal: restoring the legitimacy of *kanshousuo*   112
NICOLA MACBEAN

PART III
An assessment of the field — 131

8 Framing imprisonment studies in China: ideology, law and politics — 133
   ELISA NESOSSI AND SUSAN TREVASKES

9 Western analyses of deprivation of liberty in China — 145
   FLORA SAPIO

10 Opportunities and challenges for legislative and institutional reform of detention in China — 162
   ELISA NESOSSI, SARAH BIDDULPH, FLORA SAPIO AND SUSAN TREVASKES

Index — 171

Contributors

Sarah Biddulph is an Australian Research Council Future Fellow (2014–2018) and Professor of Law at the Melbourne Law School. She specialises in the research and teaching of Chinese law. Her research focuses on the Chinese legal system with a particular emphasis on legal policy, law making and enforcement as they affect the administration of justice in China. Her particular areas of research are contemporary Chinese administrative law, criminal procedure, labour, comparative law and the law regulating social and economic rights. Her recent publications include: *Legal Reform and Administrative Detention Powers in China* (2007, CUP); *Law and Fair Work in China: Making and Enforcing Labour Standards in the PRC*, co-authored with Sean Cooney and Ying Zhu (2013, Routledge); *The Politics of Law and Stability in China*, co-edited with Susan Trevaskes, Elisa Nesossi and Flora Sapio (2014, Edward Elgar); and *The Stability Imperative: Human Rights and Law in China* (2015, UBC Press).

Lei Cheng is an Associate Professor of Criminal Procedure Law at Renmin Law School, Renmin University of China (RUC) and Deputy Director of the Centre for Criminal Procedure and Reform at RUC. He has published widely on comparative criminal justice systems and criminal procedure reforms and he has been involved in a number of international research projects and exchanges on criminal justice. Cheng is also Deputy Secretary-General of China's Criminal Litigation Law Research Association and worked part-time as guest expert at China's Legislation body, NPC, from September 2011 to March 2012, on a revision of China's Criminal Procedure Law.

Zhiyuan Guo is an Associate Professor at the China University of Political Science and Law (CUPL) in Beijing, where she specialises in criminal procedure, evidence, international human rights law, and law and society studies. She is also a pioneer in empirical research in China. She is Deputy Director of the Centre for Criminal Law and Justice, CUPL and a Non-resident Senior Research Fellow at US-Asia Law Institute, New York University School of Law. Guo was appointed as Guanghua Visiting Scholar at NYU School of Law from 2008 to 2009 and as Sohmen Visiting Scholar at Faculty of Law, Hong Kong University in 2011. She has published several books in Chinese and also published extensively on academic journals in both Chinese and English.

Enshen Li is an associate lecturer at the TC Beirne School of Law, The University of Queensland. His research interests lie in the field of comparative criminal justice, theoretical criminology and socio-legal studies of punishment and society. He specialises in Chinese criminal justice and penal theories and their relevance to social changes in contemporary China. He has published a number of articles in leading law and criminology journals.

Nicola Macbean is the Director of the The Rights Practice, a charity working to advance the respect and protection of human rights in practice. Nicola founded The Rights Practice in 2002 and is the former Director of the Great Britain-China Centre. She was educated at the University of Cambridge, the Chinese University of Hong Kong, Fudan University and London University. She has an LLM in Human Rights and degrees in social anthropology and economics of education. Nicola is former chair of her local panel of Independent Custody Visitors and is a Trustee of BOND, the UK membership body for NGOs working in international development.

Elisa Nesossi is an Australian Research Council Research Fellow at the Australian Centre on China in the World, Australian National University. Her research interests include Chinese law and institutions, comparative criminal justice and human rights law. She has experience working for NGOs, developing projects on criminal justice and human rights within China. She is the author of *China's Pre-Trial Justice: Criminal Justice, Human Rights and Legal Reforms in Contemporary China* (2012, Wildy, Simmonds and Hill) and *The Politics of Law and Stability in China*, co-edited with Susan Trevaskes, Flora Sapio and Sarah Biddulph (2014, Edward Elgar).

Joshua Rosenzweig (B.A., Swarthmore College; M.A., University of California, Berkeley; PhD, Chinese University of Hong Kong) is an independent researcher and translator based in Hong Kong. His current research looks at the interactions between criminal justice reform and public opinion in contemporary China. From 2002 to 2011 he was a researcher for the human rights NGO The Dui Hua Foundation, where he developed the foundation's comprehensive database of information about Chinese political and religious prisoners and authored more than a dozen volumes in its series of occasional publications.

Flora Sapio is an associate at Australian Centre on China in the World, Australian National University. Her main research interests include Chinese criminal justice, administrative detention, extra-legal violence and coercion. She is the author of *Sovereign Power and the Law in China* (2010, Brill) and *The Politics of Law and Stability in China*, co-edited with Susan Trevaskes, Elisa Nesossi and Sarah Biddulph (2014, Edward Elgar).

Susan Trevaskes is a Professor and member of the Griffith Criminology Institute at Griffith University and an Adjunct Director of the Centre for China in the World (CIW) at the Australian National University. Her main research interests are in criminal justice, punishment and courts in China. Her recent books include *Courts and Criminal Justice in Contemporary China* (2007, Lexington Press), *Policing Serious Crime in China: From 'Strike Hard' to 'Kill Fewer'* (2010, Routledge), *The Death Penalty in Contemporary China* (2012, Palgrave Macmillan) and *The Politics of Law and Stability in China*, co-edited with Elisa Nesossi, Flora Sapio and Sarah Biddulph (2014, Edward Elgar). She has also published a number of papers on anti-crime campaigns, private security, public security, drug crime, public shaming events and death penalty reform.

Preface

The power to deprive people of their liberty is a defining prerogative of the state and the dominant form of punishment in most societies across the world. Chinese legislation provides for forms of deprivation of liberty in the context of criminal trials and administrative sanctions. In addition, political and social imperatives to maintain social stability and to control crime have resulted in the development of a number of extra-legal forms of detention in recent decades.

Conceptually located within broader discussions about legal and institutional reforms in contemporary China, this book offers the first comprehensive study in English of the various systems of deprivation of liberty in today's China. It explores the ways in which the systems of detention have changed since the beginning of the reform era as a result of interactions between local- and central-level institutional configurations of politico-legal power, as well as the national and global trends that have influenced the overall processes of legal reform. In this context, the authors investigate the debates and processes concerning both the expansion and contraction of state powers to detain and incarcerate for preventative and punitive purposes and examine specific legal and institutional reforms that have occurred since the 1990s, with a particular focus on twenty-first century People's Republic of China.

The volume develops three particular lines of enquiry. The first deals with the academic and theoretical debates on the subject of imprisonment and detention. These chapters explain understandings of the discourses of reform through labour in Western and Chinese scholarship and explore the difficulties encountered in this area of research. The second deals with the specific issues of criminal and administrative forms of deprivation of liberty, examining in particular the institutional and legislative dimensions, considering the relationship between reforms, and agendas shaped by social order and criminal justice policies. The third assesses the meaning of institutional reforms in the context of the changing state–society relationship in contemporary China.

Each of the chapters in the volume challenges the view that reforms simply constitute a response to either calls from below or an imposition from above. The broader thesis that runs through the ten studies in this book is that reforms of systems used to deprive citizens of their liberty are important indicators of the ideological principles that inform justice policies and state–society relations more broadly. At one level, they reflect the power struggles and negotiations involving a number of different authorities at the central and local levels, as well as actors from domestic and global civil society. At another level, they reveal the extent to which ideological principles can be modified and adapted in light of changes in legal and institutional structures.

The editors wish to express their gratitude to the Australian Centre on China in the World for its financial and logistic support for the event that has led to this publication.

Elisa Nesossi, Sarah Biddulph, Flora Sapio and
Susan Trevaskes

1 Deprivation of liberty under scrutiny[1]

Elisa Nesossi, Sarah Biddulph, Flora Sapio and Susan Trevaskes

Introduction

Since the early 1980s, the People's Republic of China (PRC) has embarked on a dramatic and ongoing experiment with legal and institutional reform (*gaige*). The aim has been the creation of an efficient and modern justice system, responsive to social and economic change and proactive in protecting the Chinese Communist Party's (CCP) hold on political power. This has meant that over approximately three decades, the topic of reform has also served as the thematic cornerstone of academic analyses in the field of Chinese law and justice. While a number of studies have developed conceptual paradigms – the 'rule of law' most notably – to explain trajectories about 'law's empire' in China (Peerenboom 2002; Lubman 2012), others have assessed reformist processes through empirical case studies (Balme and Dowdle 2009; Woo and Gallagher 2012). In this context, though, scholarly work on recent changes to the institutions that administer deprivation of liberty has visibly lagged behind.

The circumstances and experience of reform concerning detention and imprisonment[2] have been both controversial and understudied. Changes in this area of justice administration have been particularly contentious, as they usually involve strengthening and expanding the powers of police and justice functionaries, with the aim of managing problems resulting from mass movements in population, increasing crime rates, social deviance and, most controversially, political dissent. That issues related to deprivation of liberty have been understudied is perhaps also inescapable. Given their political sensitivity, until very recently institutions of detention and imprisonment have remained mostly cloaked in secrecy. As a result, the scope, significance and the internal dynamics of reforms to these systems have been less well understood than reforms in different areas of Chinese law.

In today's PRC, one of the most important and defining aspects of the various configurations of deprivation of liberty is that they span two separate justice regimes: criminal and administrative. In the criminal justice system, criminal suspects, defendants or convicted criminals may be deprived of their liberty within police stations, pre-trial detention centres (both prior to or following arrest) and prisons; they may also be subject to residential surveillance at their domicile, work units or other locations defined by the public security authorities (*Criminal Procedure Law* 2012, Articles 72–79). China also has an administrative detention system that runs in parallel with and organisationally separate from the criminal justice system. With a few exceptions such as compulsory drug rehabilitation where the justice department is responsible for the administration of detention centres, Chinese institutions of administrative detention are administered primarily by the public security organs. Police-operated detention includes administrative detention (*xingzheng juliu*), and detention for education (*shourong jiaoyu*), which includes coercive testing and treatment for sexually transmitted infections, and coercive treatment such that given to mentally ill suspects or offenders.[3] Up until the end of 2013, re-education through labour was also part of this system.

Whether for punitive, rehabilitative, or preventative purposes or for putative purposes of education and reform (transformation), the Chinese authorities have considered these institutions crucial to the control and punishment of crime and other unlawful conduct, as well as to the achievement of a modern justice system. For decades, decisions about the duration, nature and scope of detention of China's vast population of criminal suspects, convicted criminals and minor offenders have been linked intimately to social order and its importance in underpinning the smooth progress of economic development. As a result, existing law has been interpreted flexibly and has also been amended to expand the scope of targets to ensure responsiveness to the social and political dislocations that have resulted from rapid economic reform. By extension, both the law and institutions responsible for detention have also been among the most proactive in protecting CCP's hold on power. This has meant that many of those who manage facilities within this institutional behemoth have sought to maintain or even *enlarge* their already expansive powers. They have done so by emphasising their centrality to the task of maintaining social and political stability through crime control and prevention. Without explicitly acknowledging it, they have also increased the profitability of penal production to cope with growing fiscal stresses on detention facilities (Fu 2005a).

Conversely, reformers and others who advocate for stronger limits to be placed on the use of detention powers have argued that *circumscribing* rather than expanding state authority is conducive, not detrimental, to social and political stability.[4] They contend that expansive state power, especially the powers given to China's public security organs, discourages the development of procedural justice and a human rights-based system of governance. In their view, justice can and should be realised by changing the longstanding punitive official mindset, by limiting flexibility and discretion in the implementation of the law and by preventing abuses of power. Respect for fairness and justice, they maintain, lies at the heart of social and political stability. They also argue that in China politically-defined considerations about social order and stability both underpin and preserve the arbitrary powers exercised by the public security and other justice organs, and that these often eclipse legal or social considerations when deciding whether to impose a period of detention, the length of detention or incarceration and the treatment of people who are detained or incarcerated. Wide discretionary powers in this area of justice administration go hand in glove with the lack of both transparency and adequate oversight mechanisms, which invites punitive overreach and discourages prudent procedural justice-based decision-making.

This volume examines the debates that have taken place over the last decade on both the expansion and contraction of state powers to detain and incarcerate for preventative and punitive purposes and the processes by which changes in the scope of detention take place. These debates are in turn located conceptually within the broader discussions about legal and institutional reforms in contemporary China. To locate the specific studies in this volume, this chapter provides an overview of the various facilities that deprive people of their liberty and the reforms that have been developed to modernise the system.

Reforms to deprivation of liberty: an overview

A historical perspective

In Chinese legal history, deprivation of liberty was not at the heart of the punishment regime. Prior to the eighteenth century, imprisonment (*jujin*) was considered subsidiary to other punishments and was not a form of punishment per se. Rather, its main purpose was to confine wrongdoers before trial and those awaiting the execution of their sentence (Alabaster 1899). It was only at the beginning of the twentieth century that Chinese reformers, reflecting upon Western experiences and the role of detention in reforming convicts, began to perceive imprisonment as a possible alternative to harsher forms of physical punishment and started to distinguish between convicted and unconvicted prisoners. China faced many pressures to adopt a system that more closely resembled that of the 'civilised' West and many reforms approximated a gradual Westernisation of the legal and justice systems. In this process, prisons came to be placed at the centre of the Chinese penal system.

Shen Jiaben, appointed Commissioner for the Reform of the Laws (*xiuding falü dacheng*) in 1902, advocated construction of new model prisons according to international standards, first in major cities and provincial capitals, and thereafter at the county level. Well ahead of his time, Shen stressed the importance of training prison staff, the promulgation of detailed prisons rules and the collection of statistical data about criminality. He contended that different kinds of offenders should be jailed in different prisons and criminal suspects needed to be treated separately from convicts. Moreover, he pointed out that witnesses, as persons assisting in the administration of justice, should not be imprisoned, as was the practice of the time (T'ao 1966, 275–290; Guo 2005). Though highly controversial, Shen's proposals led to the promulgation of the first two sets of rules concerning pre-trial detention centres (28 January 1913) and prisons (1 December 1913). These remained in force with few modifications or additions until 1949 (Dikötter 2002, 67). New rules on pre-trial detention centres and county prisons were subsequently passed in May 1919 (Commission on Extra–Territoriality in China 1926; Dikötter 2002, 3). In the early 1930s in areas under their control, the Chinese communists created pre-trial detention centres and reform through labour institutions (*laodong ganhua yuan*) to deal with criminal suspects, offenders and, in particular, counter-revolutionaries (*fan gemin*) (Zhang 2005, 18–19).

Between the establishment of the PRC in 1949 and the 1980s, the concept of 'reform through labour' (*laodong gaizao*) was used to refer to the reform of detainees convicted of a criminal offence, unconvicted detainees, juvenile delinquents, and Chinese citizens found travelling without documents (Dutton 2005, 353). Prisons, detention centres and reform through labour institutions – the facilities within which targets of reform through labour were held – were under the jurisdiction of the Ministry of Justice (MoJ) until 1950, when they were transferred to the Ministry of Public Security (MPS).[5] The administration of reform through labour camps was regulated under the terms of the *Regulations for Reform through Labour* (*Laodong Gaizao Tiaoli*) 1954[6] which continued in force until 1994,[7] when the PRC's first *Prison Law* (*Jianyu Fa*) came into effect.[8]

From 1951, the power of re-education through labour evolved as a pragmatic and flexible response to the state's perceived need to deal with certain categories of people who were politically unreliable or socially undesirable but whose offences were not considered sufficiently serious to warrant the full force of a criminal sanction (Ma 2001, 33). Throughout its existence, re-education through labour (RETL) was conceptually twinned with reform through labour (*liang lao*). The former was used to detain people whose transgressions were adjudged not to warrant criminal prosecution and the latter to detain people convicted of a crime through the criminal justice system.

On 25 August 1955, the CCP Central Committee issued the *Directive on Thorough Elimination of Hidden Counterrevolutionaries* (*Guanyu Chedi Suqing Ancang De Fangeming Fenzi De Zhishi*) providing that 'those people who cannot be convicted of a criminal offence and politically who cannot continue to be used, where returning them to society would increase unemployment, in principle they can be sent to re-education through labour'. The targets of RETL were expanded again in the National People's Congress (NPC) Standing Committee *Resolution on the Decision of the State Council on the Question of Re-Education Through Labour* (*Quanguo Rendahui Changweiyuanhui Pizhun 'Guowuyuan Guanyu Laodong Jiaoyang Wenti De Jueding' De Jianyi*) 1957 to punish habitual offenders and those whose conduct was deemed morally unacceptable in the new socialist society, such as those involved with prostitution, gambling, the use of narcotic drugs, kidnapping and selling women and children and harmful conduct labelled 'feudal superstition'.

Since the 1980s

Administrative and criminal systems of deprivation of liberty

Since adoption of the open door and economic modernisation policies at the end of the 1970s, various forms of deprivation of liberty have been classified as belonging either to the criminal or the administrative system; however, the two systems are complementary in nature and design. In the context of the criminal justice system, post-conviction detention has served the purpose of crime control and the punishment of criminal offenders on the basis of the *Criminal Law* (*Xing Fa*) 1979 and its subsequent amendments. The *Criminal Procedure Law* (CPL) (*Xingshi Susong Fa*) – introduced in 1979, significantly revised in 1996 and again in 2012 – provides the basic guidelines for implementing the *Criminal Law*. Most notably it defines procedures, time limits and the agencies responsible for carrying out pre-trial procedures. It sets out a number of coercive measures (*qiangzhi cuoshi*) that may be used to restrain the freedom of action of criminal suspects. It also provides for post-arrest detention and imprisonment following conviction. Pre-trial coercive measures include coercive summons (*juchuan*), 'taking a guarantee and awaiting trial' (*qubao houshen*), supervised residence (also translated as residential surveillance; *jianshi juzhu*), pre-arrest detention (*juliu*) and arrest (*daibu*). Each of these coercive measures involves restriction or deprivation of personal liberty. In mid-2013, there were 1,701,344 sentenced prisoners (MoJ, 22 December 2014) and approximately 3,250,000 pre-trial detainees (Star News, 9 March 2015).

Administrative detention, at least in theory, is intended for minor offenders. It is administered primarily by the public security authorities and the rules and regulations that frame its operation are designed to limit the physical liberty of those who commit 'unlawful' acts such as prostitution, drug use or dependence and other types of misconduct that do not reach the threshold of criminality. Due to its broad scope, administrative offences are divided into four large categories: public order detention (regulated by the *Security Administrative Punishments Law* (*Zhi'an Guanli Chufa Fa*) 2006, amended in 2012) which targets minor offenders; detention for compulsory rehabilitation of drug dependent people; detention of sex workers and their clients; and, until 28 December 2013, RETL (NPC Standing Committee *Decision on Repealing Legal Rules on Re-Education Through Labour* (*Guanyu Feichu Laodong Jiaoyang Falü Guiding De Jueding*) 28 December 2013).

RETL was revived and expanded after the end of the Cultural Revolution. The December 1979 State Council *Notice Promulgating the 'Temporary Regulations of the Ministry of Public Security on Re-Education Through Labour'* (*Guowuyuan Zhuanfa Gong'an Bu 'Laodong Jiaoyang Shixing Banfa'*) defined the scope of targets to cover conduct deemed anti-socialist, conduct harming social order, vice and petty crime. After introduction of the open door and economic reform policy, the targets of RETL were increased incrementally to cover newly emerging forms of socially disruptive or unlawful conduct. Over time, RETL became a useful tool for cleaning the streets of vagrants and beggars (Biddulph 2007). The most notable expansion was in the population of drug dependent people detained under RETL. Repeat and nuisance petitioning, petty theft, fraud, and other conduct considered anti-socialist or anti-Party could conveniently fall within the amorphous bounds of RETL. The scope of RETL evolved and expanded to respond to social order challenges to policing thrown up by the rapidly changing social and economic environment. It was a particularly useful and flexible tool in policing dissent and disruptive rights-asserting conduct. For example, during the crackdown on Falungong in the 1990s, a large number of practitioners were sent to RETL for refusing to give up the practice (Human Rights Watch 2002). From the late 2000s, repeat petitioners, people involved in mass protests, groups targeted because of religious beliefs and practices, such as Tibetans and Uyghurs, could often be sent to a term of RETL (Fu 2005b, 828). RETL was also a convenient way to punish people who criticised Party and government leaders and whose conduct was construed as opposing the state but fell short of the criminal offence of harming national security. From the late 1980s, the largest increase in people sent to RETL was in drug users and drug dependent people (Biddulph and Xie 2011). The *Regulations on Public Security Organs Handling Re-Education Through Labour Cases (Gong'an Jiguan Banli Laodong Jiaoyang Anjian Guiding)* issued on 1 June 2002 by the MPS was the last consolidation of targets of RETL, though the scope of targets continued to be expanded on an ad hoc basis after that.

RETL proved to be a useful backstop for police where legal reforms in other areas restricted police investigative and interrogative powers. It was used to enable investigation to continue in cases where there is insufficient time or evidence to proceed with a criminal prosecution, particularly after the police power to detain and interrogate criminal suspects under detention for investigation (*shourong shencha*) was abolished in 1996 (Fu 2005a; Biddulph 2007, 195–206). RETL was useful to state agencies because of its flexibility, precisely the characteristic that brought it into conflict with the developing legal system and which made it an anathema to the rule of law principles of transparency, accountability and predictability. Ultimately, it was a power that could not be adequately reformed or retained and, as such, was abolished on 28 December 2013.

Trajectories of reforms

Debates on reform or lack thereof have dominated the literature on detention and deprivation of liberty. Since 1979, when scholars talk about reforms in this field, they refer mainly to either legislative or institutional changes. Policy changes have occurred less commonly, though adoption of the criminal justice policy of balancing leniency and severity marked a significant retreat from the overwhelming emphasis on severe punishment of the 'Strike Hard' (*yanda*) policy that had been in place since the early 1980s. Institutional and legislative changes have entailed expansion of administrative power in some areas, and increasingly detailed specification of mandatory procedural requirements in exercising powers and development of oversight mechanisms. Debates about the need for and shape of reform in both the criminal or administrative systems of punishment and detention in China are carried out within and between different Party and state agencies including legislative bodies, courts, police, prosecution, justice departments and prisons, and among functionaries within these individual organs. Sometimes these internal discussions between the public security and justice institutions amount to little more than attempts to increase institutional power and resources, each hoping to maintain or increase their institutional influence. As legal system reform has progressed and as the use of new media has expanded, it has become increasingly possible for others to participate in these debates, from academics and public intellectuals to citizens interested in and affected by the way these institutions of incarceration work.

However, notwithstanding the increasing participation of the wider community in discussions and debates about reforms and abuses of power, the CCP (both itself and through state enforcement agencies) retains close control over penal policy in China. The implementation of the law and changes in the justice system are subject to the dominance of a political party which frames its justice policies around the control of forces and individuals that may threaten social stability and harm the Party's legitimacy and hold on power.

While we need to be mindful of the dominance of Party policy, it is equally important to understand that the complex interactions between political and institutional players as well as the increasing plurality of voices outside state institutions have an important role in legal and institutional change. Change is no longer simply a product of top-down directives from the centre of power. Today, legislative and institutional reform can result from political opportunities taken by functionaries in the justice system and from shifting coalitions formed around particular issues, sometimes reacting to openings and sometimes responding to tensions at the central institutional levels of political authority. When discursive space opens up, institutional players at the provincial or local levels advocate for change by aligning themselves with current policies and priorities, particularly those aimed at containing social disorder and maintaining social and political stability.

Compared to the immediate post-Mao period of the 1980s, in more recent times reforms – or at least the key debates about the imperative to reform – have increasingly come to be informed by wider social forces and opinions. They have broadened to include scholars, NGOs and the general public, and have been facilitated through both the traditional and social media. In fact, over the last decade, the interest and impact of more inclusive societal debates concerning law and justice indicate just how disparate understandings are of the concepts of reform and justice among the broad community of practitioners, scholars and those who participate across China's social and traditional media. This diversity reveals changes in social values and in state–society relationships and, more specifically, in the institutional powers to control and contain socio-political problems.

The factors that have driven legislative reforms to various forms of detention over recent years vary in nature and scope. Drafting the 1996 amendments to the CPL 1979 was one key catalyst for reformist debates. Abolition of the administrative investigative power of detention for investigation and its incorporation into the coercive powers contained in the CPL was one. The case of pre-trial detention is also emblematic in this context. Indeed, both in the process of drafting and in the years that followed the enactment of the 1996 amendments, the issue of reforming pre-trial detention became more a focus for Chinese legal scholars, lawyers and members of the procuratorate who began to challenge its pervasiveness, the strict link existing between arrest and detention, the abuses of the system of residential surveillance and the monopoly over exercise of these powers by the public security authorities. These voices gradually began to articulate more clearly the view that the various measures used to deprive citizens of their personal liberty constituted serious violations of individual rights and freedom (Chen 2005; Chen 2004; Sun 2007).

Building on domestic discontent over aspects of the CPL 1996 and its implementation, the international community has also sought to shape debates about reform. In the mid-2000s, international civil society groups started to implement projects targeting pre-trial detention centres and prisons in an attempt to improve detainees' conditions of detention and enhance supervision of such institutions. In December 2004, the UN Working Group on Arbitrary Detention and, one year later, the Special Rapporteur on Torture and other Cruel, Inhuman or Degrading Treatment or Punishment, after their respective visits to China, both reported that the rules of criminal procedure and practice concerning pre-trial detention in the PRC did not conform to international laws on human rights. They also found that the period for holding criminal suspects in police custody without judicial supervision was too long both in law and practice. Hence, they recommended the restriction of the pre-trial detention period and the extension of non-custodial measures, especially for non-violent, minor or less serious crimes.

As explained in the following section, changes to the system of residential surveillance offer another example of reforms that have been driven by public discomfort with the expansive powers granted to the public security authorities in the CPL. Residential surveillance is one among the various coercive measures that are justified on the grounds they guarantee the smooth running of criminal proceedings, 'to prevent suspects from interfering with an investigation or continuing in criminal activities' (Song 2007, 11). Reforms only emerged after intense power negotiations that result in an acceptable compromise among the *gongjianfa* (the police, the procuratorate and the courts) authorities.

In a similar trajectory of reform, recent changes to the system of administrative detention and punishment have come about as a result of a coalescence of a number of political and social forces. There has been longstanding discomfort in legal and scholarly circles – both within and outside China – with the wide discretionary powers given to police to administer administrative punishment in dealing with public order infringements. It has been a matter of serious concern that public security authorities alone could make decisions affecting the lives and fate of millions of people who have not been convicted of a crime but who find themselves incarcerated administratively for stretches of time up to three years.

The most criticised of these powers was RETL. RETL had been the object of strong public feelings for quite a long time and legislative work with a view to reforming it had been ongoing since at least the 1980s. Debates about reforms of administrative detention have developed at various stages. In the 1980s and 1990s, discussions were strictly limited to internally circulated (*neibu*) public security publications. After the mid-1990s, administrative detention in general, and RETL in particular, came to be a widely debated topic both within China and internationally. The argument was that RETL was unconstitutional, abusive and extra-legal in nature. Severe and chronic abuses documented by lawyers, NGOs and international human rights organisations added weight to these criticisms. Finally, in 2012 the spectacular injustice delivered to Tang Hui when she was sentenced to 18 months RETL for her persistent petitioning galvanised public opinion and ire.[9] This case coincided with the strengthening resolve at top political levels to abandon proposals to reform and retain RETL, and instead to abolish it.

The abolition of RETL in December 2013 has been one of the most dramatic changes to the Chinese justice system in recent years and has come about largely as a result not only of media pressure and sustained domestic and international criticism, but also as a result of political jousting at the highest levels of Party power. At the time when China's media denounced widespread abuses of power and exposed cases of people incarcerated for politically motivated reasons, RETL became caught up in the politics surrounding the stability maintenance (*weihu wending*, often shortened to *weiwen*) program. With the political downfall of Zhou Yongkang and with the general failure of the Hu Jintao and Zhou Yongkang-led stability maintenance program (which ran from 2007 to 2012), the Xi Jinping leadership strategically used the abolition of RETL to draw a line in the sand between the new and the previous Party leadership's stance on stability maintenance.

An outline of reform measures

Reforming administrative detention

Reform pressure was not limited to RETL. From the 1990s pressure began to build to reform other administrative detention powers including police powers to detain sex workers and their clients and drug dependent people. The common denominator behind the decision to start legislative and institutional reform of RETL and other administrative detention measures can be found in the existence of inefficiencies and systemic abuses in the employment of these detention measures. Possibly the best-known example was the power to detain for repatriation people who came to cities without proper authorisation or documentation. The police were authorised to send these people to detention centres operated by the civil affairs departments, called detention for repatriation stations (*shourong qiansong zhan*). Systemic abuses of this power, coupled with dangerous conditions within the detention centres, culminated in a public scandal (the beating to death of a young migrant worker named Sun Zhigang) which precipitated the abolition of this power.

In the case of RETL, 'inefficiencies' consisted not only in the abuses that were widely discussed by the domestic and international press, but also in some structural features. From the 1990s there was a surge in the number of people detained under RETL and with the system unable to appropriately respond, this failure prompted its reform and eventual abolition.

As we explained above, RETL was developed largely to manage political dissent and punish minor offences. The occurrence of several crime waves throughout the 1980s and the 1990s led to the adoption of a piecemeal policing strategy based on anti-crime campaigns, which resulted in a gradual and constant multiplication of the targets of RETL. Even though RETL came to include behaviours ranging from ticket scalping to gambling and membership in political and religious groups established outside of the state's control, the main rationale behind it remained unchanged until the early 1990s (Biddulph 2007). The 1980s and the 1990s had, however, seen a steady growth of the sex trade, as well as of problems of drug dependency (Jeffreys 2004; Gao 21 July 2011).

The policing of the sex trade took place through the revival of measures substantively and procedurally very similar to those introduced four decades earlier, in the 1950s. After a series of rather ineffectual attempts at bringing the sex trade under control, in 1991 the NPC's Standing Committee *Decision on Strictly Prohibiting Prostitution and Using Prostitutes* (*Guanyu Yanjin Maiyin Piaochang De Jueding*) consolidated all previous regulatory documents and mandated the use of detention for education and RETL on recidivist prostitutes and their clients (Jeffreys 2004; Biddulph 2007). In practice, police prefer to impose a fine under the terms of the *Security Administrative Punishments Law* (*Zhi'an Guanli Chufa Fa*) 2006 (amended in 2012) as imposition of detention is costly in terms of time and police resources. The rate at which people involved in the sex trade are detained under either detention for investigation or RETL is influenced by policy imperatives, targeted campaigns at times of moral panic and the availability of detention facilities locally. Administrative detention and RETL in particular were not designed to provide any real form of education, medical care or vocational rehabilitation to sex workers. Reliance on police fines was entirely a more convenient enforcement option.

The policing of drug dependent people underwent a reform trajectory not dissimilar to that of policing the sex trade. While voluntary drug treatment had been an option available to drug users since the 1950s, in 1990 the NPC Standing Committee *Decision on Prohibiting Drugs* (*Guanyu Jindu De Jueding*) reintroduced mandatory registration at public security bureaus, administrative detention on public security charges, compulsory drug rehabilitation (*qiangzhi jiedu*) and drug rehabilitation in RETL (Article 8). Compulsory drug rehabilitation in detention centres operated by the police could last between three and six months, and be extended to a year if necessary (State Council *Measures on Compulsory Drug Rehabilitation*) (*Qiangzhi Jiedu Banfa*) 1995. Drug dependent people who relapsed after release from compulsory drug rehabilitation could receive a term of compulsory rehabilitation through labour at a RETL facility lasting from a minimum of one to three years with a possible extension of a further year for a maximum of four years (*Measures on Compulsory Drug Rehabilitation* 1995, Article 8). The 1990 NPC Standing Committee *Decision on Prohibiting Drugs* led to profound changes both in the structure of the RETL system and in the regulatory and legislative framework on drug use.

Drug users are a population whose needs are different from and more complex than those of minor offenders, sex workers and their clients. While police-run drug rehabilitation facilities in theory contained only drug dependent people, in some RETL facilities drug dependent people were detained alongside other detainees. Overcrowded and under-regulated, by the late 2000s drug rehabilitation facilities had outnumbered RETL camps. The number of registered addicts, too, had largely surpassed that of RETL detainees (Sapio 2010). The haste with which rehabilitation facilities were set up meant that many of them were fairly small in scale, and sometimes incapable of providing adequate treatment, due to either a lack of sufficient funding or of qualified personnel. Many were insecure and endangered the health and safety of detainees (Biddulph 2007). Between 1990 and 2007, nearly three million drug users transited through the compulsory rehabilitation system and, as admitted by Chinese experts, well over 85 per cent of them relapsed back into addiction after release (Liu 2005). What had made the governance of addiction even more problematic, however, was the realisation from the mid-2000s that the three million drug users who underwent compulsory treatment constituted only a small minority of the actual population of drug users, the number of which remains unknown (Qi 2008). As inmates in police-run drug detoxification centres who relapsed were sent to RETL, RETL institutions became flooded with this new category of detainees and needed to adapt quickly to provide for appropriate drug treatment. Initially such a response came through the establishment of drug rehabilitation quarters (MoJ *Standards on Modern and Civilized Re-Education Through Labour Camps* (*Xiandaihua Wenming Laojiaosuo Biaozhun*) 2004, Article 10). The spread of addiction, particularly among minor offenders, meant that by the late 2000s a majority of the population of RETL detainees consisted of habitual drug users (Fu 2009). This simple fact, coupled with the rise among the RETL population of drug-induced pathologies such as hepatitis and HIV infections, placed an insurmountable strain on the system of RETL and on RETL camps, which were not well equipped to provide drug treatment and necessary medical care.

The regulatory basis of RETL, which the *Regulations on Public Security Organs Handling Re-Education Through Labour Cases* 2002 had broadened to include conduct that was defined with reference to the *Criminal Law* 1979 (as amended), was critically out of step with the needs posed by the rapid and steady growth of the addict population within the RETL system. The system appeared flawed not only from a functional and substantive perspective, but from a procedural one as well. Over time, control over the RETL approval procedure had come to be firmly in the hands of the legal division of public security organs. The *Regulations on Public Security Organs Handling Re-Education Through Labour Cases* 2002 (as amended in 2005) set out procedures to be followed by the public security organs in investigating and determining to impose a period of detention under RETL. These regulations were supplemented by the *Regulations on the Procedures for Handling Administrative*

Cases by Public Security Organs (*Gong'an Jiguan Banli Xinzheng Anjian Chengxu Guiding*) 2004 (amended in 2006 and 2012) which introduced several improvements in the RETL approval procedure.[10] However, these regulations failed to challenge the porous boundary between administrative punishment and the criminal law and did not address the inconsistencies between criminal punishment and RETL. Nor did they effectively address the abuses to which the system was prone. If it is considered that by this time addicts were already the majority of RETL population, the procedural reform enacted in the mid-2000s failed to provide a credible and effective response to the difficulties that the RETL system was facing.

As the domestic and international debate on the abolition of RETL continued, an unexpected, although not unforeseeable, solution came from the NPC, which in 2008 promulgated the PRC *Drug Prohibition Law* (*Jindu Fa*), and from the State's Council enactment, in 2011, of the *Drug Prohibition Regulations* (*Jindu Tiaoli*). The Law and the Regulations replaced compulsory drug treatment with a more rational set of custodial and non-custodial measures, which were articulated on three levels. Recreational users, occasional users and habitual users who, if tested positive, could choose to undergo voluntary rehabilitation (*ziyuan jiedu*) (*Drug Prohibition Law*, Article 36; *Drug Treatment Regulations*, Article 11) – a measure which is voluntary and non-custodial – or, alternatively, be ordered to undergo rehabilitation in the community for three years (*Drug Prohibition Law*, Article 33). Habitual drug users who refused or were ineligible for voluntary rehabilitation became the targets of a new power, compulsory quarantine isolation for drug rehabilitation (*qiangzhi geli jiedu*) (CQDR), for an initial period of two years, which could be shortened or lengthened by one year (Biddulph and Xie 2011; *Drug Prohibition Law*, Articles 27, 38, and 43). As with the approval of RETL, the approval procedure of CQDR is among the powers of the police who, after their rehabilitation, can order addicts to receive a period of follow-up treatment in the community (*shequ kangfu*) for a maximum of three years (*Drug Prohibition Law*, Article 48). If the person relapses they can receive a further term of compulsory drug rehabilitation (*Drug Prohibition Law*, Article 38).

Prior to transfer of drug dependent people into CQDR after passage of the *Drug Prohibition Law*, the RETL system had undergone a deep structural change. In 2004, separate quarters were added to RETL facilities to hold those who had received a rehabilitation order. These quarters gradually expanded into drug rehabilitation brigades and squads. Finally, in 2008, on the eve of the promulgation of the *Drug Prohibition Law*, the closure of the existing police-operated drug treatment facilities was ordered. RETL facilities began to expand in order to receive those who had until then been held at drug treatment facilities (Sapio 2010).

If it is considered that, by the mid-2000s, the majority of RETL detainees were in need of drug treatment, the transfer of detainees from compulsory drug treatment centres to RETL facilities meant that by 2013 RETL facilities had, in practice, already been transformed into compulsory drug rehabilitation facilities. As the debate on RETL abolition went on, starting from the end of 2012 local police organs stopped issuing RETL decisions. While it is still not clear whether minor offenders were going unpunished or receiving criminal sanctions, this step signalled the demise of RETL, and its partial replacement by compulsory drug treatment. The abolition of RETL, and the re-designation of some RETL facilities as compulsory drug treatment centres, took place from mid-November 2013.

Reforming pre-trial detention centres

In contrast with the dramatic changes described above in relation to administrative detention, neither the legislation nor the institutional structure of pre-trial detention institutions has changed significantly since the early 1990s. As in other areas of the criminal justice system, denunciations of maladministration in pre-trial detention centres and cases of death in custody have brought to light problematic areas in the way pre-trial detention centres are regulated and administered. These injustices have fuelled debates about legislative and institutional reforms. However, to date, proposals for reforms have not translated into concrete changes. In the 2000s, attempts to reform the current system have focused on two main areas: first, legislation, in the form of the amendment of the State Council *Regulations on Criminal Detention Centres* (*Kanshousuo Tiaoli*) 1990; and secondly, the institution administering pre-trial detention, with the recommendation that authority over pre-trial detention centres be transferred from the MPS to the MoJ. These reform priorities were formalised and publicised in 2009 in the aftermath of the media revelations of the 'hide and seek' (*duo mao mao*) case (see for example, Liu and Zhang 21 February 2009; Luo 27 February 2009; see also Chapter 6 and 7 of this volume) and a number of other unnatural deaths (*feizhengchang siwang*) in custody.

Legislative reforms: from the Regulations 1990 to a detention centre law?

In today's PRC, the State Council *Regulations on Criminal Detention Centres* 1990 and the 1991 *Methods of Implementation of the Regulations on Criminal Detention Centres* (*Kanshousuo Tiaoli De Shishi Banfa*) 1991 regulate the work of the police in detention centres as well as the conditions under which detention should be carried out (Nesossi 2012). The 1990 *Regulations* are supplemented by more than fifty rules, notices and opinions – not counting local legislation – issued by the MPS (sometimes jointly with other ministries, the Supreme People's Court and the Supreme People's Procuratorate) to regulate all the various aspects of pre-trial detention. The *Regulations* 1990 have remained untouched ever since their promulgation, and have become obsolete in light of subsequent developments in the criminal justice field and the introduction of new technologies and managerial techniques in places of detention. Adopted well before the promulgation of the *Criminal Law* 1997, the CPL 1996, the *People's Police Law* (*Renmin Jingcha Fa*) 1995, the *Lawyers Law* (*Lüshi Fa*) 1996 (amended in 2007) and other fundamental PRC laws, the *Regulations* 1990 often contradict these laws in both spirit and substance. A document of its times, the *Regulations* 1990 tend to be vague, ambiguous, broadly worded, and replete with (now) outmoded terms and politically laden references. For example, 'criminal' (*renfan*) is used instead of its contemporary term 'criminal suspect' (*fanzui xianyiren*), *ganjing* (colloquialism for police) is used instead of people's police (*renmin jingcha*), and 'reform through labour' (*laodong gaizao*) used instead of prison (*jianyu*).

In March 2000, the Bureau for the Management of Prisons and Criminal Detention Centres of the MPS (*Gong'an Bu Jiansuo Guanli Ju*) established a small working group (*gongzuo xiaozu*) for the purpose of reforming the *Regulations* 1990. All the major justice departments were consulted in the process; such consultation led to a re-drafting of the *Regulations*, with a revised version including 100 articles (compared to the 52 articles in the 1990 version). In December 2008, the plan to reform the *Regulations* and to strengthen the supervisory role of the procuratorate was officially inserted in the *Central Political Committee Opinions on Several Issues on Deepening Reforms of the Judicial System and Working System* (*Zhongyan Zhengfa Weiyuanhui Guanyu Shenhua Sifa Tizhi He Gongzuo Jizhi Gaige Ruogan Wenti De Yijian*) issued by Central Political Committee of the CCP (Cheng 2014, 42). These reform priorities were formalised and made public in 2009 in the aftermath of the 'hide and seek' case. During that year, reforms to the *Regulations* 1990 were included in the discussion agenda of the State Council and the annual session of the NPC (Cheng 2014, 60). While up to that point legislative reform was primarily intended to be an amendment to the *Regulations* 1990, from then on a number of scholars started to seriously contemplate the option of drafting a new law, the *Criminal Detention Centres Law* for promulgation by the NPC. On 24 January 2011, the proposal for the amendment of the *Regulations on Detention Centres* drafted by the MPS was submitted to the State Council and, at the time of writing, neither the amendment or the *Criminal Detention Law* have yet been passed.

Institutional reforms: from the MPS to the MoJ?

In 1983, the MoJ acquired jurisdiction over prisons, but pre-trial detention centres remained under the control of the organs of public security. At the time, the Central Political–Legal Committee (*zhongyang zhengfa wei*) considered whether both prisons and pre-trial detention centres could be transferred to the MoJ, but the idea was soon dismissed. Because of the 'Strike Hard' campaign that was ongoing at the time, the police felt the need to maintain their stronghold on at least one form of criminal detention without having to rely on the newly re-established MoJ (restored in 1979 after its dissolution during the Maoist period) to facilitate the process of co-ordination between investigation, arrest and detention.

On the whole, the problem of institutional reform relates precisely to the double function given to the organs of public security: that of conducting investigation and, at the same time, detaining individuals. This has meant that places of detention have also become places of investigation, where abusive practices against detainees – such as extraction of confession through torture (*xingxun bigong*) – could be easily condoned or concealed in the guise of obtaining evidence.

In 2009 and 2010, the national media reported more than ten cases of 'unnatural deaths' in detention facilities, which raised public indignation and fuelled intense debates (China Daily 20 April 2009). At this point in time, scholars and officials from the MPS and the Supreme People's Procuratorate (SPP) were mobilised to make specific suggestions on how to strengthen the existing legal framework of such institutions, improve the conditions for those held within detention centres and make places of detention more transparent through better monitoring and supervision. On 15 April 2009, the MPS held its first ever national meeting focused on detention supervision since the founding of the PRC; in addition, the MPS and the SPP organised a major investigation into legal implementation in pre-trial detention centres, stressing the need to protect the rights and the physical integrity of detainees. On 20 July 2009, the MPS issued the *Advice for Further Enhancing and Improving Detention Supervision by Public Security Departments* (*Guanyu Jin Yi bu Jiaqiang He Gaijin Gong'an Jianguan Gongzuo De Yijian*) (Nesossi 2014). From June 2009 to January 2010, the MPS Bureau for the Administration of Prisons and Detention Centres opened up detention centres to external visits and invited media, Party officials, members of the NPC, family members and lawyers to visit pre-trial detention centres. Approximately 2,100 pre-trial detention centres opened up their doors to external visits in an attempt to enhance a system of transparent operation and strengthen external supervision.

Reforming prisons

In comparison to reforms to the system of pre-trial detention and administrative detention, changes to the prison system have attracted less public attention. Calls for reforms have not been widely discussed in the public sphere and have primarily attracted the attention of prison scholars and officials working within the Chinese penitentiary system.

The first *Prison Law* (*Jianyu Fa*) of the PRC was introduced in 1994. A decade later, scholars and officials involved in prison administration around the country started to debate the inadequacies of such legislation and to put forward proposals for reform. Reformist voices have been asking for a clearer status assigned to the *Prison Law* in the Chinese legal system. Critics contend that since the Law 1994 was issued by the NPC Standing Committee and not the NPC itself, the Law may not be considered a 'primary law', that is, on a par with the *Criminal Law* and the CPL. Moreover, critics maintain that the *Prison Law* 1994 is inconsistent in many places with other criminal justice legislation. In addition, it lacks specificity in relation to the rights and duties of police guards, management procedures, financial matters and administration of punishment. In discussions on how to strengthen existing legislation, reformers have proposed supplementary *Regulations on Prison Organisation* and *Regulations on Prison Police*, though these proposals have failed to attract significant public attention.

Seven articles of the *Prison Law* 1994 were revised in October 2012 to make the legislation consistent with the amended CPL 2012. This revision has not attracted particular attention among scholars or the media. It is considered to be fairly limited in scope and generally unsatisfactory, as it fails to address the main problems in the *Law* 1994 (Han 2013). Prison scholars and officials calling for reforms to the *Prison Law* 1994 would have hoped that new legislation could also improve the institutional structure of prisons and their relations with other institutions and forms of punishment. They have asked for a better system of supervision and an improved collaboration with the *gongjianfa* authorities and with governmental authorities at the local level responsible for supporting activities of reform and social reintegration of prisoners (Xie 2009). At the time of writing, this process had not yet begun and reforms appear stalled.

Focusing on reform in this volume

This volume assesses the myriad factors that contribute to reform of detention and incarceration institutions, and examines the related political and social implications of reform. In doing so, it challenges the view that in China the process of reform constitutes a unilateral response to either calls from below or impositions from above. The studies in this book understand 'politics' in the context of reform to be a multifaceted affair. Thus, they ask: what do these dynamics reveal about the nexus existing between law, justice and politics in contemporary China?

Notwithstanding their relevance to the contemporary Chinese system of justice and governance, to date any detailed academic analyses of detention facilities in China have been fairly limited in scope. With the exception of a number of studies on imprisonment and penal policies in traditional and modern China (Dutton 1992; Dikötter 2002; Mühlhahn 2009), this area of research has been fairly sparse. For many decades, penal policies and the circumstances explaining institutions and conditions of detention have been extremely opaque because of their political sensitivity. The increased openness and transparency in relation to the issue of detention and the paucity of robust academic research related to the experience of deprivation of liberty in the PRC open up opportunities for sustained research in the area. This book aims to address some of the shortcomings in the field by providing a foundation for understanding recent reforms to legal regulations and operation of detention and incarceration facilities with three main focus points. The first relates to administrative punishment; the second concerns the area of criminal justice; and the third relates to the scholarly literature on reform. These concerns are the subject of the three main parts in this volume.

Part I focuses on administrative detention and punishment. We determined to discuss these topics upfront as these are the areas that, for over thirty years, have been subject to sustained public attention and criticism both within and outside China and have been subject to the most dramatic changes. The chapters examine the various problematic issues and the challenges concerning recent reforms to China's infamous system of RETL. All the authors here are in favour of a substantial restructuring of the system of administrative detention, but each demonstrate different aspects of scepticism about the feasibility of any revolutionary new reformist attempts to abolish the forms of administrative punishment and non-custodial punishment that have now largely replaced RETL. The ending of RETL raises as many questions as it resolves. While it has been widely celebrated, it is important to note that administration punishment, as a system, has not been abolished. RETL's abolition has shifted the problems characterising the original system of RETL to different areas of administrative detention. A number of the authors see this problem as inherent to the context of the current legal and institutional structures, which continues to see significant social and political value in punishing illegal behaviour and minor crime outside the auspices of the formal criminal justice system.

Sarah Biddulph's study sets the scene in this initial part of the volume by assessing the meaning and significance of abolishing the system of RETL. She argues that the ending of RETL has been hailed as a major step toward strengthening both human rights and the rule of law. However, there remains uncertainty about the long-term impact of its abolition on punitive powers more broadly. She points out that in addition to hoped-for improvements in the protection of rights under China's version of the rule of law, there are a number of institutional consequences. One of those has been to transfer the burden and cost of punishment of minor offenders onto the criminal justice system and local governments and justice agencies who are responsible for implementing the system of community corrections.

RETL was abolished without engagement with the broader debates that featured in the years prior to its abolition about the values and priorities the legal system should reflect. While this may not be surprising in view of Party–state's priorities, abolition of RETL does not give any promise that other administrative powers will be reformed in the same way. Instead, the reforms, if any, that might be made to powers such as detention for education of sex workers will depend on their own particular circumstances and a consideration of three core questions. First, is there popular and international criticism of the power such that it can be abolished in a way that is politically advantageous or at least not disadvantageous? Second, can the power be abolished in a way that does not have a significant impact on public order? Finally, is there an alternative available form of punishment, or has there been a decision that this form of punishment no longer needs to be applied to that conduct?

Li Enshen's chapter delves into the issue of community corrections (*shequ jiaozheng*) as an alternative to the system of administrative detention. He combines a detailed analysis of the legislative and institutional frameworks with a socio-political assessment of the difficulties surrounding the implementation of the system of community corrections. He explains that in China today this burgeoning system lacks sufficient legal justification, social support and financial resources and, crucially, is institutionally inconsistent with China's *hukou* (household registration) system.

The last chapter in Part I, by Guo Zhiyuan, shifts the lens to a different area of administrative detention. It addresses the system of mental health institutions in contemporary China and the debates related to the enactment of a *Mental Health Law* in 2012. The author focuses in particular on the problematic issues of involuntary deprivation of liberty and compulsory treatment and she examines relevant legal reforms taking into account both the letter of the law and a number of preliminary empirical findings. She concludes by advancing further proposals for reform related to compulsory treatment and involuntary hospitalisation, and by advocating for a change in public attitudes toward psychiatric patients.

Part II of this book focuses on other areas of detention in the criminal justice system. It builds on the debates outlined in Part I and provides an in-depth analysis of key problematic issues raised by attempts to reform the existing criminal justice system. The focus on detention in this second part of the book covers two key areas where recent controversy has driven reform: residential surveillance and pre-trial detention.

In Chapter 5, Joshua Rosenzweig analyses the system of residential surveillance; he considers its scope and the problems raised by its implementation. Rosenzweig places particular emphasis on the debates surrounding residential surveillance in the context of the 2012 amendment of the CPL. In a similar fashion to other detention practices analysed in this volume, the development of residential surveillance has been influenced significantly by socio-economic changes and crime-fighting activities that have been connected with the Party-state's obsession with social and political stability. According to Rosenzweig, residential surveillance was originally intended as a fairly lenient and non-coercive alternative to pre-trial detention, similar to house arrest in Western countries. However, over time, it developed in its own right as a distinctive and highly coercive measure. In recent years, both foreign and domestic scholars have voiced their discomfort with the nature and scope of such changes and have found that the public consultation process during the final drafting stage of the 2012 reforms to the CPL was a propitious time to express their concerns and advocate for its abolition. Rosenzweig explains that residential surveillance was indeed substantially revised but retained in the CPL 2012 and today includes two quite distinct measures. The law justifies both an 'ordinary form of residential surveillance' intended primarily as a tool for reducing pre-trial detention, and an 'exceptional' non-residential form used to deal with offenders considered by the authorities to be serious threats to the socio-political order.

Chapters 6 and 7 are complementary since they examine the system of pre-trial detention, in particular the amendment of the relevant legislation – the 1990 *Regulations on Criminal Detention Centres* – and the reform of the institution of pre-trial detention itself. In Chapter 6, Cheng Lei and Elisa Nesossi provide an introduction to the institutional system of pre-trial detention centres. They consider the history, the legislative and institutional framework of Chinese pre-trial detention centres. In addition to offering an insider view on the historical development of the institution, they examine the developments that have occurred in the aftermath of the 'hide and seek' accident that exploded in the media in 2009. They also consider the numerous suggestions for reforms, with a particular focus on the draft of a *Criminal Detention Law* and the debates surrounding the passage of the authority administering pre-trial detention from the MPS to the MoJ.

Written from the perspective of a scholar and NGO practitioner, Nicola Macbean's chapter considers the factors that have contributed to the crisis of legitimacy facing China's pre-trial detention institutions. In particular, it looks at the recommendations advanced by reformers and the contours of policy response. Macbean argues that various scandals involving brutality and death in custody have brought pre-trial detention institutions to centre stage of the process of reforms. The terms of both legislative and institutional reforms in this area are indeed influenced by imposing human rights principles and laws, overseas practice and greater domestic awareness of the reality of pre-trial detention centres. She argues that the reform process has in part been facilitated by internationally funded pilot projects focused on specific areas like complaints mechanisms, monitoring by the people's procuratorate and local citizens, and improved access to lawyers. By emphasising the urgency of the problems associated with detention, she also claims that the various scandals helped to establish within China ideas about minimum standards of treatment in detention and detainees' rights to safety. To conclude, she advocates for the creation of a more sophisticated narrative concerning pre-trial detention, one that establishes the rights of the criminal suspects to a presumption of innocence.

Part III of the book assesses the question of deprivation of liberty from the point of view of scholarly literature and theory.

Chapters 8 and 9 offer an overview of the existing Chinese and Western literature on the topic of deprivation of liberty in China. These two chapters analyse respectively key Chinese and Western issues and debates in the area and demonstrate that these two have unfolded in parallel, as two separate discourses and approaches. Elisa Nesossi and Susan Trevaskes (Chapter 8) focus on the domestic Chinese literature on imprisonment. They highlight the inevitable link existing between national criminal justice policy and its impact on institutions of punishment today, and observe how in recent years, new topics, narratives and concepts have emerged and unfolded in the area of prison discourse. They trace discursive shifts that reflect new conceptual approaches that have imposed on the system; further, they acknowledge how these are influenced by the broader dynamics of change in Chinese politics and society. Their chapter is in two parts. The first discusses the move from Marxist-based discourse of 'reform through labour' in the 1980s and early 1990s to the more legal and penology-focused approaches after the promulgation of the *Prison Law* 1994. The second part focuses on more recent Chinese literature, surveying a study in a key (practitioner-oriented) specialised journal, *Prison Review* (*Jianyu Pinglun*). They discuss an exemplar study of the contemporary literature written by three prison officials that provides an insight into current Chinese thinking about the nature of policy-driven reform that affects both prisoners and the prison system. Nesossi and Trevaskes engage with this 2013 study, to understand the relationship between the country's current 'foundational' criminal justice policy called 'balancing leniency and severity' and recent prison policy and practice.

Flora Sapio's reflections in Chapter 9 discuss the limits of conventional Western approaches toward the Chinese correctional system. She explains how these views have generated a 'Gulag narrative' whereby individual depictions of Chinese incarceration have tended to be employed as examples of 'living hell on earth'. Sapio argues that since the early days of the PRC, conventional Western narratives have been constructed to create a relatively stereotyped and orientalised image of China and the Chinese, serving political and geo-strategic imperatives. This literature was initially used to justify the imposition of foreign extra-territorial powers at the end of the nineteenth century. Later, it was employed during the Cold War to orientalise the Communist enemy and, since the 1990s, to justify the exportation of human rights values to the authoritarian regime. To mediate such biased and exotic accounts, Sapio advocates a change in perspective – a shift in approach that this volume attempts to realise. Sapio's examination encourages Chinese and Western scholars alike to develop their analysis by exploring this area through the conceptual prisms of criminology and penology, two interpretative grids that may explain the Chinese circumstances in a more discipline-specific way.

Chapter 10, by Nesossi, Biddulph, Sapio and Trevaskes, offers a final reflection on the issues that create opportunities and contribute to define future challenges. The chapter concludes by advocating that contemporary scholarship should look critically behind cosmetic changes and understand the deeper forces that drive reforms in China's contemporary justice system.

Conclusion

Various forms of detention and incarceration belonging to both the criminal justice and administrative systems exist in the PRC to deprive criminal suspects, offenders and wrongdoers of their physical liberty. Social order and stability are primary political concerns in China and it is in this context that detention and imprisonment have become the hallmark of a heavily politicised justice system where crucial political and institutional battles are played out. The studies in this volume develop from the understanding that in China today the Party and the state institutions that control and punish crime remain closely interconnected; this means that law, its implementation and its development are subject to the Party's policy and institutional dominance.

The existing literature in the area of Chinese detention and incarceration indicates that while some of the contemporary forms of detention and incarceration have been widely discussed and explored both domestically and internationally, others remain less well understood. Scholarship on some areas of administration detention such as RETL is highly nuanced and detailed and covers expansive ground. In contrast, there has been very little work outside China on prisons since Seymour and Anderson's work published in the late 1990s. And it was only in the early 2000s that a small number of Chinese scholars and officials began to examine other facilities, such as pre-trial detention centres, and to detail the conditions in which prisoners and detainees were living. Therefore, it has only been in the last decade or so that many issues concerning detention have been subject to public scrutiny within China, generating calls for reforms. In the process, the legislative authorities have amended some areas of the relevant legislation and established new alternative systems of control.

While scholars have gained more knowledge and access to institutions of detention, to date there has been no sustained study of the recent changes. This volume is the first to centre on the theme of reform to this regime. It is neither intended as a tool to advocate for reforms in the existing detention powers in view of rule of law and human rights principles, nor as an account of what some commentators might see as barbaric punitive practices in China. Written at a time when places of detention are becoming increasingly open, transparent and accessible to external observers, this book is primarily an attempt to explain the complexities in the dynamics of the current process of penal reforms, and the factors which make the need for institutional restructuring in this area both timely and compelling. It does so by bringing together analyses and reflections by both Western and Chinese scholars set around the theme of reform over the last decade or more. We expect it to generate an enriching and constructive dialogue about the nature of reform and change in China that was largely absent in earlier studies.

Notes

1. A longer version of this chapter is published in *China Law and Society Review* (2017).
2. The section 'Use of Terms' of the *Body of Principles for the Protection of All Persons under Any Form of Detention or Imprisonment* 1988 sets a standard in the relevant terminology adopted internationally. Accordingly, 'detention' refers to the condition of 'any person deprived of personal liberty except as a result of conviction for an offence'. 'Imprisonment' indicates the condition of 'any person deprived of personal liberty as a result of conviction for an offence'.
3. Detention for repatriation (*shourong qiansong*) was part of the system until 2003, when it was abolished.
4. For a discussion of these types of arguments in relation to re-education through labour see Biddulph 2012.

5 These changes were introduced by two internal documents, both of which were issued in 1950: the Ministry of Justice and the Ministry of Public Security *Decision on Prisons, Reform through Labour Team, Detention Centres* (*Guanyu Jianyu, Laodong Gaizao Dui He Kanshousuo De Jueding*) and the *Instructions for the Transferring of Prisons, Detention Centres and Reform through Labour Team to the Ministry of Public Security (Guanyu Jianyu, Kanshousuo, He Ladong Gaizao Dui Yizhuanggui Gong'an Bumen Lingdao De Zhishi)* (Dutton 2005, 353). As noted by Dutton, the passage of places of detention from the control of the Ministry of Justice to the Ministry of Public Security initiated a struggle between these two branches of the Chinese government that partially resolved only in 1983 when the Ministry of Justice regained control over the prison system.
6 A partial translation of the text of the 1954 *Regulations* may be found in Cohen (1968, 365–68).
7 According to a 1979 resolution by the NPC Standing Committee, all laws and regulations enacted after 1949 were to remain in effect if not in conflict with the Constitution and other laws or regulations (see NPC Standing Committee *Resolution on the Problem of the Legal Effectiveness of Laws and Decrees Enacted Since the Establishment of the People's Republic of China* (*Quangguo Renmin Daibiao Dahui Changwu Weiyuanhui Guanyu Zhonghua Renmin Gongheguo Yilai Zhiding Falü, Faling Xiaoli Wenti De Jueyi*) 1979).
8 The *Regulations on Reform through Labour* were lastly abrogated by the State Council *Resolution on Repealing Some Administrative Regulations Issued Before the End of the Year* 2000 (*Guowuyuan Guanyu Feizhi 2000nian De Yiqian Fabude Bufen Xingzheng Faguide Jueding*), adopted on and effective from 6 October 2001.
9 The mother of an underage rape victim, Tang, protested outside local government buildings, claiming that police had falsified evidence in order to mitigate the punishment of men who had kidnapped and raped her eleven-year-old daughter, forcing her into prostitution. In August 2012, the police sentenced Tang to 18 months' detention at a RETL facility in Yongzhou, Hunan province, for 'seriously disturbing social order and exerting a negative impact on society'. A public outcry helped secure her speedy release. In April 2013, the Yongzhou court rejected Tang's claim for compensation but in July she won her case on appeal and was compensated RMB 2,941.
10 See also the *Regulations on Public Security Organs Handling Re-Education Through Labour Cases* (*Gong'an Jiguan Banli Laodong Jiaoyang Anjian Guiding*) 2002 (amended in 2005), which provided for procedural rules specifically related to RETL. See also the discussion in Biddulph 2007.

References

Alabaster, Ernest, 1899. *Notes and Commentaries on Chinese Criminal Law, and Cognate Topics. With Special Relation to Ruling Cases. Together with a Brief Excursus on The Law of Property, Chiefly Founded on the Writings of the Late Sir Chaloner Alabaster*. London: Luzac & Co.
Balme, Stéphanie and Dowdle, Michael W., eds. 2009. *Building Constitutionalism in China*. New York: Palgrave Macmillan.
Biddulph, Sarah. 2007. *Legal Reform and Administrative Detention Powers in China*. Cambridge, UK: Cambridge University Press.
Biddulph, Sarah. 2012. 'Between Rhetoric and Reality: The Use of International Human Rights Norms in Law Reform Debates in China.' In *Narrative and Legal Transfers: Informing Law and Development*, edited by John Gillespie and Pip Nicholson, 143–78. Cambridge, UK: Cambridge University Press.
Biddulph, Sarah and Xie Chuanyu. 2011. 'Regulating Drug Dependency in China: The 2008 PRC Drug Rehabilitation Law.' *The British Journal of Criminology* 51(6): 978–96.
Chen Ruihua. 2004. *Wei Jue Jiya Zhidu De Shizheng Yanjiu* (*An Empirical Study of the System of Pre-Trial Detention*). Beijing: Beijing daxue chubanshe.
Chen Weidong. 2005. *Jiya Zhidu Yu Renquan Baozhang* (*The System of Detention and Protection of Human Rights*). Beijing: Zhongguo jiancha chubanshe.
Cheng Lei. 2014. *Kanshousuo Lifa Wenti Yanjiu* (*On the Legislation About Detention House*). Beijing: Zhongguo fazhi chubanshe.
China Daily. 20 April 2009. 'State Cleans House over Detentions.' Available at http://www.chinadaily.com.cn (accessed 16 February 2016).
Cohen, Jerome A. 1968. *The Criminal Process in the People's Republic of China, 1949–63: An Introduction*. Cambridge, MA: Harvard University Press.

Commission on Extraterritoriality. 1926. *Report of the Commission on Extra-territoriality in China.* London: H.M. Stationery Office.

Dikötter, Frank. 2002. *Crime, Punishment and the Prison in Modern China.* New York: Columbia University Press.

Dutton, Michael R.1992. *Policing and Punishment in China: From Patriarchy to the People.* Cambridge, UK: Cambridge University Press.

Dutton, Michael. 2005. 'Toward a Government of the Contract: Policing in the Era of Reform.' In *Crime, Punishment and Policing in China*, edited by Børge Bakken, 189–234. Lanham: Rowman and Littlefield.

Fu Hualing. 2005a. 'Punishing for Profit. Profitability and Rehabilitation in a *Laojiao* Institution.' In *Engaging the Law in China. State, Society, and Possibilities for Justice*, edited by Neij J. Diamant, Stanley Lubman and Kevin J. O'Brien, 213–29. Stanford: Stanford University Press.

Fu Hualing. 2005b. 'Re-Education Through Labor in Historical Perspective.' *The China Quarterly* 184: 811–31.

Fu Hualing. 2009. 'Dissolving *Laojiao*.' *China Rights Forum* 1: 54–8.

Gao Qiang. 21 July 2011. 'Guowuyuan Jiedu Tiaoli Sui Dabu Chuangxin Dan Xiaoqu Dongtai Guankong Reng Yaoyao Wu (Despite the Big Innovation in the State Council's Drug Prohibition Regulations, Abolition of Dynamic Control is Still Remote).' Available at http://www.jhak.com/jlzm/zm/2011-07/21/content_6133.html (accessed 16 February 2016).

Guo Chengwei. 2005. *Qing Mo Ming Chu Xingsu Fadianhua Yanjiu* (Studies on Criminal Procedure Codification at the End of the Qing Dynasty and the Early Period of the Republic of China). Beijing: Zhongguo gong'an daxue chubanshe.

Han Shuqin. 2013. ' "Jianyu Fa" Xiugai Ying Zhu Zhong Jiejue De Ruogan Wenti (Several Major Problems that Needed To Be Solved in the Revision of the Prison Law).' *Henan Sifa Jingguan Zhiye Xueyuan Xuebao* (Journal of Henan Judicial Police Vocational College) 11(1): 27–9.

Jeffreys, Elaine. 2004. *China, Sex and Prostitution.* London: Routledge.

Human Rights Watch. 2002. *Dangerous Meditation: China's Campaign Against Falungong.* New York, Washington, London, Brussels: Human Rights Watch.

Liu Jinpeng. 2005. 'You Gao Fuxilü Dui Woguo Xianxing Jiedu Tixi De Sikao (Considering China's Drug Rehabilitation System from the Perspective of the High Relapse Rate).' *Fanzui Yu Gaige Yanjiu* (Crime and Reform Research) 7: 24.

Liu Ziqian and Zhang Wenling. 21 February 2009. 'Yunnan Jingfang Tongbao Duo Mao Mao Shijian. Cheng Li Wan Youxi Fasheng Yiwai (Yunnan Police Notify about the Accident of Hide and Seek. A Guy Called Li Had an Accident while Playing).' *Zhongguo Qingnian Bao* (China's Youth Daily). Available at http://news.sina.com.cn/c/2009-02-21/032717258307.shtml (accessed 16 February 2016).

Lubman, Stanley. 2012. *The Evolution of Law Reform in China: An Uncertain Path.* Cheltenham: Edward Elgar.

Luo Jieqi. 27 February 2009. 'Guanfang Tongbao 'Duo Mao Mao' Shijian Diaocha Jieguo (Officials Notify about the Results of the 'Hide and Seek' Accident).' *Caijing*. Available at http://www.caijing.com.cn/2009-02-27/110075141.html (accessed 16 February 2016).

Ma Longhu. 2001. 'Dui Woguo Laodong Jiaoyang Zhidu De Lixing Fenxi (Analysis of the Rationality of My Country's System of Re-Education Through Labour).' *Zhengfa Luncong* (Collected Essays on Politics and Law) 6: 33–5.

Ministry of Justice. 22 December 2014. 'Zhongguo Jianyu Zuifan Jiaoyu Gaizao Fazhan Qingkuang (The Developmental Trend of Education and Reform of Convicted Offenders in China).' *Zhongguo Qingnian Bao* (China's Youth Daily). Available at http://www.moj.gov.cn/sfxzjlzx/content/2014-12/22/content_5895340_2.htm (accessed 16 February 2016).

Mühlhahn, Klaus. 2009. *Criminal Justice in China: A History.* Cambridge, MA: Harvard University Press.

Nesossi, Elisa. 2012. *China's Pre-Trial Justice: Criminal Justice, Human Rights and Legal Reforms in Contemporary China.* London: Wildy, Simmonds and Hill.

Nesossi, Elisa. 2014. 'Detention, Stability and "Social Management Innovation".' In *The Politics of Law and Stability in China*, edited by Susan Trevaskes, Elisa Nesossi, Flora Sapio and Sarah Biddulph, 219–43. Cheltenham: Edward Elgar.

Peerenboom, Randall. 2002. *China's Long March toward Rule of Law*. Cambridge, New York: Cambridge University Press.

Qi Dan. 2008. *Zhi'an Zhixu Guanli Zhuanlun* (*Special Discussion of the Management of Public Order Administration*). Beijing: Zhongguo renmin gong'an daxue chubanshe.

Sapio, Flora. 2010. *Sovereign Power and the Law in China*. Boston and Leiden: Brill.

Seymour, James D. and Anderson, Richard. 1999. *New Ghosts, Old Ghosts. Prison and Labor Reform Camps in China*. Armonk: M. E. Sharpe.

Song Yinghui. 2007. *Xingshi Susong Fa*. Beijing: Tsinghua Daxue chubanshe.

Star News. 9 March 2015. 'Xiao Rui: Kanshousuo Boli Gong'an, Yueshu Jingquan Caineng Baozhang Renquan (Xiao Rui: Only by Separating Pre-Trial Detention Centres from the Police, and Limiting Police Powers Can Human Rights Be Guaranteed).' *Sohu*. Available at http://star.news.sohu.com/20150309/n409517709.shtml (accessed 16 February 2016).

Sun Lianzhong. 2007. *Xingshi Qiangzhi Cuoshi Yanjiu* (Study of the Criminal Coercive Measures). Beijing: Zhishi changquan chubanshe.

T'ao Lung-Sheng. 1966. 'Shen Chia-Pen and Modernization of Chinese Law.' *Shehui Kexue Luncong* (Social Sciences Forum) 25: 275–90.

Woo, Margaret Y.K and Gallagher, Mary E. 2012. *Chinese Justice: Civil Dispute Resolution in Contemporary China*. Cambridge, New York: Cambridge University Press.

Xie Liping. 2009. 'Guanyu "Jianyufa" Xiugai He Wanshan De Sikao (Reflections on the Revision and Perfection of the "Prison Law").' *Zhongguo Sifa* (Justice of China) 2: 23–5.

Zhang Xuehua, ed. 2005. *Xiandai Gong'an Kanshousuo Lingdao Shiwu Quanshu* (The Complete Book of Concrete Issues of Contemporary Detention Centres for Public Security Leaders). Tianjin: Tianjin dianzi chubanshe.

Part I
Administrative detention

2 What to make of the abolition of re-education through labour?

Sarah Biddulph[1]

Introduction

In 1979 two of the first laws to be passed in the People's Republic of China's (PRC) era of reform and opening up were the *Criminal Law* (*Xing Fa*) and the *Criminal Procedure Law* (*Xingshi Susong Fa*) 1979. While a number of legislative instruments had been in place prior to 1979 that authorised arrest and criminal punishment, this was the first time in the history of the PRC that comprehensive codes of criminal law and procedure had been passed. Of course, the lack of legislation had not prevented the dispensation of criminal justice. In fact, the system of punishments was not limited to criminal punishment, but also included a very extensive array of punitive administrative powers. At that time, and continuing into the reform period, the public security organs (the 'police') exercised (and continue to exercise) a wide range of administrative power that empowered them to sanction crime and other conduct considered to be harmful to social order. These powers were mostly not defined by law, or were poorly defined if they were. They lacked any detailed description either of their scope or the procedures to be applied in their exercise. Needless to say, the use of these powers was not under any effective supervision and abusive practices were common. So passage of criminal and criminal procedure laws in 1979 was not the end of the process of legalisation of punishments, but was merely one step in a still incomplete process of subjecting punishments to rules.

As legal reform has progressed, one by one these administrative powers have been abolished. This chapter discusses the abolition of one of these powers, re-education through labour (RETL) (*laodong jiaoyang*). It evaluates the significance of its abolition. It also considers what impact this abolition might have on the shape of the Chinese sanctioning system and on the principles reflected in China's version of the rule of law more broadly. Re-education through labour was not the first administrative power exercised by the police to be abolished in the reform era. So, before discussing abolition of RETL, this chapter considers the ways in which these other administrative powers were abolished as these also provide some keys to evaluating the significance and impact of abolition of RETL.

History of the abolition of administrative detention powers

First to go was the power of detention for investigation (*shourong shencha*).[2] It was formally established in 1961 as a power to detain, investigate and repatriate unauthorised rural migrants in cities. After 1975 this power was used by the police to detain for interrogation people who were suspected of going from place to place committing crime, committing many crimes, being a member of a criminal gang, or who were suspected of committing a crime where their name and address could not be established (see discussion in Biddulph 2007, 10–11).

These people could be detained for interrogation for up to thirty days, or with an extension, up to three months (Ministry of Public Security 1985, *Notice on Strictly Controlling the Use of Detention for Investigation Measures*, Article 3). In practice this power was used well outside its nominal scope to include people who were mentally ill, alcoholics, people who co-habited illegally or who breached family planning regulations and people involved in economic disputes. Many were detained for extended periods, with some unfortunate people still in detention after ten years or even longer (Cui 1993, 93; Zhang 1993; Ministry of Public Security *Notice on Urgently Rectifying the Abuse of Detention for Investigation Measures* 1992). Being detained under this power was terrifying and unsafe, with many confessing to crimes purely to get themselves transferred out of this form of detention and into the regular criminal justice system. In practice the police used detention for investigation as a substitute for the coercive investigation powers set out in the *Criminal Procedure Law* 1979. One estimate was that between 80–90 per cent of people convicted of criminal offences had first been taken in to detention for investigation (Zhang 1993, 20; see also Zhang and Li 1994, 58).

Detention for investigation was abolished at the time of passage of the 1996 amendments to the *Criminal Procedure Law* (see Gu 1996 and discussion in Biddulph 2007, 338–9). In exchange for giving up this detention power, the Ministry of Public Security managed to negotiate inclusion of compensatory provisions into the amended *Criminal Procedure Law 1996*. The *Criminal Procedure Law* 1996 made provision for extended detention prior to formal arrest of the categories of people who had originally fallen within the scope of detention for investigation (Article 69(2)) and lowered the standard of evidence required for an application for arrest to be approved (Article 60). An interpretation of *Criminal Procedure Law* 1996 Article 128(2) by the Ministry of Public Security (1998) enabled the calculation of time for detention not to commence until the true name and address of a person suspected of committing a crime had been ascertained. While such an interpretation was not foreshadowed in the law, it was tolerated (Wang 2000, 93–5).

When detention for investigation was abolished, one commentator suggested that the police would be required to change their traditional approach to obtaining evidence through interrogation of suspects and to develop new investigation and interrogation methods (Cui 1996, 36–7). It was hoped that this legislative reform would push the police towards developing more sophisticated investigation techniques that were not solely reliant on obtaining a confession from a suspect in custody as basis for a criminal prosecution. However, that the use of torture to obtain confessions continues to be a serious problem nearly twenty years later, and detention of suspects for excessive periods has not been eradicated, demonstrates that legal reform alone is not sufficient to bring about changes in policing practice.

The power of detention for repatriation (*shourong qiansong*, also called custody and repatriation, C&R) was the second administrative detention power to be abolished in 2003. This power was used from 1949 but was formalised in 1961 (Ministry of Public Security *Internal Work Party Group Report on Urgently Preventing Free Population Movement Approved by the CCP Central Committee* 1961). It was originally combined with detention for investigation discussed above (Fan and Xiao 1991, 142). This power was designed to prevent rural migrants from entering cities as well as to investigate suspected criminal or counter-revolutionary offences (Cui 1993, 90–1; Fan and Xiao 1991, 142–3). The power to detain and repatriate migrants (ostensibly the welfare aspects of the original combined detention power) was separated from the criminal investigation aspects of detention for investigation after 1975 (Cui 1993, 91). Detention for repatriation was used to house and forcibly repatriate migrant workers and others who did not have permission to reside in the city (State Council *Measures for Detention for Repatriation of Urban Vagrants and Beggars* 1982 Article 2).

In theory detention under this power should not exceed thirty days (Ministry of Civil Affairs, Ministry of Public Security *Implementing Regulations for the Measures for Detention for Repatriation of Urban Vagrants and Beggars (For Trial Implementation)* 1982 Article 13). Police delivered people to detention centres that were operated by the local civil administration. As with other forms of detention, detainees were required to work (Ministry of Civil Affairs *Notice on Several Issues on Strengthening the Work of Detention for Repatriation* 1994). This power transformed into a flexible way to 'clean the streets' ahead of important events and visits, to round up migrants, vagrants, sex workers and mentally ill people with nowhere to go. Some people were forcibly repatriated, some released after conclusion of the event or visit or, often in the case of sex workers, after paying a fine to procure their release. Abuse of this power and of detainees in detention centres was rife. In the same way as detention for investigation above, the scope of detainees expanded well beyond that originally intended, people were held for extended periods and the conditions in detention were abusive and unsafe (Human Rights in China 1999; Liu 2001; Wang 2002; Xie 2000).

A number of factors coincided to seal the fate of this power. Calls to reform or abolish it provided the background against which other factors combined. First was the change of leadership to Hu Jintao and Wen Jiabao and adoption of a more people-oriented governance focus. Second was the public uproar that arose after the beating death in custody of Sun Zhigang in early 2003. As Hand notes, Sun Zhigang, a young university graduate pursuing a career in Guangzhou, was the 'ideal figure to capture public attention . . . and focus it on abuses in the C&R system' (Hand 2006, 137). In addition to the public furore over this death in custody, a group of three scholars presented a petition to the National People's Congress (NPC) Standing Committee asserting the unconstitutionality and illegality of this power. A further petition was presented calling for an investigation into the handling of Sun Zhigang's case and the operation of the system of detention for repatriation (Hand 2006, 124). The perpetrators and other people held responsible for Sun Zhigang's death were quickly prosecuted and convicted. Shortly after that the State Council (2003) issued the *Measures on the Administration of Aid to Vagrants and Beggars Having no Means of Livelihood in Cities* (*Chengshi Shenghuo Wuzhuo De Liulang Qitao Renyuan Jiuzhu Guanli Banfa*). The measures were issued on 18 June 2003 and were implemented on 1 August 2003, effectively abolishing detention for repatriation. These measures substituted for the old detention power a system to provide for the shelter and welfare of vagrants and beggars in the city. It was purported to be voluntary, so that residents could enter and leave these facilities at will (Article 5). Hand reports that abolition of detention for repatriation was met with great enthusiasm by academics, the media and the general public (Hand 2006, 128–9). Police, especially those responsible for maintenance of social order in urban areas, were less enthusiastic. For a period after abolition of detention for repatriation, in many cities the number of itinerants on the streets increased dramatically, with police enforcement activities noticeably absent.

Finally, after years of criticism and debate probably the most infamous of the administrative detention powers, RETL, was abolished on 28 December 2013. This occurred as a result of the passage by the NPC Standing Committee of the *Resolution on Abolishing Laws and Regulations on Re-Education through Labour* (*Quanguo Renda Changweihui Guanyu Feichu Laodong Jiaoyang Falü Guiding De Jueding*).

The abolition of each of these powers shares some similarities. Abolition followed extensive public, official and international criticism about the extent of abuse under these powers and the lack of any effective controls over their use and misuse. Each of these powers clearly lacked proper legislative authorisation as they were not sufficiently established by a law passed by the NPC or its Standing Committee. For the latter two, this illegality was made explicit in Article 8 of the *Legislation Law* (*Lifa Fa*) 2000. With social, political and legal reforms, they were all becoming less and less defensible on the grounds either of efficiency, or that they reflected China's particular situation or 'national spirit' (*guoqing*). There are some differences as well between the ways in which each was abolished. Detention for investigation was largely incorporated into the revised *Criminal Procedure Law* 1996. Detention for repatriation was replaced by a welfare measure, which purported to represent the original intent of the power. RETL was abolished without its functions being clearly substituted by another power. What happens after abolition of RETL is not yet clear and is still evolving.

What is the significance of abolition of RETL and what are the implications for further reforms of the system of coercive and punitive powers? What does abolition of RETL suggest in terms of further reforms of police administrative powers and to law reform more generally? These are questions examined in this chapter. To give up a coercive power it would be naive to think that concern for integrity of the legal system and protection of citizens' rights is in itself a sufficient motivation. The discussion above suggests that at least three practical and policy issues also arise for consideration in understanding both the reasons for and implications of the abolition of RETL.

- The first is the nature of the pressure for reform, both internal to government and Party as well as from the general public and international sources. Can the abolition be done in a way that is politically advantageous, or at least not disadvantageous?
- The second consideration relates to the perceived impact on public order. Can the power be abolished in a way that does not adversely affect public order, or at least keeps that impact within acceptable limits? Here two sets of issues are pertinent. The first is to examine what are currently considered to be the threats to social order and whether RETL was seen as effective in maintaining order. The second is to consider the overall powers remaining for dealing with related public order issues.
- Third has there been social or policy change that removes the need and/or desire to punish some or all of the conduct that was originally targeted? If not, then which measures are being put in place to cover the gaps left by abolition of RETL?

These three issues are considered in section three of this chapter. Finally, in section four the chapter concludes with some thoughts on the implication of abolition of RETL more broadly for legal regulation of state coercive powers.

Abolishing RETL: three considerations

Pressure for reform

There is no doubt that throughout the reform era RETL was one of the most publicly debated and controversial of police detention powers. Both internationally and domestically, RETL was the subject of sustained criticism for being arbitrary and abusive. It lacked proper legal basis, enabled imposition of disproportionately harsh punishment on minor offenders, decision-making was partial and opaque and there was a lack of any credible measures for supervision or control over its imposition. In fact these criticisms have been so well rehearsed over many years that I do not intend to repeat them here (see for example: Amnesty International 1991; 2006; 2013; Human Rights in China 2001; Human Rights Watch 2002; and Hung 2003). In 2012, there was a case of imposition of a term of RETL on Tang Hui on the grounds of 'seriously disrupting social order and having a negative impact on society' for her ongoing petitioning activities demanding serious punishment of the men responsible for kidnapping, raping and forcing her daughter into prostitution (Xinhua Net 10 August 2012). Although Tang Hui was subsequently released, the public furore focused attention on the wide-open potential for abuse of RETL. Further public pressure followed with the exposé in the *New York Times* of a letter secreted into a packet of Halloween decorations purchased in the USA and made by an inmate in the Masanjia RETL camp. This letter highlighted long hours of work and abusive conditions in the camp (Jacobs 11 June 2013).

In addition, RETL had become increasingly inconsistent with the developing principles of legality articulated in the law and finally came to be seen by interested actors (including the police and justice department) as being unconstitutional and unlawful. In particular, the *Legislation Law* 2000 (as amended in 2015) Article 8(5), the *Administrative Punishments Law* (*Xingzheng Chufa Fa*) 1996 (as amended 2009) Article 9(2) and the *Administrative Compulsion Law* (*Xingzheng Qiangshi Fa*) 2011 Article 10 all require that powers for deprivation of personal liberty must be authorised by 'law', defined by the *Legislation Law* Article 7 as laws passed by the NPC or its Standing Committee. The *Administrative Compulsion Law* Article 11 further provides that it is not permitted for the scope of targets, conditions and types of administrative coercive measures to be expanded by way of administrative or local regulation. Even though there had been some debate about whether RETL should be characterised as a 'punishment' or a 'coercive measure' and so which law was applicable, these laws, taken together, gradually backed RETL into a legal black hole. There was a clear need for legislation to provide proper authorisation for any power to deprive a citizen of their liberty. The urgency of efforts to draft and obtain the consensus necessary to pass legislation to regulate RETL demonstrated official appreciation of the legal vulnerability of RETL (discussed in Biddulph 2015, 211–2).

Abolition of RETL has been widely applauded as a long-overdue step and necessary for progress to be made towards rule of law. Police agree that it is a necessary consequence of legal developments, but consider that they are not properly prepared for the challenges its abolition will bring in fulfilling their responsibilities to ensure public order. Since its abolition there have been some complaints that police capacity to maintain social order has been weakened, that the social order situation has deteriorated and morale of local police has fallen (Zou 2014). Others contend that social order has not been adversely impacted by its abolition (Huang and Zhou 2014, 32). The only reservation expressed by the Committee on Economic, Social and Cultural Rights in its concluding observations on China's second periodic report in June 2014 was to ensure that RETL was completely abolished throughout China and that no alternative or parallel powers were established to act as a substitute for RETL (Committee on Economic Social and Cultural Rights 23 May 2014, para 22). From the perspective of pressure to reform and praise for effecting this reform, abolition of RETL has been very positive and politically advantageous.

Impact on public order

The second set of considerations draw our attention to questions about whether RETL could be abolished in a way that did not have a seriously negative impact on public order. A number of factors combined. The first was a breakdown of the consensus about the effectiveness of RETL in maintaining social order and changes in official evaluations about the types of conduct that seriously undermined social stability. The second was that legal and institutional changes made prior to abolition of RETL reduced the numbers of people in RETL camps and transferred many to alternative forms of punishment.

Changing perceptions about the effectiveness of RETL in maintaining social order

One of the assumptions, often asserted and accepted without question within China, was that RETL was effective in maintaining social order and that it was a successful way of dealing with troublemakers and crime (see, for example, Chu 2009). This argument formed an important plank in supporting the positions of those calling for reform that fell short of abolition of RETL. There were a small number of scholars and officials who put the opposite argument: RETL was an historical anachronism and was so embedded in the political culture of the 1950s that it was no longer needed (Feng et al. 2008, 246; Wang 1997, 32; Wu 2008, 62). A small number of public intellectuals advanced the argument that RETL was arbitrary and productive of injustice and that it was these elements that produced instability rather than preserved stability. Their argument was that abolishing RETL would benefit social order and stability through improving social justice and the lawfulness of government conduct (Hu et al. 2007). As the proponents of retention and reform of RETL liked to point out, these opposition views were in the minority (Chu 2009, 49).

In public, the tide started to turn against this consensus view around the time of the decision by the Central Political–Legal Committee in early 2013 to designate RETL as one of the four priority areas for reform in the political–legal system (Cui and Liu 7 January 2013). More voices joined those asserting that RETL was a historical anachronism. Professor Mou Yuchuan in late 2012, for example, stated that the original objectives of RETL had been transformed and its effectiveness now was lost (Mou 21 October 2013). In January 2013 an editorial in *Southern Metropolis Daily* reported that at the Guangdong People's Congress meeting, the Guangdong Police Chief, Xie Xiaodan, rejected the 'instrumental value' of RETL. He also opposed the use of RETL in cases involving repeat and nuisance petitioners and people who criticise Party and government officials. His argument was grounded in the view that people who petition because they do not trust the law should not be punished by RETL but should have their dispute returned to legal channels for resolution (Nandu.com 25 January 2013; *Southern Metropolis Daily* 25 January 2013).[3]

This specific re-evaluation of the effectiveness of RETL in preserving social order should also be seen in the context of a broader shift in views about the types of conduct that undermine social order and cause social harm. From the early 1980s people committing crime had been identified as the new class of 'enemy' whose conduct undermined the program of economic modernisation and social stability and who were targeted for severe punishment (Deng 1980; 1993, 176–7). The 'Strike Hard' policy of dealing out severe and swift punishment to targeted serious criminal offences gave practical effect to this priority. It was against the background of the 'Strike Hard' against crime that the use of RETL expanded from the early 1980s.

However, alongside the social and economic transformations provoked by economic reform, social order problems were also becoming more complex. By the early 2000s, senior police and political leaders began to focus more directly on public protest and other forms of disruptive behaviour as posing a serious threat to social order and stability (Trevaskes 2013, 62). From 2003 greater policy and policing focus was placed upon mass incidents as undermining social stability. Trevaskes documents five main conflicts identified as being the main causes of mass incidents: between rich and poor; government officials and the masses; people from urban and rural areas; Han and ethnic minorities; and people from different regions within China (Trevaskes 2013, 66). By their nature these conflicts arise out of structural social and economic conflicts and are less amenable to resolution purely by the imposition of harsh punishments. The harm to social and political stability caused by mass incidents required a concerted multi-faceted Party–state response, within which the use of punitive powers such as RETL was only one component.

Limiting the numbers of people entering RETL

In addition to these attitudinal changes, a number of practical changes reduced the number of people placed in RETL. Prior to abolition of RETL, compliance with procedural rules internally within public security organs was gradually tightened, thus limiting the number of RETL cases being examined and approved. In 2005 the Ministry of Public Security issued the *Opinion on Further Strengthening and Improving the Work of Examination and Approval of Re-Education Through Labour* (*Gong'an Bu Guanyu Jinyibu Jiaqiang He Gaijin Laodong Jiaoyang Shenpi Gongzuo De Shishi Yijian*) which strengthened procedural rules and expanded the scope of the internal hearing procedure (*lingxun*) that had originally been inserted into the decision-making process in the 2002 Ministry of Public Security *Regulations on Public Security Organs Handling Re-Education Through Labour Cases* (*Gong'an Jiguan Banli Laodong Jiaoyang Anjian Guiding*). Instead, police were encouraged to initiate criminal prosecutions where the conduct was amenable to criminal prosecution. A number of changes in sentencing practice were also set out in the 2005 opinion to bring time limits for detention into line with a draft *Law on the Correction of Misdemeanours* (*Weifa Xingwei Jiaozhi Fa (Cao'an)*). This was originally anticipated to be the law that would implement reforms to RETL. It included a provision to limit the period of detention to eighteen months. Police sentencing practice had changed (in what they had thought would be in advance of passage of this law) to favour imposition of sentences of no more than eighteen months.

Finally, in 2013, in the year following the Central Political–Legal Committee announcement that it intended to reform RETL, a number of local areas decided not to impose RETL on certain categories of people. In Guangdong these included nuisance petitioners and people criticising government and Party leaders, in Yunnan it was those suspected of minor conduct threatening national security, nuisance petitioners and people who criticised government and Party leaders, and in Chongqing it was sex workers (Biddulph 2015, 215).

Transferring drug dependent people from RETL to other forms of detention

In terms of total numbers, legislative reform to the treatment of drug dependent people probably had the most significant impact on the numbers of people actually in detention under RETL. As problems of drug use and dependence increased in China, RETL was increasingly used to detain and punish drug dependent people. In some areas, such as Guangdong, it was estimated that more than 80 or 90 per cent of detainees in RETL were drug dependent (Li and Huang 2008). By 2008, many RETL camps were specifically designated for the detention of drug dependent people (Biddulph and Xie 2011). Overall, at the time the *Drug Prohibition Law* (*Jindu Fa*) was passed in December 2007 (effective on 1 June 2008), a significant proportion of detainees in RETL were drug dependent. Subsequently, sex workers, people committing minor offences such as petty theft or repeated public order infringements, including as picking quarrels and causing trouble, and nuisance petitioners were also strongly represented in the population of detainees (for example, see Zou 2014, 36).

The first significant institutional change occurred with passage of the *Drug Prohibition Law* in 2007. This is an omnibus law dealing with both the supply and demand side of illicit drugs, including punishment of drug offences, as well as treatment for drug dependent people. Measures that may be taken for drug rehabilitation include voluntary rehabilitation in medical or other approved drug rehabilitation facilities, registration of drug users, and a range of compulsory orders for people determined to be drug dependent.

The *Drug Prohibition Law* 2008 instituted two compulsory, non-custodial orders: community rehabilitation (*shequ jiedu*), overseen by the local street or village committee for a period of three years (Article 33), and recovering health in the community (*shequ kangfu*), also for a period of three years. The latter is an order imposed on a person after they have undergone compulsory drug rehabilitation in a detention centre (Article 48). It may be served in the community or in a closed facility, such as a 'giving up drugs and recovering health camp' (Article 49; see also the discussion in Biddulph and Xie 2011). The law also merged two pre-existing administrative detention powers used for compulsory rehabilitation of drug dependent people. The first was coercive drug rehabilitation for between three and six months in detention centres operated by the public security agencies. The second was RETL for a period of between one and three years with a possible extension of one year, imposed by the police where coercive drug rehabilitation had failed: this was operated by the justice department (NPC Standing Committee *Decision on Prohibiting Illicit Drugs* 1990, paragraph 8). The new power which replaces these two pre-existing powers, the compulsory quarantine for drug rehabilitation (CQDR, *qiangzhi geli jiedu*), is a form of administrative detention of drug dependent people for an initial period of two years, with the possibility of early release after one year for those who reform well and extension of one year for those who do not reform well (Article 47). The *Drug Prohibition Law* 2008 authorises the police at county level to impose this period of detention (Article 38).

The *Drug Prohibition Law* 2008 retains the pre-existing procedures for imposing a term of administrative detention which are largely parallel (though not identical) to the procedures for imposing a term of RETL. It provides that the decision is to be imposed by the police at county level upon determination that the person is drug dependent. A person dissatisfied with a decision to send them to CQDR may commence either administrative review, which considers the lawfulness and appropriateness of the decision, or administrative litigation, which enables a court to examine the lawfulness of the decision (Article 40). The only involvement that a court has in this decision-making process is to consider the lawfulness of the decision after it has been made, and then only if the detainee or their representative challenges the lawfulness of the police decision.

The power to register drug dependent people strengthens the surveillance capacity of the police over this group. Connecting the register to resident identity cards enables police to keep track of the movements of drug users and drug dependent people and to carry out random drug tests.

After passage of this law, many detainees in RETL camps were transferred to CQDR centres. In some areas where specialist RETL camps for drug dependent people had been established, this merely required changing the name on the front gate of the detention centre. In other areas, where drug dependent detainees were admixed with people detained for other reasons, physical transfer of people was required. As a result of this law the number of people in RETL dropped dramatically.

By the end of 2013, when abolition of RETL was formally implemented, the people remaining in RETL in most provinces had shrunk to very small numbers. When the doors of the remaining RETL camps were opened, there were not floods of people left to be released. So the immediate, physical impact of abolishing RETL on social order had been minimised by reducing the number of people detained in RETL over the previous years.

But the discussion above of the ways the population of RETL camps was reduced does not mean that impact of abolition of RETL on the policing of social order was negligible. RETL for many years had provided a convenient way for police to respond flexibly to social order problems as they developed and were identified. By removing this power, a degree of flexibility was also removed. The section below discusses the remaining institutional structure for punishment of offences and emergence of other, including illegal, forms of detention to deal with some problems, such as repeat petitioning, that were a thorn in the side of local governments.

Policy or social changes removing the need to punish or capacity to punish in other ways

Abolition of RETL does not suggest that there has been a decision no longer to punish the conduct that was previously targeted for punishment under that power. This section broadens the focus of inquiry to examine the system of punishments more generally and the available alternative powers that might be brought to bear on conduct originally punished under RETL. It discusses recent reforms, primarily to the criminal law, to include certain types of conduct that had previously been punished by way of RETL.

First it is necessary to locate RETL in the overall punishments regime. Conceptually, RETL was seen as occupying an intermediate space between the criminal justice system and the administrative punishments system enacted by the *Security Administrative Punishments Law (Zhi'an Guanli Chufa Fa)* 2006 (as amended in 2012) (SAPL). However, such a conception is not universally accepted. Some scholars have argued that there is no gap in the system of punishments. They argue that a system of punishments comprising administrative punishments under the SAPL and criminal punishments under the *Criminal Law* 1979 (as amended) already covered the whole range of offending conduct that should be punished and so the system of regulation of punishments was already gap free. So, after its abolition, punishment of conduct originally the target of RETL could, according to this argument, to an extent be disaggregated and diverted into either the criminal justice system (for more serious offences) or the administrative punishments system (for less serious offences). In fact, this was one of the influential proposals for reform of RETL; to deal with some of the more minor offending through existing administrative sanctions regime and the more serious offending through the criminal justice system (Jiang and Yuan 1990; Liu 2010; Zhang 2009).

This question of the structure of the punishment system was not resolved by abolition of RETL and there continues to be discussion about whether this intermediate space exists, and if so whether it needs to be filled and with what. One suggestion is that it should be filled by the 'security punishment' (*bao'an chufen*), a type of preventative detention used against repeat minor offenders or others considered to pose a risk to society (Liu 2013). Another is the creation of a category of 'minor crime' or even the passing of the draft *Law on the Correction of Misdemeanours* that had originally been intended to reform (but maybe now could replace) RETL (Wang et al. 2014, 140). Yet another is to adjust the administrative and criminal punishment systems to catch those forms of conduct not currently targeted, effectively to fill the gap left by abolition of RETL (Liu 2013; Song 2015; 113–4; Zou 2014).

For conduct to be punished under alternative administrative or criminal punishment systems without the need to change the law, conduct previously punished by RETL should also at the same time have been punishable under other powers. As the discussion below shows, there is a degree of overlap (but not a complete overlap) between the scope of conduct punishable under RETL and conduct punishable by other criminal and administrative punishments. Over time, the scope of people and conduct that fell within the purview of RETL expanded as the forms of socially disruptive and unacceptable behaviour changed. This flexibility in terms of scope of the power was one of the factors that made RETL convenient for law enforcement officials and an anathema to basic rule of law principles. It also ensured that for some types of proscribed conduct, police had discretion to impose one of a range of punishments of differing degrees of severity. Recent changes in the criminal law, discussed below, have lowered the threshold for certain offences that were previously targeted by RETL and increased the degree to which RETL and the criminal law overlap.

At the outset RETL was primarily designed to target people who were politically unreliable. The *Directive on Thorough Elimination of Hidden Counter-Revolutionaries* (*Guanyu Chedi Suqing Ancang Fangeming Fenzi De Zhishi*) issued by the Chinese Communist Party (CCP) Central Committee on 25 August 1955 provided that 'for those people who cannot be convicted of a criminal offence and politically who cannot continue to be used, where returning them to society would increase unemployment, in principle they can be sent to re-education through labour.' Almost immediately the process of expansion of the scope of RETL began. The *Resolution on the Decision of the State Council on the Question of Re-Education Through Labour* (*Guowuyuan Guanyu Laodong Jiaoyang Wenti De Jueding*) approved in 1957 by the NPC Standing Committee, the NPC Standing Committee *Supplementary Regulations of the State Council on Re-Education Through Labour* (*Quanguo Renmin Daibiao Dahui Changwu Weiyuanhui, Guowu Yuan Guanyu Laodong Jiaoyang De Buchong Guiding*) 29 November 1979 and the Ministry of Public Security *Temporary Regulations on Re-Education Through Labour* (*Laodong Jiaoyang Shixing Banfa*) which were issued by the State Council on 21 January 1982, each progressively expanded the scope of targets to cover social order infringements, vice, petty crime and conduct deemed to be anti-socialist.

This process of incremental expansion of the scope of RETL continued after introduction of the open door and economic reform policy to cover newly emerging forms of socially disruptive, unlawful or otherwise proscribed conduct. On 1 June 2002 the Ministry of Public Security issued the *Regulations on Public Security Organs Handling Re-Education Through Labour Cases* to consolidate and further expand the scope of RETL. Through the years, the State Council, central level ministries and commissions and local governments issued a plethora of regulatory instruments that both fragmented the legal basis of RETL and expanded the scope of targets on an ad hoc basis.

Under the 2002 regulations, targeted conduct could now conceptually be seen as lying somewhere between administrative infringements punished under the *Security Administrative Punishments Law* 2006 and offending punished under the *Criminal Law* 1979 (as amended). It could be characterised as either conduct constituting a public order administrative infringement but which was carried out repeatedly or was particularly serious, or criminal offending that was too minor to be prosecuted or where a decision had been made not to continue a criminal prosecution (Xie 2013, 110–14). The former included repeated minor troublemaking and sex workers and their clients who had been punished repeatedly. The latter included 'picking quarrels and causing trouble' and petty theft. Conduct of those that could be understood to fall generally within the purview of dissent such as democracy and rights activists, members of banned religious groups such as Falungong, and repeat petitioners could be pushed into either category.

Alternative administrative powers

RETL was seen as targeting offending that was more serious than that which warranted imposition of administrative punishments under the *Security Administrative Punishments Law* 2006. Nevertheless, the SAPL does target a wide range of conduct that constitutes a minor public order infringement. It authorises the police to impose administrative punishments of warning, fine, administrative detention, or revocation of licenses issued by public security organs (Article 10). The SAPL also allows for confiscation of contraband in accordance with relevant laws (Article 11) and adoption of protective temporary detention measures for people who are intoxicated (Article 15). The maximum accumulated period of administrative detention cannot exceed twenty days (Article 16).

A range of other powers exists that empowers police to investigate and detain people disturbing public order. For example, police can also exercise powers to detain a person for questioning (*liuzhi panwen*) for a maximum period of 48 hours under the *People's Police Law* (*Renmin Jingcha Fa*) 1995, or forcibly remove a person from a scene if they pose a threat to public order or security (Article 8). The *Administrative Compulsion Law* 2011 Article 9(1) authorises police to take a number of compulsory measures for temporary restriction of personal liberty to protect order and public health, and for example compulsory testing and treatment for sexually transmitted infections.

'*Big RETL*'

In addition, there remain a number of administrative powers for detention of minor offenders that are regulated in ways similar to RETL. These powers have been referred to as RETL-type powers (*lei laodong jiaoyang*) or 'Big RETL' (*da laojiao*) – a term used by Liu Renwen (see, for example, Liu 2014, 13). As they are in fact punitive powers that involve deprivation of personal liberty for extended periods, there is increasingly a view that it is inappropriate for these powers to remain unreformed. A number of powers, discussed below, fall within this envelope.

Sex workers and their clients were one group previously detained under RETL. In the run-up to its abolition, in some places such as Chongqing, a decision was made that it was not appropriate to punish sex workers with RETL. However, abolition of RETL does not exempt sex workers and their clients from punishment as alternative administrative powers to detain and punish them already exist. The SAPL 2006 Article 66 empowers police to impose a fine of up to RMB 5,000 and/or up to fifteen days administrative detention. Transgressions may also be punished by imposition by the police of a period of administrative detention for education (*shourong jiaoyu*) of between six months and two years in camps run by the police.

While detention for education is authorised by the NPC Standing Committee *Decision on Strictly Prohibiting Prostitution and Using Prostitutes* (*Guanyu Yanjin Maiyin Piaochang De Jueding*) 1991, it does so in particularly formalistic terms that are arguably inconsistent with at least the spirit if not the text of the *Legislation Law* 2000. Paragraph 4.2 of the 1991 Decision authorises detention for education in the following terms:

> Those who prostitute or use prostitutes may be coercively gathered up by the public security organs in conjunction with other relevant departments to carry out legal and moral education and to engage in productive labour to give up this evil habit. The time limit [for detention] is between six months and two years. The State Council will pass specific measures [for implementation].

In 1993, the State Council passed the *Measures for Detention for Education of Prostitutes and Clients of Prostitutes* (*Maiyin Piaochang Renyuan Shourong Jiaoyu Banfa*) providing only slightly more regulatory detail. These Measures were revised in 2011 and stipulate that detention for education may be approved by the public security bureau at county level or above (Article 8). These Measures describe detention for education as an 'administrative compulsory education measure to gather up prostitutes and their clients to carry out legal and moral education, organise them to participate in productive work and to carry out testing and treatment for sexually transmitted infections' (Article 2). The 2011 Measures at Article 7 provide that apart from punishment under SAPL Article 66, sex workers and their clients whose conduct is insufficient to warrant RETL may be punished with detention for education. It exempts sex workers under fourteen years old, those who are pregnant or nursing a child under one year old, those with a serious infectious disease that is not a sexually transmitted infection and people who have been kidnapped and sold into prostitution. The almost entire lack of legal definition of the targets of this form of 'compulsory education measure' allows the police very broad discretion as to the penalty they might impose. Preferred policing practice has been to impose fines rather than detention unless a concerted crack-down has been ordered (Biddulph 2007, 175). A recent illustration (beginning in February 2014) of such a crack-down has been waged in Dongguan (Wong 6 March 2014). In May 2014, high profile actor Huang Haibo was detained for six months; this suggests that the use of this form of punishment is not in abeyance.

Another in the category of 'Big RETL' is the power to impose a period of administrative detention on minors who have committed offences that are not punishable as criminal offences under the power of detention for re-education (*shourong jiaoyang*). The *Criminal Law* 1979 (as amended) (Article 17(4)) stipulates that where a person cannot be criminally punished because they are not yet sixteen years old, the family may be ordered to subject them to discipline or where necessary they may be given detention for education. This provision is repeated in Article 39 of the PRC *Law on the Protection of Minors (Weichengnian Ren Baohu Fa)* 2006. The period of detention is between one and three years and may be approved by the county level public security bureau (Ministry of Public Security 1982, *Notice on the Scope of Juvenile Offenders to be Taken in and Detained in Juvenile Correctional Facilities (Gong'an Bu Guanyu Shaonianfan Guanjiaosuo Shouyang, Shourong Fanwei De Tongzhi)*. The scope of detainees is given more detailed description in the *Notice on Issues of Detention for Education of Juvenile Offenders under 14 years old* (*Guanyu Dui Buman Shesi Sui de Shaonian Fanzui Renyuan Shourrong Jiaoyang Wenti De Tongzhi*) issued by the Ministry of Public Security in 1993 (Sun 2013, 37). It authorises the use of detention for education for juveniles under fourteen years old who have committed a serious crime (for example, murder, armed robbery, or causing explosions) but who are too young to be subject to criminal sanction. In practice, detention for education is primarily imposed on offenders between fourteen and sixteen years old (Sun 2013, 37). This power suffers from the same legal shortcomings as RETL did – that is, there is no proper legal basis for the power, decision-making is in the hands of the police and there are no proper procedural safeguards or oversight mechanisms in place. The detention facilities in which detention for education may be served vary from place to place and may include juvenile prison, work study schools (*gongdu xuexiao*) and, before its abolition, RETL (Zhang 2014, 285).

Other administrative powers exist which on the face of it are directed towards well-defined conduct and situations. However, in practice they provide a degree of flexibility to local authorities who may have incentives to detain people illegally for reasons not related to the targeted conduct, particularly where the procedures for applying the power are ill-defined and mechanisms for oversight and accountability weak or non-existent. These include detention and interrogation of Party officials suspected of corruption (*shuanggui*) (Liu 12 May 2014) and the power of involuntary commitment in psychiatric hospitals. Whether recent legal reforms under the *Mental Health Law* (*Jingshen Weisheng Fa*) 2012 to strengthen protections for involuntary commitment will be sufficient to curb abusive practices by local agencies remains to be seen (Munro 2000; LaFraniere and Levin 11 November 2010).

Shuanggui is not officially a legally sanctioned criminal investigation power, but instead is exercised by the Party Discipline Inspection Committee to detain Party officials for interrogation who are suspected of breaching Party discipline (that is, suspected of corruption) (Sapio 2008). This power has been used extensively to investigate official corruption and often these cases are transferred into the criminal justice system where a decision has been made to prosecute and sufficient evidence has been obtained.

Criminal justice reforms

At the more serious end of the punishment spectrum a number of changes have been made in criminal law, procedure and practice that, taken together, have made it more feasible to deal with some categories of minor criminal offences through the criminal justice system. These reforms to the Chinese criminal justice system began prior to abolition of RETL. They include expanding the scope of matters that fall within the definition of crime, expanding the scope of matters that may be dealt with by summary procedure and instituting non-custodial sentences for minor crimes.

Expanding the scope of some crimes

Prior to abolition of RETL a number of changes were made in the 8th amendment to the *Criminal Law*, passed in 2011, to lower the threshold for conviction of a number of minor criminal offences. Of these, a number correspond to categories of people targeted for RETL. A (non-exhaustive) list includes:

- Article 133 on traffic offences to include the offence of driving while exceeding the limit of alcohol and dangerous car racing;
- Article 141 to lower the threshold for punishments for producing or selling fake medicines by removing the requirement that the fake medicine seriously endangers health;
- Article 143 to increase the scope of liability for breaching food safety standards or adding non-food or hazardous materials to foodstuffs;
- Article 205 to expand the scope of the crime of falsely issuing invoices;
- Article 210 to increase the scope of offences for stealing invoices to include carrying or using counterfeit invoices;
- Article 226 to expand the categories of the offence of forcing or intimidating someone to engage in sex work or to provide or accept a service, to include voting, participate or withdraw from an auction, transfer or acquire shares in a company or enterprise or other property, to engage in or refrain from engaging in designated production activities;
- Article 264 to increase the scope of theft to include pickpocketing, committing thefts many times or committing burglary;
- Article 274 to increase the scope of the crime of extortion of public or private property to include committing the offence many times; and
- Article 293 to increase the scope of the crime of picking quarrels and causing trouble to include assembling other people many times to pick quarrels or cause trouble.

The reforms to expand the scope of Article 293 add further flexibility to an offence that has been labelled a 'pocket' offence, so-called because its vague definition enables a wide range of conduct to be stuffed in (Zhang 4 February 2015). The pocket offences that have been attracting significant attention since the abolition of RETL include 'picking quarrels and causing trouble' (*xunxin zishi zui*) (Article 293) and 'gathering a crowd to disturb social order' (*juzhong raoluan shehui zhixu zui*) (Article 290). Human rights NGOs have noted the dramatic upswing in conviction of rights lawyers, civil society activists and other people engaged in conduct construed as opposing the state under these offences (Dui Hua 22 January 2014). Lowering the threshold for these crimes does not completely cover the scope of minor crimes previously punished under RETL, but does go some way in that respect. Of course, pursuing a criminal prosecution is not as institutionally convenient as imposing RETL was, because of the involvement of a number of agencies; police, procuratorate and courts. Each have their own powers and institutional interests. For a criminal prosecution the police must obtain sufficient evidence for the procuratorate to decide to accept the file, approve an arrest and initiate a prosecution. For political cases where there is insufficient evidence or the conduct does not readily fall within one of the categories of crime set out in the law there must be coordination between the courts, procuratorate and police to secure a conviction, which requires political will and coordination work to be carried out among the different agencies.

Expanding non-custodial punishments

Much attention has been given to the criminal punishment of community correction, which provides a mechanism for non-custodial punishment of offenders guilty of minor crimes. While community correction cannot act as a complete substitute for RETL, because it is applied when a person has been convicted of a criminal offence, its inclusion in the 2011 revisions to the *Criminal Law* expands the array of punishments that may be imposed in respect of minor crimes. Community corrections was linked to the post-RETL punishments regime in the *Decision on Major Issues on Comprehensively Deepening Reform* (*Zhonggong Zhongyang Guanyu Quanmian Shenhuo Gaige Ruogan Zhongda Wenti De Jueding*) approved by the 3rd Plenary session of the 18th CCP Central Committee on 12 November 2013 in the following terms: 'repeal the system of RETL, perfect the laws for punishment and correction of unlawful conduct and criminal offences, perfect the system of community corrections' (Section IX point 34).

The number of people given this form of punishment has increased dramatically. In November 2014, the Deputy Minister of Justice, Zhang Sujun, was reported to state that since the beginning of trials in selected locations from 2003, there had been a total of 2,113,000 people punished under the system of community corrections (Chinanews 5 November 2014).

Community correction may be imposed in a range of different circumstances. Under the *Criminal* Law 1979 (as amended) a person may be sentenced to community corrections and ordered to serve their sentence out of custody when an offender has been sentenced to the criminal punishment of control (Article 38), given a suspended sentence (Article 76) or granted parole (Article 85). An order to serve a sentence out of prison under community correction must be issued by a court with inputs from the procuratorial office in each of China's more than 680 prisons and according to the procedures specified in the 2014 revisions to the *Provisions on Working Procedures in Prisons for Proposing Commutation and Parole* (*Jianyu Tiqing Jianxing Jiashi Gongzuo Chengxu Guiding*) (Chinanews 5 November 2014).

Criminal procedure reforms

The 2012 reforms to the *Criminal Procedure Law* have expanded the jurisdiction to try matters with a single judge using summary procedure to basic level courts (Article 208). Summary procedure may be used in cases where the facts are clear and the evidence sufficient, the defendant confesses to the crime and raises no objection to the charges, and the defendant does not object to summary procedure (Article 208). Such reforms enable expeditious processing of criminal trials where the main facts are not in contention, or at least where the defendant does not raise any objections to the evidence and the charges. Summary procedure is not confined to and does not perfectly correspond to the prosecution and trial of minor crime. However, expansion to basic level courts makes its use attractive in trials of minor offences where evidence is clear and uncontested. Initial research suggests that the number of offences tried using summary procedure has expanded dramatically (Fang 2014). It is beyond the scope of this chapter to address any questions that might arise about the impact this dramatic expansion of summary procedure might have on the administration of justice and protection of the procedural rights of defendants. It is enough to note here that this reform enables courts to deal with straightforward matters quickly and would go some way to addressing concerns that diversion of people originally dealt with by RETL into the criminal justice system would increase caseloads to the extent that it would overwhelm the capacity of courts to deal with minor crime.

Areas of flexibility in the criminal justice system

The criminal law and procedure also contain a number of areas of flexibility that enable creative use of existing powers to punish certain categories of conduct not obviously amenable to criminal conviction. The first is the criminal coercive power of detention which enables the police to detain for interrogation a major criminal suspect (*Criminal Procedure Law* 1979 (as amended) Article 80). The police may detain the person for three days before applying for an arrest or releasing the person. Police may apply for an extension of between one to four days in 'special circumstances'. If the person is suspected of committing crimes in different places or of involvement in a gang, detention for thirty days can be authorised. The procuratorate must determine whether to approve an arrest within seven days (*Criminal Procedure Law* 1979 (as amended) Article 89). The police thus have a number of days before their decision to detain is subject to scrutiny by the procuratorate. Such a device, however, is not as flexible as the administrative powers that have been abolished. If an application for arrest is made, it may not be in the institutional interests of the procuratorate to cooperate by approving an application for arrest where the circumstances and evidence are manifestly inadequate to support an arrest.

Conduct no longer punished and unintended consequences

In the year leading up to the abolition of RETL, some local changes suggested that certain categories of conduct previously labelled troublemaking behaviour would no longer be punished. In both Yunnan and Guangdong, for example, three categories of people were publicly excluded from the scope of RETL. They were people suspected of minor conduct threatening national security, repeat and nuisance petitioners, and people criticising government and Party leaders (Nandu.com 25 January 2013; *Southern Metropolis Daily* 25 January 2013; *Yunnan Information Daily* 7 February 2013; Zhou et al. 16 July 2013). However, the uproar over the discovery and subsequent closure of an illegal 'Education and Reprimand Centre' (*xunjie zhongxin*) in Luoyang city (Henan) in 2014 raises the prospect that incentives still exist for local governments to deal coercively with nuisance and repeat petitioners. The existence at local levels of this and other forms of illegal compulsory and punitive detention including 'legal education bases' (*fazhi jiaoyu jidi*) (Liu 12 May 2014), may be an unintended and unwelcome consequence of abolishing RETL without also removing the perceived need to punish certain groups.

Implications

What then are the implications of this reform? In addition to hoped-for improvements in rights protection under China's version of the rule of law, there are a number of institutional consequences.

Abolition of RETL has removed a power that the police have found to be a flexible and useful tool to address an array of emerging problems of disruptive conduct and dissent in the reform era. An arbitrary and abusive power has been abolished. While alternative powers exist to punish much conduct targeted for RETL, institutional discretion has been restricted. In the area of minor crime, for example, police must still provide a brief of evidence to the procuratorate that is sufficient to meet standards for arrest and prosecution. Under RETL, the police did not have to convince another agency that punishment was required. In some areas, such as repeat petitioning and other forms of conduct perceived to oppose the Party–state, categories of crime must be strained to cover such conduct. If that cannot be done, the consequence is that the person should not be punished. In this area, where local governments retain incentives to suppress or punish such conduct, the temptation to establish ad hoc and illegal forms of detention and punishment has already proven to be strong. The problem with illegal forms of detention is that they are precisely that, illegal, and so not subject to any legal or practical constraints.

With the expansion of community corrections as a form of non-custodial punishment for minor crime, there has been a transfer of responsibilities and burden of resources and costs onto the local government and local justice agencies. Not only does the local government shoulder the responsibility of community corrections, but the creation of compulsory community-based drug treatment orders in the *Drug Prohibition Law* 2008 also imposes a substantial burden on local authorities. The shortfall in local government budgets to perform their ever-increasing scope of responsibilities casts a shadow of doubt over the extent to which they are willing or able to allocate needed resources into administering these community-based orders.

Debates about RETL before its abolition raised broader issues about the values that should be reflected in China's punishments regimes and in governance more generally. Questions of how ideals of justice and the protection of human rights should be instantiated were extensively debated in the lead up to abolition of RETL. Some academics argued that reforms should be guided by a rights-centred interpretation of China's international obligations under the *International Covenant on Civil and Political Rights* 1976. Such a reading would place the protection of personal liberty at the heart of these human rights protections. Thus, it was argued that a broad interpretation should be taken of principles such as proportionality and procedural justice (Wu 2008, 61–2).

In the end, RETL was abolished without any definitive engagement with these broader arguments about justice and human rights, or with the conceptual structure of the punishments system. The broader impact on the conceptual structure and values of the system of punishments remains to be worked through. In just the same way, detention for repatriation was abolished without explicitly addressing the issues of the power of the NPC Standing Committee to review the constitutionality of powers that had been raised by the academic petition letters (Hand 2006, 149). Detention for investigation was not so much abolished as incorporated into the criminal justice system by inclusion into the *Criminal Procedure Law* 1996 of the elements of flexibility demanded by the police when interrogating those categories of criminal suspects formerly targeted by detention for investigation. The pattern that emerges is one of incremental reforms to abolish or reform those areas of worst abuse. It is not surprising that the Party–state has chosen not to take these opportunities to articulate broad principles of rights and justice against which the whole sanctioning system can be judged. Rather it has retained the flexibility of dealing with problems in the composition of coercive powers on a case by case basis.

Finally, the question arises about the fate of the other administrative powers that fall into the category of 'Big RETL'. In particular, questions have been raised about the fate of detention for education of sex workers. I would suggest that the same three factors, discussed above in relation to RETL, could usefully be applied to this question. That is, is there popular and international criticism of the power such that it can be abolished in a way that is politically advantageous, or at least not disadvantageous? Can the power be abolished in a way that does not have a significant impact on public order? And finally, is there an alternative available form of punishment, or has there been a decision that this form of punishment no longer needs to be applied to that conduct?

The prominent media coverage of the detention of the actor Huang Haibo in 2014, discussed above, suggests that there is increasing attention being paid to this form of detention, but this public awareness and concern starts from a very low base. However, similar to RETL, and despite the minimal legislative reference to this power in the NPC Standing Committee's *Decision on Strictly Prohibiting Prostitution and Using Prostitutes* 1991, I would argue that substantively this power suffers from the same problems of unconstitutionality and illegality as RETL. The political implications of abolition and the question of whether there has been a change of official views about the need to punish such conduct suffer from the persistently heavy moral overtones of sex work as a form of vice that is destructive of the social fabric. In the *Decision on Some Major Questions in Comprehensively Moving Forward Governing the Country According to Law* (*Guanyu Quanmian Tuijin Yifa Zhiguo Ruogan Zhongda Wenti De Jueding*), adopted on 23 October 2014, the CCP Central Committee emphasised the need to strengthen citizens' morality and the role of the Party and rule of law in this task. It may be that the arguments based on illegality outweigh these moral overtones. In saying this, the Party-state is fettered in its decision-making by the official and popular view, not unique to China, that legalising conduct is a signal that the conduct is socially and politically acceptable. Sex work and soliciting sex are unlawful and also punishable under the SAPL, but abolition of the alternative detention power would signal that this conduct is viewed as a minor infringement. It remains to be seen whether the Party-state is ready to send this signal.

Notes

1 This research was supported by ARC grants FT130100412 and DP 0988179.
2 In other places this power has been translated as 'shelter and investigation'. The term *shourong* literally means 'to receive' or 'take in' or 'gather up'. I remain unwilling to translate *shourong* as 'shelter' as in substance what happens is that a person is taken into a form of detention and not given 'shelter'. To ensure consistency in translation I have translated all other detention powers that include the term *shourong* in their name as detention.
3 The article is also translated in the *Dui Hua Human Rights Journal* at http://www.duihuahrjournal. org/search/label/reeducation%20through%20labor

References

Amnesty International. 1991. *China: Punishment Without Crime*. London and New York: Amnesty International Publications.
Amnesty International. 2006. 'Abolishing "Re-education Through Labour" and Other Forms of Punitive Administrative Detention: An Opportunity to Bring the Law into Line with the International Covenant on Civil and Political Rights.' Available at https://www.amnesty.org/en/documents/ASA17/016/2006/en/ (accessed 16 February 2016).

Amnesty International. 17 December 2013. 'China: "Changing the Soup but Not the Medicine?": Abolishing Re-Education Through Labour in China.' Index number: ASA 17/042/2013. Available at https://www.amnesty.org/en/documents/ASA17/042/2013/en/ (accessed 16 February 2016).

Biddulph, Sarah. 2007. *Legal Reform and Administrative Detention Powers in China*. Cambridge, UK: Cambridge University Press.

Biddulph, Sarah. 2015. *The Stability Imperative: Human Rights and Law in China*. Vancouver: UBC Press.

Biddulph, Sarah and Xie Chuanyu. 2011. 'Regulating Drug Dependency in China: The 2008 PRC Drug Rehabilitation Law.' *The British Journal of Criminology* 51(6): 978–96.

Chinanews. 5 November 2014. 'Sifabu Fubuzhang: Shequ Jiaozheng Fa Cao'an Songshengao Zheng Wanshan (Deputy Minister of Justice: The Draft Community Corrections Law for Examination Has Been Completed).' Chinanews.com.

Chu Huaizhi. 2009. 'Cong Guoqing Chufa Sikao Laodong Jiaoyang Shedu Gaishan (Reflections on the Reform of the System Re-Education Through Labour from the Perspective of China's National Conditions).' *Zhongguo Sifa* (Justice of China) 3: 49–50.

Committee on Economic Social and Cultural Rights. 23 May 2014. 'Concluding Observations on the Second Periodic Report of China, Including Hong Kong, China and Macao, China.' E/C.12/CHN/CO/2.

Cui Ming. 1993. 'Shourong Shencha De Lishi, Xianzhuang Yu Chulu (The History, Present Situation and Prospects of Detention for Investigation).' In *China's Contemporary Crime and Law*, edited by Ming Cui, 90–8. Beijing: Qunzhong chubanshe.

Cui Qingxin and Liu Yizhan. 7 January 2013. 'Zhongguo Jiang Tuijin Laojiao, Huji Deng Zhidu Gaishan (China Will Promote Reform of Re-Education Through Labour, Household Registration Etc Systems).' Xinhua net.

Cui Xin. 1996. 'Xingshi Susong Fa Xiugai Hou Gong'an Gongzuo Mianling De Xingshi Ji Renwu (The Situation and Tasks of Public Security Work after Revision of the Criminal Procedure Law).' *Gong'an Xuekan* (Public Security Studies) 3: 36–8.

Deng Xiaoping. 1980. 'The Present Situation and the Tasks Before Us.' In *Selected Works of Deng Xiaoping (1975–1982)*, edited by Lenin Bureau for the Compilation and Translation of Works of Marx, Engels and Stalin under the Central Committee of the Communist Party of China, 224–58. Beijing: Foreign Languages Press.

Deng Xiaoping. 1993. 'Uphold the Four Cardinal Principles, 30 March 1979.' In *Selected Works of Deng Xiaoping (1975–1982)*, edited by Lenin Bureau for the Compilation and Translation of Works of Marx, Engels and Stalin under the Central Committee of the Communist Party of China, 166–91. Beijing: Foreign Languages Press.

Dui Hua. 22 January 2014. 'Criminal Detention as Punishment in the Post-RTL Era.' *Dui Hua Human Rights Journal*. Available at http://www.duihuahrjournal.org/2014/01/criminal-detention-as-punishment-in.html (accessed 16 February 2016).

Fan Chongyi and Xiao Shengxi eds. 1991. *Xingshi Susong Fa Yanjiu Zongshu Yu Pingjia* (Summary and Appraisal of Criminal Procedure Law Study). Beijing: Zhongguo zhengfa daxue chubanshe.

Fang Meng. 2014. 'Xin Xingsufa Shishi Hou Jianyi Chengxu Kaizhan Xianzhuang, Cunzai Wenti, Yuanyin Ji Wanshan Duice (Current Situation, Existing Problems, Causes and Perfection of Summary Procedure since the Implementation of New Criminal Procedure Law-A Case Study of Q County in Sichuan Province).' *Guizhou Jingguan Zhiye Xueyuan Xuebao* (Journal of Guizhou Police Officer Vocational College) 4: 35–40.

Feng Ruirui, Liu Yanhai and Dai Ying. 2008. 'Lun Feichu Laodong Jiaoyang Zhidu De Biyaoxing (Discussing the Necessity of Abolishing Re-education through Labour).' *Fazhi Yu Shehui* (Legal System and Society) 18: 246.

Gu Angran. 1996. 'Explanation of the Revision of the PRC Criminal Procedure Law.' Delivered at the 4th Plenary Session of the 8th NPC on 12 March 1996. In *Zhonghua Renmin Gongheguo Quanguo Renmin Daibiao Dahui Changwu Weiyuanhui Gonggao* (Gazette of the Standing Committee of the National People's Congress of the PRC), 85.

Hand, Keith. 2006. 'Using Law for a Righteous Purpose: The Sun Zhigang Incident and Evolving Forms of Citizen Action in the People's Republic of China.' *Columbia Journal of Transnational Law* 45: 114–95.

Hu Xingdou, Liu Renwen, Zhu Shunzhong and He Xiaopeng. 2007. 'Shiyue Tan: Laojiao Zhidu De Hefaxing Weiji (October Talks: The Crisis in Legitimacy of the System of Re-Education Through Labour.' *New Century Weekly* 31: 64–7.

Huang Jianshui and Zhou Fuyin. 2014. 'Laojiao Zhidu Feizhi Hou Ruogan Wenti De Falü Sikao (Some Legal Thoughts on Several Questions After Abolition of the System of Re-Education Through Labour).' *Henan Gongye Daxue Xuebao* (Journal of Henan University of Technology) 10(4): 29–32.

Human Rights in China. 1999. *Not Welcome at the Party: Behind the 'Clean-Up' of China's Cities-A Rreport on Administrative Detention under Custody and Repatriation*. New York: Human Rights in China.

Human Rights in China. 2001. *Re-Education Through Labour (RTL): A Summary of Regulatory Issues and Concerns*. Hong Kong: Human Rights in China.

Human Rights Watch. 2002. *Dangerous Meditation: China's Campaign Against Falungong*. New York, Washington, London, Brussels: Human Rights Watch.

Hung, Veron Meiying. 2003. 'Reassessing Re-Education Through Labour.' *China Rights Forum* 2: 35–41.

Jacobs, Andrew. 11 June 2013. 'Behind Cry for Help from China Labor Camp.' *New York Times*.

Jiang Qihan and Yuan Kaiying. 1990. 'Laodong Jiaoyang Wenti Shulue (Discussion of Problems of Re-Education through Labour).' *Gong'an Yanjiu* (Public Security Studies) 4: 46–8.

LaFraniere, Sharon and Levin, Dan. 11 November 2010. 'Assertive Chinese Held in Mental Wards.' *New York Times*.

Li Lan and Wu Huang. 2008. 'Dangqian Woguo Jizhong Jiedu Moshi Zhi Bijiao (A Comparison Between Current Different Models for Giving Up Drugs in China).' *Henan Sifa Jingguan Zhiye Xueyuan Xuebao* (Journal of the Henan Professional College of Judicial Police) 6(2): 81–3.

Liu Renwen. 2001. 'Shourong Qiansong Gongzuo Buyi Jixu Baoliu (It Is Not Appropriate to Preserve Detention for Repatriation).' *Falu Lunwen Ziliao Ku* (Repository of Legal Thesis Materials).

Liu Renwen. 2010. 'Zhi'an Juliu Yu Laodong Jiaoyang Naru Xingfa De Sikao (Consideration of Bringing Public Order Detention and Re-Education Through Labour into the Criminal Law).' *Zhongguo Jianchaguan Xueyuan Xuebao* (Journal of the China Procurators College) 18(1): 94–100.

Liu Renwen. 2013. 'Laojiao Zhidu De Gaige Fangxiang Yingwei Bao'an Chufen (The Direction of Reforms to the System of Re-Education Through Labour Should Be Security Punishments).' *Faxue* (Law Science) 2: 5–11.

Liu Renwen. 12 May 2014. 'Sheke Yuan Zhuanjia: Laojiao Huoyi Xunjie Zhongxin De Xingshi Fusheng (CASS Expert: Re-Education Through Labour or Its Reincarnation as Admonition Centres and the Like).' ifeng.com.

Liu Renwen. 2014. 'Bao'an Chufen Yu Zhongguo Xingzheng Jujin Zhidu De Gaige (Security Punishments and the Reform of China's Administrative Detention System).' *Fazhi Yanjiu* (Rule of Law Studies) 6: 13–20.

Mou Yuchuan. 21 October 2013. 'He Xuefeng: Feichu Laojiao Zhidu, Tian Ye Bu Hui Ta Xialai (He Xuefeng: The Day Re-Education Through Labour Is Abolished the Sky Will Not Fall).' *Forum: Jimen Juece*.

Munro, Robin. 2000. 'Judicial Psychiatry in China and Its Political Abuses.' *Columbia Journal of Asian Law* 14: 1–125.

Nandu.com. 25 January 2013. 'Piping Shi Tuidong Guojia He Shehui Jinbu Zhennengliang (Criticism Is a Resource for State and Social Progress).' *Nanfang Dushi Bao* (Southern Metropolis Daily).

Sapio, Flora. 2008. 'Shuanggui and Extra-legal Detention in China.' *China Information* 22: 7–37.

Song Ying. 2015. 'Hou Laojiao Shidai Shourong Jiaoyu De Xingszhi Ji Yu Xingfa Xianjie Wenti Tanjiu (An Exploration of Problems of the Nature and Convergence with Criminal Punishment of Detention for Education after Abolition of Re-Education Through Labour).' *Xibu Faxue Pinglun* (Western Region Law Review) 1: 112–21.

Southern Metropolis Daily. 25 January 2013. 'Criticism Is a Positive Force for Promoting the Progress of the Nation and Society.' *Dui Hua Foundation*. Available at http://www.duihuahrjournal.org/search/label/reeducation%20through%20labor (accessed 16 February 2016).

Sun Hongri. 2013. 'Wei Chengnian Ren Shourong Jiaoyang Zhidu Ruogan Falü Wenti Yanjiu (A Study of Several Legal Issues on the System of Detention for Education of Juveniles).' *Fazhi Yu Shehui* (Legal System and Society) 8: 37–9.

Trevaskes, Susan. 2013. 'Rationalizing Stability Maintenance Through Mao's Not So Invisible Hand.' *Journal of Current Chinese Affairs* 42(2): 51–77.

Wang Faqiang. 1997. 'Tan Laodong Jiaoyang Zhidu De Cunfei (Discussing Preservation or Abolition of Re-Education Through Labour).' *Faxue Zazhi* (Juridical Science Journal) 4: 32.

Wang Jiancheng. 2000. 'Qiangzhi Cuoshi (Coercive Measures).' In *Xingshi Susongfa Shishe Wenti Yanjiu* (Research on the Issues in Implementation of the Criminal Procedure Law), edited by Guangzhong Chen, 78–99. Beijing: China Law Press.

Wang Kexian. 2002. 'Shourong Qiansong Zhidu Yingyu Feizhi (The System of Detention for Repatriation Should Be Abolished).' *Guangxi Zhengfa Guanli Ganbu Xueyuan Bao* (Journal of Guangxi Administrative Cadre Institute of Politics and Law) (June): 72–3.

Wang Yufang, Fu Shanshan and Du Bing-hua. 2014. 'Laojiao Shi Yu Leixing Yanjiu – Jiyu Laojiao Anjian De Shizheng Fenxi (Study of the Types of Re-Education Through Labour Cases – An Empirical Analysis of Cases).' *Huadong Jiaotong Daxue Xuebao* (Journal of East China Jiaotong University) 15(4): 134–41.

Wong, Edward. 6 March 2014. 'Red Lights Dim in China's Sin City.' *New York Times*.

Wu Baohong. 2008. 'Guanyu Laodong Jiaoyang Zhidu De Falü Sikao (Legal Consideration of Re-Education Through Labour System).' *Tongling Xueyuan Xuebao* (Journal of Tongling College) 6: 59–62.

Xie Chuanyu. 2000. *Zhi'an Xingzheng Cuoshi Tonglun (General Discussion of Public Security Administrative Measures)*. Beijing: Zhongguo gong'an daxue chubanshe.

Xie Chuanyu. 2013. *Weihai Shehui Xingwei De Zhicai Tixi Yanjiu (On the Sanction System of Offences)*. Beijing: Falü chubanshe.

Xinhua Net. 10 August 2012. 'Mother of Underage Rape Victim Released from Chinese Labor Camp.' Available at http://news.xinhuanet.com/english/china/2012-08/10/c_131775435.htm (accessed 16 February 2016).

Yunnan Information Daily. 7 February 2013. 'Yunnan Zanting San Zhong Xingwei Laojiao Shenpi Chouhua Lingdao Ren Xingxiang Bu Zai Laojiao (Yunnan Suspends Examination and Approval on Three Types of Conduct, Vilifying the Image of Leaders Will No Longer Be Given Re-Education Through Labour).' *Renmin Wang*.

Zhang Chuanwei. 2009. 'Cong Ganga, Dianfu Zouxiang Xinsheng: Laodong Jiaoyang Gaizao Wei Shequ Jiaozheng Zhi Fenxi (From Embarrassment and Subversion to Rebirth: An Analysis of the Reform of Re-Education Through Labour to Community Corrections.' *Beijing Xingzheng Xueyuan Xuebao* (Journal of Beijing Administrative College) 1: 80–5.

Zhang Hao. 2014. 'Lun Woguo Shourong Jiaoyang Zhidu Cunzai De Wenti Ji Qi Wanshan (Discussing Existing Problems with My Country's System of Detention for Re-education and Its Reform).' *Jingying Guanlizhe* (Managers Journal) 4: 285–6.

Zhang Jianwei and Li Zhongcheng. 1994.'Lun Feichu Shourong Shencha (Discussing the Abolition of Detention for Investigation).' *Zhongwai Faxue* (Peking University Law Journal) 3: 55–9.

Zhang Qianfan. 4 February 2015. 'Yanshen Dao Wangluo Yanlun De 'Xunxin Zishi (Extending 'Picking Quarrels and Causing Trouble' to Internet Speech).' FT Chinese Web. Available at http://www.ftchinese.com/story/001060493?full=y (accessed 16 February 2016).

Zhang Xu. 1993. 'Lun Shoushen De Chulu Yu Daibu De Gaige (Discussing the Way Out for Detention for Investigation and Reform of Arrest).' *Xiandai Faxue* (Modern Legal Science) 2: 20.

Zhou Qingshu, Zhang Han and Song Shijing. 16 July 2013. 'Tang Hui: Liang Yifan Sixing Fuhe Jiu Bu Shangfang (Tang Hui: Will Not Petition Again After the Review of the Death Penalty on Two Suspects.' *Beijing News*.

Zou Yutong. 2014. 'Laodong Jiaoyang Zhidu Feizhi Dui Jiceng Gong'an Gongzuo De Yingxiang Ji Duice – Yi Hulunbei'er Diqu Wei Li (Effects on Local Level Public Security Work of the Abolition of Re-Education Through Labour and Counter-Measures – Using Hulunbeir as an Example).' *Shanxi Jingguan Gaodeng Zhuanke Xuexiao Xuebao* (Journal of Shanxi Police Academy) 22 (4): 34–8.

3 China's socialisation of administrative offenders in the community
An unrealistic agenda?

Enshen Li

Introduction

Administrative detention has long been an indispensable penal measure in China's justice and social control system. Created in the 1950s, it was originally designed to deal with individuals who commit minor deviant acts, such as prostitution, drug abuse and public order offences (Biddulph 2007). These are handled solely by the police through administrative procedures, and governed by administrative regulations. Separate from the formal criminal penal system, the administrative detention mechanism contains a variety of administrative coercive approaches that form a vertical framework in which different types of minor offenders are subject to different types of confinement.

Many human rights activists and organisations have been critical of China's use of administrative detention due to its shaky legal basis of depriving offenders' freedom as well as the blatant violation of detainees' human rights during incarceration (Amnesty International 31 August 1991; China Human Rights Strategy Group November 2001; Human Rights in China February 2001; Human Rights Watch 7 January 2010). The ways in which these custodial measures have been maladministered are diverse, including the arbitrary deprivation of offenders' liberty (Amnesty International 1 March 1996), the use of administrative detention to bypass the procedural requirements of the *Criminal Procedure Law* (*Xingshi Susong Fa*) 1979 (amended in 1996 and 2012) (Peerenboom 2004), and the denial of offenders' rights to seek redress from the courts (Dong 1997). In the meantime, how to legalise and rationalise administrative detention has elicited a broad range of reform proposals in legal academia. Most arguments call for an incorporation of administrative minor offences into the formal criminal justice system (Chu 2005; Zhang 2003). In doing so, it is said that defaulters who are subjected to administrative detention would have procedural protections set out under the *Criminal Procedure Law* 1979 (amended in 1996 and 2012), and the legal foundation for depriving citizens' liberties would be justified by such law (Peerenboom 2004). Other legal professionals contend that a specific law is needed to better formalise the implementation of administrative detention and legitimise deprivation of the individual's liberty (Zhang 2001). However, given the reality that the drafting of a law that specifically targets minor offenders, for example, the *Law on the Correction of Misdemeanours* (*Weifa Xingwei Jiaozhi Fa (Cao'An)*),[1] is cumbersome and time-consuming, some experts suggest the alternative idea that the administrative detention power could be transferred from the police to the judiciary to meet the requirements of impartiality and neutrality (Chu 3 June 1999).

In addition, scholars observe that administrative detention does not truly reform behaviour, nor does it reduce the high recidivism rates among administrative offenders (Li 2010). Rather, the incarceration of perpetrators alienates them from their society, community and family, thereby hampering the social forces that may help them address drug abuse or prostitution, or socially harmful behaviours. To a great extent, incarceration furthers the social and mental marginalisation of minor offenders, and hinders them from reintegrating into society (Li 2010).

In this context, the Chinese authorities have begun to re-assess the lawfulness and appropriateness of administrative detention and the effectiveness of this measure in rehabilitating offenders (Chen 2001; Li 2012). Since the 2000s, a number of policy changes have been made, showing that China has begun to rethink its far-reaching ideology and practice of administrative coercive penalty. For example, a new system of community drug treatment was enforced to primarily target drug addicts while coercive drug rehabilitation was reformed and downgraded as a last resort. More recently, the infamous system of re-education through labour (RETL) (*laodong jiaoyang*) was abolished, with community corrections being advocated to play a more vital role in China's justice system. These penal shifts reflect the state's new inclination to adopt a community-based penal system to handle minor offenders in lieu of punitive detention.

However, this altered tenet that underlines the rehabilitative ideal raises some immediate questions as to the practicality of accommodating administrative offenders into the community-based penal system. Given the uniqueness of the contemporary Chinese legal culture and social condition, is the Chinese community penalty a proper alternative to administrative detention? More specifically, are social resources and forces in the Chinese neighbourhood adequate to provide what administrative offenders need for their rehabilitation and remoulding? Is the full enforcement of community penalties contradictory with any legal or institutional mechanisms in force in contemporary China?

This chapter examines the legal, institutional and philosophical impediments the Chinese community penal system has to face in the process of replacing administrative detention. It argues that while China endeavours to prompt the socialisation of administrative offenders in the community, the legal deficiencies of community approaches create a general obstacle for this practice to be fully implemented in China. The difficulty of imposing community penalty on minor offenders also lies on the characteristic features of China's contemporary socio–economic landscape. In particular, institutional conflict with the *hukou* system, shortage of community resources and lack of social recognition shape the most disturbing factors that discourage this new instrument from functioning as a well-operated program centring on education and persuasion.

China's reform of administrative detention: a shift towards community penalty

The Chinese administrative detention system has developed alongside the Chinese criminal penal system since the founding of the People's Republic of China. Unlike criminal punishment, which targets criminality to serve the purpose of crime control, administrative detention targets offences that are not serious enough to warrant prosecution and criminal sanction. Depicted as a penal approach to tackle the 'non-antagonistic' contradiction, an internal conflict between the people (Biddulph 2004), administrative detention is theoretically employed to reform offenders as their corrupt conduct and mentality are deemed 'correctable' (Biddulph 2007; Shaw 1998). Over time, four coercive measures have become the major components of the Chinese administrative detention system: public order detention (POD) (*xingzheng juliu*), detention for education (DE) (*shourong jiaoyu*), coercive drug rehabilitation (CDR) (*qiangzhi jiedu*)[2] and RETL. While POD applies to those who commit public order offences with minimal harm to society, the three remaining compulsory measures are mainly imposed on prostitutes, drug users and those who commit serious administrative offences when public order penalties are too lenient and criminal punishments are too harsh. As the most severe form of administrative detention, RETL also targeted repeat offenders, ranging from habitual public nuisance offenders to recidivist prostitutes who have failed to comply with compulsory education or treatment in previous detention periods.

The extensive imposition of administrative detention has drawn massive criticism from the international human rights regime and legal scholars. The Western democratic states and highly publicised NGOs, such as Human Rights Watch, used strategies of shaming, accusation and stunning to describe administrative detention as contrary to fundamental human rights standards, and being punitive and arbitrary. They contended that this harsh system deprives offenders from their basic legal and human entitlements while in custody (Human Rights Watch 7 January 2010). In the meantime, the Chinese experts perceive administrative detention as a system that is at odds with the dogmas of legality and justice (Zou 2002). A number of substantial and procedural problems, such as lack of effective supervision (for example, unfettered exercise of police power), conflict with fundamental laws and limited legal recourse of offenders, were seen as the most flawed aspects of the implementation of administrative detention (Peerenboom 2004; Hung 2003).

Some questions have also been raised over the effectiveness of administrative detention as a means of reducing or eliminating offending behaviour. Although defined as a rehabilitative tool, administrative detention seldom serves a corrective and educative purpose.[3] Rather, it is literally employed as a 'second line of defence' (Biddulph 2007, 139) that focuses on punishment and control of offenders for maintaining social order with little regard to the correction of their socially disruptive conduct. Recidivism rates of administrative offences affirm the uselessness of administrative detention in preventing misconduct. For example, estimates based on statistical surveys from the 1990s place prostitute recidivism following release from DE or RETL at between 50 to 60 per cent nationwide (Gil et al. 1994).[4] A large number of prostitutes 'go straight back to the game once completing their compulsory education at reformatories' (Anderson and Gil 1998, 255). Likewise, one report on the recidivism of drug addicts revealed that an estimated 60 to 95 per cent of detoxed patients in China relapse within one year (Lu and Wang 2008).

Not surprisingly, a vigorous and longstanding debate has been evident in China's legal scholarship about how to reform the administrative detention system. In particular, with the principle of 'rule of law' becoming the leading philosophy of legal practice and the 'harmonious society' (*hexie shehui*) discourse becoming the priority policy of political agenda (Fan 2006), managing administrative offenders in a less harsh and more humanitarian fashion has become the consensus between the political elites and the legal apparatus. As such, China has begun to seek more effective and people-oriented methods to deal with minor offenders, especially those who are physically, psychologically and socially disadvantaged. Illustrative examples include the establishment of a community-based drug detoxification program and the elimination of RETL.

In 2008, the *Drug Prohibition Law* (*Jindu Fa*) came into effect to replace obsolete drug regulations. The highlight of this legislation is the introduction of a new detoxification system which underlines China's changed attitudes towards drug use and abusers. By re-defining drug users as not only administrative offenders but also as patients and victims who need medical and psychological assistances, the *Drug Prohibition Law* 2008 reveals a 'human-centred' rhetoric whereby reform is based 'on the mechanism of drug treatment and rehabilitation in accordance with the principle of humanity' (Office of China National Narcotics Control Commission 2008, Section IV). Accordingly, the old drug rehabilitation system that relied heavily on CDR was repealed. A brand new three-tiered scheme that focuses mainly on the psychological and social aspects of drug-dependence treatment has been established. The new system consists of three rehabilitation pathways, namely voluntary rehabilitation (*ziyuan jiedu*), community rehabilitation (*shequ jiedu*) and compulsory quarantine for drug rehabilitation (*qiangzhi jiedu*) (Biddulph and Xie 2011). Of these three measures, community rehabilitation is specified as the prioritised means to handle drug abusers.

China's ideological shift towards the rehabilitative handling of minor offenders is also exemplified by the most recent decisions to abolish RETL and reinforce the community corrections system. On the Third Plenum of the 18th Chinese Communist Party Congress held in November 2013, the government resolved among a raft of legal reforms to remove RETL (Zhai 28 December 2013). One month later, in December, the Standing Committee of the National People's Congress officially announced the elimination of this coercive measure. Meanwhile, the government proposed to strengthen the use of community corrections as a major penal form in future penal practice (Zhai 28 December 2013).

Introduced in 2003, China's community corrections operate as an independent intermediate penalty, aiming to target criminal offenders whose crimes are minor and cause minimal social harm, and those who have repented after incarceration and display no further intention to harm society (*Notice on Implementing Experimental Work of Community Corrections (Guanyu Kaizhan Sheque Jiaozheng Shidian Gongzuo De Tongzhi*) 2003, Section 2).[5] Although the authorities do not articulate that community corrections will become a substitute for RETL (*Xinjing Newspaper* 6 January 2014), the new policy implies that this correctionalist penal approach will play a role in the aftermath of the removal of RETL. In fact it points to a new direction for the broad-based reform of China's administrative detention system, downplaying the imposition of administrative coercive measures while upgrading community-based tools as the primary instrument to handle minor offenders.

Practical obstacles: is placing administrative offenders under the community penalty feasible?

China embarking on accommodating administrative offenders in the community does not rule out the critical question of whether community penalties can really be used as a regular measure to serve the purposes of correction and education. In particular, Chinese community penalty is still at the preliminary stage and its implementation varies considerably due to cultural, economic and social diversity in different locales across the country. To understand the difficulty of remoulding administrative offenders in Chinese communities, one needs to carefully look into the factors that impede this practice in an interdisciplinary perspective, spanning socio-legal and eco-cultural contexts.

Legal impediments to replacing administrative detention with community-based penalties

China's use of community corrections emerged in 2003 with the issuance of the *Notice on Implementing Experimental Work of Community Corrections*. Six prefectures were initially chosen to commence this pilot project, which was soon expanded on a national scale in the following years (Wang 2008). In 2004, the Ministry of Justice issued the *Provisional Measures of Judicial and Administrative Organs in Administering Community Correction Work* (*Sifa Xingzheng Jiguan Jiaozheng Gongzuo Zanxing Banfa*) to function as a temporary operational guide for community corrections. In 2012, the *Measures for the Implementation of Community Corrections* (*Shequ Jiaozheng Shishi Banfa*) was promulgated and systematically institutionalised across the country. The official rhetoric characterises community corrections as a non-custodial penal measure, and places emphasis on correcting minor offenders' criminal orientation and behavioural vices by means of ideological and labour reform (*The Notice on Implementing Experimental Work of Community Corrections* 2003, Preface).

In a similar way, community drug treatment was established in 2008 to help addicted individuals overcome drug addiction (Biddulph and Xie 2011). It seeks to target the high rate of recidivism that resulted from traditional anti-drug measures, by maximising addicts' social capital and community supports. China's community drug treatment consists of two independent but interconnected schemes: community rehabilitation and recovering health in the community (*shequ kangfu*). While the former is viewed as an official detoxification channel, the latter is utilised as a follow-up program of compulsory quarantine rehabilitation, facilitating the post-detoxification recovery of drug addicts in the community.

Community rehabilitation and recovering health in the community are conceptualised as community-based measures to socialise delinquents; the approaches are very similar in their legal prescriptions and practical implementations. First, the operation of these community-based programs is carried out by administrative bodies at the sub-district level and supervised by the law enforcement institutions. For example, Section 2 of the *Measures for the Implementation of Community Corrections* 2012 states:

> the judicial and administrative offices are responsible for management and organization of community corrections . . . the people's procuratorates are responsible for the legal supervision of the implementation of community corrections . . . the police are responsible for handling those who re-offend or [found to be] violating the regulations of public order while serving community corrections.

Likewise, according to Article 33 of the *Drug Prohibition Law* 2008, drug treatment in the community is carried out by the sub-district administrative offices and the people's governments of towns and villages. However, Section 4 of the *Drug Prohibition Regulations* (*Jindu Tiaoli*) – the supplementary rule of the *Drug Prohibition Law* enacted in 2011 – reveals that

> the public security organs above county level . . . are responsible for the registration and dynamic management of drug addicts; . . . the management of the facilities of community drug treatment; and are responsible for providing guidance and assistances [sic] of community rehabilitative work.

Second, both minor criminals under community corrections and drug addicts under community drug treatment are required to attend compulsory educational programs and labour work while serving their 'sentences'. Section 15 of the *Measures for the Implementation of Community Corrections* stipulates that those who are placed under community corrections ought to regularly participate in the study groups to enhance their public morality, legal knowledge and consciousness of repentance. In the meantime, they must undertake a certain amount of labour in the community to 'repair social relationship[s], cultivate social responsibility, collective conception and sense of discipline' (Section 16). Likewise, drug addicts are required to take part in education-centred correctional programs, such as study for drug-related knowledge and occupational skills training (Section 18). During community drug rehabilitation in particular, community agencies are allowed to arrange physical exercise and manual labour for addicts as part of their rehabilitative treatment (Section 42).

It is these legal settings and practical operations that unveil the true nature of China's community penalties; these turn out to be rather different than the official rationale. More specifically, community corrections and drug treatment, while defined as correction-oriented measures, rarely serve the stated objectives of rehabilitation and therapy. Rather, they are more like a different form of compulsory penalty to control offenders, identical to the law enforcement measures employed for certain coercive approaches in the Chinese criminal justice system.

The coercive character of community penalties is first demonstrated by the deprivation of offenders' liberty during the exercise of correctional schemes and detoxification treatments. While both community corrections and community drug treatment are designed as non-incarcerative means aimed to preserve offenders' social linkages, the practices require them to be subject to a variety of restrictive rules that literally control their mobility in the community. Section 11 of the *Measures for the Implementation of Community Corrections* illustrates that offenders under community corrections should frequently report to the authorities in regards to their attendance at study, community services and social activities. To ensure that offenders are remanded within the orbit of the community, offenders are not allowed to leave the city or county in which they live without approval (Section 13). If offenders do need to leave their residences due to medical reasons or family incidents, they should apply to the appropriate judicial and administrative bodies seven days in advance for permission (Section 13). Once approved, offenders must return to their communities within one month (Section 13). If offenders breach these rules, they will receive a warning from the community authorities and may be further penalised by the police for breaching public order regulations (Sections 23 and 24).

In many respects, community drug treatment entails a similar level of confinement of drug abusers in the neighbourhood. To highlight the compulsoriness of this measure, Section 14 of the *Drug Prohibition Regulations* 2011 states that drug addicts must report to the sub-district administrative offices and the people's governments of towns and villages within fifteen days of being issued a notice regarding community detoxification. Failure to report without a proper reason is considered a refusal to undertake community detoxification. Similarly, Section 40 of the *Drug Prohibition Regulations* 2011 stipulates that drug addicts released from coercive quarantined detoxification must report to the sub-district administrative offices and the people's governments of towns and villages within fifteen days of being issued a notice of community drug rehabilitation. While setting up a mandatory deadline for drug addicts to commence their detoxification, the legislation establishes a number of obligatory requirements imposed on drug addicts. Section 19 of the *Drug Prohibition Regulations* 2011 provides that in the process of detoxification programs, addicts should obey the following rules: (1) execute the community detoxification agreement; (2) periodically undertake medical tests upon the request of the police; and (3) submit a written report if planning to leave the city or town for more than three days where the community detoxification is being undertaken.

The compulsory nature of community penalties also shows in the ways community correctional programs are managed by the authorities. Although local judicial and administrative bodies are legally assigned to carry out correctional and educational activities, their actual work focuses more on control and punishment than rehabilitation and persuasion, due to a wide range of factors. For example, many community penalty enforcers concede that Chinese communities are neither financially prepared nor resourced to carry out the legislated approaches (Wang 2008). Due to the lack of fiscal support from local governments and the heavy daily workload imposed on the authorities, community-level judicial and administrative officers are mostly incapable of mobilising the required social capital to organise systematic educational and correctional programs. To make their jobs easier, they tend to simply follow the existing working models for implementing non-custodial criminal justice measures set out in the Chinese *Criminal Procedure Law* 2012 – for instance, residential surveillance (*jianshi juzhu*) and bail (*qubao houshen*).[6] Therefore, many operational similarities can be identified in the practice of community-based penalties and non-incarcerative criminal instruments, including (1) requiring the regular attendance of offenders to report their activities; (2) restricting the range of certain offenders' mobility; (3) reporting to the police instantly upon being called; and (4) organising offenders to assume productive labour and community service.

In many under-developed localities, it is not uncommon for local governments to deploy former prison police and officers from local police stations to deal with offenders in the community (Wang 2007). Assigning the handling of offenders to retired public security personnel relieves judicial and administrative agencies of the heavy burden of oversight. Moreover, local governments argue that former police officers are more experienced than administrative officers and social workers when it comes to ensuring that offenders will not get into trouble, be involved in accidents or lose contact with authorities (Yang 2005). For example, the police adopt a 'reporting' system to guarantee that drug addicts are under close surveillance and do not leave their designated mobility areas. In the operation of community drug treatment, the police require drug abusers to submit to frequent requests for drug tests during their service in the neighbourhood. The communities in Shanghai, for instance, carry out at least twenty-eight urine tests during the three-year detoxification treatment (*Temporary Measures on Implementing Detoxification Approaches in the Drug Prohibition Law (Guanyu Guanche Zhixing 'Zhonghua Renmin Gongheguo Jingdu Fa' Youguan Jiedu Cuoshi De Zanxing Banfa*) 2008, Part 5.4(1)).[7] While the first twelve are mandatory in the first year, the police randomly perform the remainder in the second and third years (Zhang et al. 2009). During the first year of treatment, drug addicts are obliged to take urine tests every month or one-and-a-half months to assess their progress under community therapeutic programs. Those who refuse to accept the test or intentionally delay it may be sent to coercive quarantined detoxification (Zhang et al. 2009). This control strategy reflects a general rationale of the authorities in administering community penalties; the focus is on coercion and incapacitation of offenders to minimise risks they represent to the society. As a consequence, the fundamental aspects of education and correction that require more professional capability and understanding are mostly neglected.

Perhaps a more substantial legal obstacle to incorporating administrative offenders into the community-based penal system lies in the legal deficiencies of community-based penalties. China's legal context classifies illegal conduct into two categories, namely criminal and minor offence. While criminal conduct is punished by the formal criminal justice system, minor offence is handled by the administrative penal system. Article 13 of the Chinese *Criminal Law (Xing Fa)* 1979 (as amended) characterises crimes as all acts that:

> [E]ndanger the sovereignty, territorial integrity, and security of the state; split the state; subvert the political power of the people's democratic dictatorship and overthrow the socialist system; undermine social and economic order; violate property owned by the state or property collectively owned by the labo[u]ring masses; violate citizens' privately owned property; infringe upon citizens' rights of the person, democratic rights, and other rights; and other acts that endanger society, are crimes if according to law they should be criminally punished. However, if the circumstances are clearly minor and the harm is not great, they are not to be deemed as crimes.

Accordingly, criminality in China appears to be a combination of 'criminal characterisation' and 'criminal quantity' (Chu and Wang 2000). While 'criminal characterisation' concerns the nature of illegal conduct, 'criminal quantity' refers to the degree of severity of a particular act and an assessment which is characterised as the vital factor in determining whether the offender should be sanctioned criminally or administratively (Pei 2007).

Unlike the specified stipulation of a criminal act, minor offences lack a clear definition in the criminal legislation. Instead, the *Security Administrative Punishments Law* (*Zhi'an Guanli Chufa Fa*) (2006 as amended in 2012) (SAPL) sets forth several categories of infringement that are considered as minor offences:

> with regard to an act of disrupting public order, encroaching upon the right of the person, the right of property or impairing social administration, if it is socially harmful and constitutes any crime as provided for in the Criminal Law of the People's Republic of China, it shall be subject to criminal liabilities. If it is not serious enough to be subject to a criminal punishment, it shall, in accordance with this law, be subject to public security punishment by the public security organ (Article 2).

Therefore, minor offence refers to behaviour conducted with minor criminal intention, resulting in petty socially damaging consequences. The administrative laws and regulations have described drug abuse, prostitution and social order infringements as minor offences that are supposed to be handled outside the criminal regime, as they are not serious enough to warrant criminal prosecution.

Such legal characterisations rule out the hypothesis of accommodating administrative offenders under the system of community corrections on a legislative basis as they conceptualise China's community corrections as a criminal sanction (*Notice on Implementing Experimental Work of Community Corrections* 2003, Preface). The primary task of this instrument is to cope with criminals in the community in lieu of imprisonment and ensure that punishment is smoothly implemented through community corrections in light of the *Criminal Law* 1979 (as amended), the *Criminal Procedure Law* 1979 (as amended in 1996 and 2012) and other relevant laws (*Notice on Implementing Experimental Work of Community Corrections* 2003, Preface). Clearly, it stresses the nature of community corrections as a new method of penalty in the criminal justice system, targeting those who violate the *Criminal Law* 1979 (as amended). Therefore, this measure lacks a solid legal foundation to seamlessly cover offenders who are targets of the administrative detention system, a parallel penal system in China's legal mechanism. In addition, the Chinese government requires community corrections for only limited offences. Only five categories of criminals are eligible to serve their sentences in the community: probationers, parolees, those sentenced to control, those deprived of political rights and those permitted to temporarily serve their sentences outside prison (*Notice on Implementing Experimental Work of Community Corrections*, Section 2). These offenders are considered to have committed trivial crimes with minimal harmful intention. Regardless of the resemblance in legal definition of minor criminals and administrative offenders, this legal categorisation places prostitutes, drug addicts and social order offenders outside the scope of community corrections as their offending does not meet the threshold of 'criminal quantity'.

Community drug treatment targets minor administrative offenders. The law requires that it deals exclusively with one specific offender: drug abusers. The *Drug Prohibition Law* 2008 and the *Drug Prohibition Regulations* 2011 establish a clear leadership system and a detailed working mechanism and corresponding social support system surrounding the need to detoxify drug addicts. Although drug abusers share similar social and psychological roots of their offending with other categories of minor offenders in China, this neighbourhood-based measure is not accessible to prostitutes, public order offenders and those subjected to administrative detention.

Institutional deficiencies and limits

Over the last decade, community penalties have been widely used in the majority of Chinese provinces and municipalities, including in both developed and undeveloped localities. The operations thus vary significantly from place to place in accordance with different local conditions and cultural characteristics. Some earlier pilot cities such as Beijing and Shanghai have developed a set of original educational programs that fit well with their own community cultures (Wang 2008). Other follow-up locales have borrowed the pioneers' experience in designing their own community correctional programs and are carrying them out in accordance with their regional advantages (Wang 2008). However, despite the fact that the community penal system has begun to play a role in the Chinese legal system, its practice in each locale shares some common institutional deficiencies and procedural limits. These weaknesses not only impact on the balanced growth of this mechanism in China but, more importantly, obstruct the integration of administrative offenders into this system at the current stage.

The conflict with the hukou system

The *hukou* system was first implemented in Chinese cities in 1951, with the officially stated purpose of maintaining social order, safeguarding the people's security, and protecting their freedom of residence and movement (Liu 2005). All Chinese nationals' personal *hukou* are classified as either urban (non-agricultural) or rural (agricultural); these also pertain to urban and rural populations respectively. Each individual is required to register one and only one place of residence (Liu 2005). For urban residents, the unit of registration is a household, while the unit of registration for rural people can be a commune, a village or a state farm (Xia and Wang 2002). Only through proper government authorisation – the *hukou* conversion process – can one permanently change his or her *hukou* location or categorisation from rural to the urban (Chan and Buckingham 2008). There is a general consensus among both legal and sociological scholars that the *hukou* system has long served as an important mechanism in distributing resources and determining life chances in China (Li 2001; Wu and Treiman 2004). The designation of non-agricultural status entitles the bearer to enjoy state-provided welfare, including permanent employment, medical insurance, housing, pensions and educational opportunities for children (Windrow and Guha 2005). Agricultural status, however, denies residents access to most state benefits, in particular urban community and social resources (Chan and Buckingham 2008). While the *hukou* system has created a class-divided society in China by rendering urban residents first-class citizens and rural residents second-class citizens (Chan and Buckingham 2008), it has made community penalties a selectively accessible program available only to those who have local *hukou* status. The *Drug Prohibition Law* 2008 stipulates: 'a person is to serve their community drug treatment in the place of their household registration or their permanent residential address under the supervision of either the local street committee in urban areas or the village government in rural areas' (Article 33). Although community corrections regulations do not determine eligibility in terms of offenders' *hukou* and residential status, most cities and provinces choose to receive only those offenders who have a local *hukou* and residential location. Beijing, for example, specifically instructs that community corrections only apply to criminal offenders who hold Beijing *hukou*, and non-Beijing *hukou* offenders should return to their registered residences to serve their community sentences (Tang 2004). Likewise, Hunan Province expressly states that those who are eligible to be held under community corrections must have Hunan *hukou* or have resided in Hunan permanently or for a long period of time (*Temporary Measures on Evaluating Targets of Community Correction in Hunan Province* (*Hunanshen Shenqu*

Jiaozheng Duixiang Kaohe Zanxing Banfa) 2002).[8] Although Shanghai has more or less opened the door of community corrections to rural–urban migrants in the last few years, the overwhelming majority of offenders in Shanghai neighbourhoods are still local *hukou* holders and permanent residents (Shanghai Community Corrections Office 2012).

Indeed, as far as the implementation of community correctional programs is concerned, those who are registered with a local *hukou* are easier to regulate and control due to their lifelong familial and social ties in the local neighbourhood. Meanwhile, local governments are more willing to reserve their limited resources for local *hukou* offenders over migrants or temporary residents from outside regions. This entry standard, however, produces another critical obstacle to placing administrative offenders in the community penal system, particularly in some modern and big cities where community correctional schemes are properly developed and well operated.

Much evidence shows that prescribed administrative offenders in China, namely prostitutes, drug addicts and social order breakers, are mostly part of a 'floating population' (*liudong renkou*) that lacks a local *hukou* (Wang 2004). Since 1978, Deng Xiaoping's economic reform has encouraged large-scale population mobility nationwide (Wu and Li 1996). With under-employment in the rural labour force, farmers have been motivated to seek jobs outside the agricultural sector (Li 1996). The enormous number of agricultural workers that have moved to cities and towns has created a new migrant class, rural labourers (*nongmingong*), pursuing better employment opportunities and fortunes in the urban region. However, rural labourers with agricultural *hukou* have diminished chances of holding a job in the state sector and are more likely to be self-employed or experience periods of unemployment (Lin 2009). Even if they are temporarily employed, they normally undertake heavy and cheap labour for their daily income due to their low-level education attainment and lack of advanced skills and human capital (Rozelle et al. 2002).

The difficulty of finding stable, well-paid employment, coupled with the tension resulting from increasing urban–rural income inequality, contributes heavily to administrative offences by rural–urban migrants in China. For instance, it is documented that many female rural labourers, motivated by the need to find employment, choose to sell sex to earn money in cities (Gil et al. 1996). Shanghai-based research shows that more than 71 per cent of prostitutes were rural women in the 1990s (Wang 1999). Regional prostitutes come from poor, overpopulated or remote and mountainous provinces, such as Sichuan and Hunan (Ren 1999). Most prostitutes have either only completed middle school or dropped out of school in their adolescence (Gil et al. 1996). Selling sex is their only source of income.

Drug addicts and prostitutes share various general features in terms of their social and behavioural profiles. In the reform period, most drug addicts are of the younger generation, with low educational levels and limited job skills (Zhao et al. 2004). The vast majority of surveyed drug abusers remain jobless for lengthy periods (Sun et al. 2001) and more than three-quarters of drug addicts are only primary or middle school graduates (Liu et al. 2004). They have never had legal and scientific education about the dangers of drugs, nor have they received guidance on how to avoid possible drug interactions (Tang 2001). More notably, most detained drug abusers in cities are rural labourers with low education attainment and wages (Bai et al. 2008). For example, one statistical study conducted in Beijing in 2007 shows that among 598 detained drug users across three districts, 64.7 per cent were rural labourers, whereas only 35.3 per cent were urban residents holding local Beijing *hukou* (Yang 2010).

The existing literature shows that the high rates of public order offences in cities can be attributed to the large number of rural labourers who do not possess adequate skills, struggle to find stable jobs, and fail to adjust to urban living and social environments (Curran 1998). This hypothesis is particularly supported by a survey undertaken on the issue of

Table 3.1 Statistical summary of administrative offences and crimes committed by floating people in Beijing

	1996 (Year)	2005 (Year)	Rate of increase
Administrative Offences	9725 (Person)	47648 (Person)	4.9
Committed Crimes	8025 (Person)	17104 (Person)	2.1

crime committed by the floating population in Beijing. In this study, researchers explored the behavioural and social characteristics of rural offenders in Beijing in 1996 and in 2005. Their findings show that the percentage of the floating population committing crimes had been growing since the mid-1990s, reaching the pinnacle of 61 per cent in 2005 (Wang et al. 2007). Although the report does not provide the precise percentage of 'floaters' who were involved in public order offences, it states that the number of rural labourers detained for public order transgressions is much higher than the number of those detained for criminal activities and other local public order offenders who had a Beijing *hukou*. Table 3.1 shows the number of administrative offences and other crimes in both 1996 and 2005 (Wang et al. 2007, translated by the author).

Inapplicability of community penalties in rural society

Although the implementation of community penalties has been greatly encouraged over the last decade, their practice has been largely limited to cities and towns where social and human resources are sufficient to bolster the execution of correctional programs. In contrast, many rural communities have difficulty formally initiating this mechanism. The reasons are multifaceted. First, rural community corrections suffer significantly from a lack of human resources, including professional workers and law enforcement personnel. In China's most rural regions, local judicial and administrative departments house a small number of government-employed staff together with some part-time social workers (Beijing Fengtai Justice Bureau 2011). Apart from the roles and responsibilities related to community corrections, they are required to undertake a considerable amount of regular legal service activities and neighbourhood mediation (Beijing Fengtai Justice Bureau 2011). For example, in Fengqiao Town, the first village to experiment with community corrections in China's rural society, only two officially employed justice workers and fourteen casual officers are assigned to specifically carry out community corrections. Faced by more than thirty minor criminals, they are often frustrated and find it impossible to keep up with daily management and time-consuming educational activities (Kong 2005).

Secondly, scarce funds to perform correctional programs discourage community penalties from being a regular tool to handle minor offenders in the Chinese countryside. The cost of implementing community penalties is usually excluded from rural governments' financial budgets and the actual practice is mostly financed by temporary and residual funds allocated by the local justice bureau (Feng et al. 2006). The distribution of capital, however, is discretionary and random in light of the varied implementation needs (Kong 2005). This means that many rural towns do not have separate furnished offices for community workers to carry out their duties (Wu and Ma 2011). The grassroots officials are usually not equipped with the same uniforms, working license or relevant identification or badges for enforcement of community-based penalties (Wu and Ma 2011). This lack of financial support is in part due to a strong urban-biased development policy that promotes urbanisation in contemporary Chinese society. It is also attributable to the general destitution of China's most rural areas, where people are still struggling to fight poverty. They are not only economically poor, but also poor in cultural and social services.

Thirdly, the cultural and environmental contexts in contemporary rural China are likely to act as a hindrance to establishing community-based penalties in the countryside. Although since the late 1970s China's economic reforms have fundamentally reshaped the social and economic fabric of the rural regime, some far-reaching ideological roots have remained intact. Having been influenced by Confucian ideals for thousands of years, rural society in China functions more through customary standards and traditional moral values than law (Liu 1998). Virtue, morality and community rules that have long been the foundations of Confucian traditions eclipse law and order in the regulation of rural communities (Fei 2006). As such, peasants adopt a plain version of standards to discern 'good and bad' and deeply believe that 'bad people' should be severely punished to serve the purposes of retribution and deterrence (Wu and Ma 2011).

Such a philosophy is inconsistent with the legal spirit of community-based penalties. As an alternative measure to handle administrative offenders, community-based punishment advocates education, rehabilitation and rescue. It emphasises 'remoulding' to help offenders reintegrate into society rather than punishing them to serve the goal of crime control. Therefore, the exercise of this tool requires a relaxing and forgiving environment, as well as participants who possess high levels of legal understanding and consciousness so that they may appreciate the significance of this social treatment. Yet the current state of rural education indicates that the number of well-educated people in China's rural population is comparatively low, and few people have received formal, quality legal education (Tan 2003). Although China has established a nine-year compulsory educational system and propagated public legal education in the rural region, the availability and affordability of educational attainment have always been challenged by rural poverty and low educational investment. Tian and Wang (2005) found that in the total employed rural population in 2004, 35.9 per cent were illiterate or semi-illiterate and 37.2 per cent had only completed primary school.

Social rejection and discrimination

Another major obstacle to incorporating administrative offenders into the community lies in the rejection, discrimination and fear of the general public against socially and morally harmful behaviours. In contemporary China, public attitudes towards drug use and prostitution are discriminatory and hostile (Liu and Ma 1999; Yang and Li 2007). Abusing drugs, from the perspective of the public, is an unethical form of behaviour that contradicts social values and morality. Rather than gaining sympathy, drug addicts more frequently face great hostility from the community and even their own families and friends (see for example, *Shanghai Youth Daily* 26 June 2006). A research survey was conducted in 2006 to observe the general attitude of Shanghai community residents towards drug addicts. The statistics collected from 9,400 people show that among these interviewed residents, 32 per cent despise drug addicts and 13 per cent are fearful of drug addicts (*Shanghai Youth Daily* 26 June 2006). This phenomenon is not unique to this part of China. Yang and Li's (2007) study conducted in Gansu Province shows that 92 per cent of residents feel very unsafe around drug addicts and are unwilling to make contact with them due to the fear of potential risk of contracting HIV/AIDS-related illnesses.

Due to the high level of social denial and discrimination, almost every administrative officer and social worker in community drug treatment encounters a great deal of resistance from addicts and faces indifferent attitudes from addicts' families. For example, Qi Linde, the head of the social worker station of community detoxification in the Shanggang Subdistrict, Pudong District (Shanghai), has observed:

> When we are trying to build . . . [a] close relationship with drug addicts, they tend to be distant with us in order to keep their privacy. They usually leave the houses very early and come back very late to avoid . . . contact with social workers. It is pretty common that we have to pay 7 or 8 visits to see our targets just . . . [to see them] once (*Bund Picture* 30 June 2004).

Yuan Zheng, one of Qi's colleagues, has had his offer of help refused many times by addicts' families. He shared an account of such a refusal:

> Once I went to one addict's house to check on his detoxification progress. The addict's mother wouldn't let me in but simply told me her son went out for work. I knew that person did not have a job at the moment. Eventually, I found out that at that day the addict stole his mother's money to purchase drugs and she might think all we have done to help him is absolutely useless!

This uncooperative attitude is attributed to two factors. On the one hand, drug addicts are unwilling to or are worried about accepting social workers' assistance due to their fear of being exposed as drug users. They fear public stigmatisation through direct discrimination. On the other hand, many families show sceptical and unfriendly attitudes towards social workers and their requests for cooperation. This is in part because most families have long since abandoned drug addicts due to an intolerance of their behaviour. But mainly, other family members are afraid of being involved in the matter of drug abuse, as it may tarnish the family's reputation.

The public holds some similar attitudes towards prostitution. Despite the modernisation of Chinese society where people have accepted that 'to be rich is glorious' (Rojek 2001), popular culture still portrays prostitutes as women who sell their souls for 'dirty money' (Li 2000). In Liu and Ma's (1999) study regarding public attitudes towards prostitution in Wuhan City, 91.3 per cent of 159 interviewed residents characterised prostitution as a morally unacceptable behaviour and 87 per cent of residents objected to proposals to decriminalise prostitution and establish a red light district, arguing that the legalisation of prostitution would exacerbate declining moral and social values (Liu and Ma 1999).

In contrast, the general attitudes towards public order offenders are relatively mild. This is because public order offenders in China commit transgressions that are not serious enough to be criminalised. They break the law due mainly to their intuitive–impulsive consciousness or certain unexpected sporadic incidents (Petersilia 2001). Most of these offenders are later found to express shame and remorse for their past conduct and long for social forgiveness and acceptance (Karstedt 2002). However, with enormous migration waves from rural areas to urban territories over last decades, the continuously increasing rates of public order offences have raised public concern over the issue of social security. Inflowing rural labourers have contributed statistically to this social unease. As such, they are frequently portrayed negatively in the media and perceived as a direct threat to social stability (Wong et al. 2007). In effect, there is a tendency in some modern and large Chinese cities for local residents to blindly and wilfully blame rural migrants for the worsening of public order and safety (Wang 2001). To show their unwelcoming attitude, local residents have begun to treat migrant workers unpleasantly, including verbal disrespect or deliberate avoidance.[9]

Not surprisingly, the behavioural patterns and socio-cultural attributes of drug abusers, prostitutes and public order offenders produce the greatest social hindrance to achieving the proposed community socialisation. It is not uncommon that local residents, especially urban inhabitants, often object to accepting alien individuals and groups in their community in an effort to maintain 'purity' and 'integrity'. In a society where populist punitiveness still dominates public opinion in respect of punishment (Bakken 2011), most people are concerned that they and their society could become victims if offenders are not heavily penalised and imprisoned to realise the goals of retribution and deterrence (Lin and Yang 1999). Over the last few decades, although the Chinese penal system has gradually brought in elements of education and rehabilitation to its practice, the principle of severe punishment (*zhongxing zhuyi*) has not been eliminated but rather reinforced in some stern government-sponsored anti-crime activities, such as the 'Strike Hard' (*yanda*) campaigns since the 1980s. The public preference for adopting a disciplinary and punitive society clearly contradicts the ideological and constitutive nature of community penalties. Many residents are worried that the use of community corrections represents benevolence and kindness that will impinge on the authority and justice of law, hence giving offenders a second chance to commit further crimes (Dan 2007).

Conclusion

Over the last decade, China has endeavoured to reform its administrative detention system by gradually transferring administrative offenders to social treatment in the community. Indeed, community-based programs that abound with positive social factors and rich social resources may serve in theory as a better instrument to correct and rehabilitate administrative offenders. However, the reality reveals that simply placing them in the neighbourhood can hardly achieve this ultimate goal as planned, considering the legal, economic and social dynamics and conditions in contemporary China.

Despite being described as a penal form that represents a correctionalist ideal, the legal stipulations emphasise the coercive nature of community penalties that in actuality serve the purposes of incapacitation and control of offenders. In addition, the lack of a legal foundation for community penalties to jurisdictionally accommodate minor offenders casts considerable doubt on their enforceability and in supplanting administrative detention. Perhaps the most alarming factors in the practice of this instrument spring from institutional and social aspects. Foremost, the genuinely widespread use of community penalties will not be realisable without the eradication of social and spatial stratification, as well as rural–urban inequalities. More precisely, the *hukou* system that divides Chinese people into two different categories – 'the haves' and 'the have-nots' – has formed an invisible wall which limits most administrative offenders' access to the services of community-based measures. While a small number of urban offenders may be placed under community treatment, the substantial population of rural offenders are most likely to be left unsupervised and uncared for, due to the lack of the effective community correctional mechanisms in rural communities. Furthermore, social rejection and avoidance generates an environment where community programs are functionally misunderstood and locally repulsed. Such a general attitude shows a negative perception towards behaviours and individuals that endanger social order and morality. In addition, urban people also have feelings of superiority and resentment towards the rural population and view them as potential lawbreakers and a drain on urban community resources.

Notes

1 The discussion of enacting the *Law on Correction of Misdemeanours* to displace re-education through labour was first initiated in 2005. The drafting of this law was officially incorporated in the state's legislative agenda in 2010. However, there have been no updates since.
2 In 2008, coercive drug rehabilitation merged with drug treatment under re-education through labour to become a new form of compulsory measure for addicts; it was termed compulsory quarantine for drug rehabilitation (*qiangzhi geli jiedu*).

3 Reviewing the characteristics of administrative detention reveals that this instrument is very similar to criminal imprisonment, which is largely carried out in the form of mandatory productive labour, promoting the exploration of the individual's ideological outlook and personal faults that lead to repentance and reform (Li 2010).
4 The latest recidivism rates concerning prostitution are not available, due to the secrecy concerning such issue within China.
5 The Notice was issued jointly by the Supreme People's Court, the Supreme People's Procuratorate, the Ministry of Public Security, and the Ministry of Justice on 10 July 2003.
6 See Article 65 and Article 72 of the *Criminal Procedure Law* 2012 setting out the circumstances under which bail and residential surveillance may be imposed.
7 The *Measures* 2008 were issued by the Shanghai Public Security Bureau to detail the detoxification measures set out in the *Drug Prohibition Law* 2008 and to interpret them in the context of the Shanghai communities.
8 This regulation was issued by the Hunan Public Security Bureau in 2011 to formulate and strengthen the daily management of offenders under community corrections. It establishes a scoring system to evaluate offenders based on their performances and activities in the neighbourhood.
9 For example, in *Kuandaishan* – one of the most popular Internet forums in Shanghai – many local Internet users call rural migrants 'hard disk' (*yingpan*). This term is derived from a well-known brand of computer hard disk, Western Digital (WD), the first letters of which coincide with Chinese *pinyin* of rural regions (*waidi*).

References

Amnesty International. 31 August 1991. 'China: Punishment Without Crime.' Index number: ASA 17/027/1991. Available at https://www.amnesty.org/en/documents/asa17/027/1991/en/ (accessed 16 February 2016).
Amnesty International. 1 March 1996. 'China: No One Is Safe: Political Repression and Abuse of Power in the 1990s.' Index number: ASA 17/001/1996. Available at http://www.amnesty.org/en/library/asset/ASA17/027/1991/en/6ec5f3dd-f941-11dd-92e7-c59f81373cf2/asa170271991en.pdf (accessed 16 February 2016).
Anderson, Allen F. and Gil, Vincent E. 1998. 'China's Modernization and the Decline of Communitarianism: The Control of Sex Crimes and Implications for the Fate of Informal Social Control.' *Journal of Contemporary Criminal Justice* 14: 248–61.
Bai Junwei, Shi Wenya and Qu Youming. 2008. 'Beijingshi Fengtaiqu 120 Li Zaiya Xidu Renyuan Aizibing Xiangguan Xingwei Diaocha. 2008. (Research on AIDS-related Behaviours of 120 Drug Abusers in Beijing Fengtai District).' *Zhongguo Jiankang Jiaoyu* (*Chinese Health Education*) 24: 193–194, 197.
Bakken, Børge. 2011. 'China, a Punitive Society?' *Asian Criminology* 6: 33–50.
Beijing Fengtai Justice Bureau. 2011. 'Nongcun Diqu Kaizan Shequ Jiaozheng Gongzuo De Diaocha (Research on Implementing Community Correction in the Rural Area).' *Renmin Tiaojie (People's Mediation)* 11: 33–35.
Biddulph, Sarah. 2004. 'The Production of Legal Norms: A Case Study of Administrative Detention in China.' *UCLA Pacific Basin Law Journal* 20: 217–77.
Biddulph, Sarah. 2007. *Legal Reform and Administrative Detention Powers in China*. Cambridge, UK: Cambridge University Press.
Biddulph, Sarah and Xie Chuangyu. 2011. 'Regulating Drug Dependency in China: The 2008 PRC Drug Prohibition Law.' *The British Journal of Criminology* 51(6): 978–96.
Bund Picture. 30 June 2004. 'Social Workers: The Non-Governmental Path for Anti-Drug Action in Shanghai.' Available at http://news.sina.com.cn/c/2004-06-30/16273568260.shtml (accessed 16 February 2016).
Chan, Kam Wing and Buckingham, Will. 2008. 'Is China Abolishing the Hukou System?' *The China Quarterly* 195: 582–606.
Chen Ruihua. 2001. 'Laodong Jiaoyang de Lishi Kaocha yu Fansi (The Historical Examination and Rethinking of Re-Education Through Labour).' *Zhong Wai Faxue* (Peking University Law Journal) 6: 657–73.

China Human Rights Strategy Group. November 2001. 'Human Rights in China, Promoting Human Rights in China.' Available at http://www.hrichina.org/sites/default/files/publication_pdfs/hric-strategy.pdf (accessed 16 February 2016).

Chu Kuizhi. 3 June 1999. 'Lun Jiaoyang Chuyu De Helixing (The Rationality of Re-Education Treatment).' *Fazhi Ribao* (*Legal Daily*): 6.

Chu Kuizhi. 2005. 'Yilun Laodong Jiaoyang Zhidu Gaige (The Discussion of Re-education Through Labour Reform).' *Zhongguo Sifa* (*Justice of China*) 5: 27–9.

Chu Kuizhi and Wang Yongle. 2000. 'Zailun Woguo Xingfazhong Fanzui Gainian De Dingliang Yingsu (The Further Review of Quantity Factor of the Criminality in Chinese Criminal Law).' *Faxue Yanjiu* (*Chinese Journal of Law*) 2: 34–43.

Curran, Daniel. 1998. 'Economic Reform, the Floating Population, and Crime: The Transformation of Social Control in China.' *Journal of Contemporary Criminal Justice* 14: 262–80.

Dan Weili. 2007. *Shequ Jiaozheng: Lilun Jichu Yu Zhidu Goujian* (*Community Corrections: Its Theoretical Basis and Institutional Construction*). Beijing: Zhongguo gong'an daxue chubanshe.

Dong Baigao. 1997. 'Woguo Sifa Jiguan Duochong Zhineng Gaige Zhi Sikao (Thoughts on Reforming the Multiple Responsibilities System of China's Judicial Organs).' *Zhongguo Faxue* (China Legal Science) 4: 24–31.

Fan, Cindy. 2006. 'China's Eleventh Five-Year Plan (2006–2010): From "Getting Rich is Glorious" to "Common Prosperity".' *Eurasian Geography and Economics* 47(6): 708–23.

Fei Xiaotong. 2006. *Xiangtu Zhongguo* (*Rural China*). Shanghai: Shanghai renmin chubanshe.

Feng Weiguo, Wei Hua and Liu Yanling. 2006. 'Shequ Jiaozheng De Zhongguo Shijian: Xianzhuang, Wenti Yu Duice (The Chinese Practice of Community Correction: Current Situation, Problems and Resolutions).' *Zhongguo Jianyu Zazhi* (China Prison Journal) 2: 137–42.

Gil, Vincent E., Wang, Marco, Anderson, Allen F. and Lin, Guao Matthew. 1994. 'Plum Blossoms and Pheasants: Prostitutes, Prostitution, and Social Control Measures in Contemporary China.' *International Journal of Offender Therapy and Comparative Criminology* 38: 319–37.

Gil, Vincent E., Marco Wang, Anderson, Allen, Lin, Guo Matthew and Wu, Zongjian Oliver. 1996. 'Prostitutes, Prostitution and STD/HIV Transmission in Mainland China.' *Social Science and Medicine* 42(1): 141–52.

Human Rights in China. February 2001 'Re-Education Through Labour (RTL): A Summary of Regulatory Issues and Concerns.' Available at http://www.hrichina.org/sites/default/files/publication_pdfs/hric-rtl.pdf (accessed 16 February 2016).

Human Rights Watch. 7 January 2010. 'Where Darkness Knows No Limits: Incarceration, Ill-Treatment and Forced Labour as Drug Rehabilitation in China.' Available at http://www.hrw.org/sites/default/files/reports/china0110webwcover_0.pdf (accessed 16 February 2016).

Hung, Veron Mei-Ying. 2003. 'Improving Human Rights in China: Should Re-Education Through Labour Be Abolished?.' *Columbia Journal of Transnational Law* 41: 303–26.

Karstedt, Susanne. 2002. 'Emotions and Criminal Justice.' *Theoretical Criminology* 6: 299–317.

Kong Yi. 2005. 'Zhongguo Nongcun Shequ Jiaozheng De Kunhuo—Yi Fengqiao Weili (The Plight of China's Rural Community Correction — Fengqiao Case).' *Jiangxi Gong'an Zhuanke Xuexiao Xuebao* (Journal of Jiangxi Public Security College) 5: 85–7.

Li Cheng. 1996. 'Surplus Rural Laborers and Internal Migration in China: Current Status and Future Prospects.' *Asian Survey* 36(11): 1122–45.

Li Enshen. 2010. 'Prisonization or Socialization? Social Factors Associated with Chinese Administrative Offences.' *UCLA Pacific Basin Law Journal* 27: 213–60.

Li Jieyu. 2012. 'Shourong Jiaozhu Zhidu Zhi Jiantao Yu Guizhi (The Examination and Regulation of Detention for Education—A Reassessment of 'Administrative Compulsory Law').' *Hubei Jingguan Xueyuan* (Journal of Hubei University of Police) 6: 27–30.

Li Lin. 2001. 'Towards a More Civil Society: Mingong and Expanding Social Space in Reform-Era China.' *Columbia Human Rights Law Review* 33: 149–88.

Li Yinhe. 2000. 'Maiyin Feizuihua (Non-Criminalization of Prostitution).' *Renmin Gong'an* (People's Police) 18: 9.

Lin Maorong and Yang Shirong. 1999. *Jianyuxue—Fanzui Jiaozheng Yuanli He Shiwu* (Penology— The Principles and Practices of Correcting Criminals). Taipei: Wunan chubanshe.
Lin Shuangchuan. 2009. 'Nongmingong Jiuyenan Tanxi (Exploring the Employment Difficulties of Rural Labourers).' *Renmin Luntan* (People's Political Science) 4: 26–7.
Liu Wei, Jie Jihua and Guo Benyu. 2004. '104 Li Hailuoyin Yilaizhe Fuxi Yuanyin Diaocha (Analysis on Reasons of 104 Heroin Dependents Relapse).' *Linchuang Xinshen Jibing Zazhi* (Journal of Clinical Psychosomatic Disease) 4: 278.
Liu Xinhui and Ma Li. 1999. 'Wuhanshi Shehui Renqun Dui Maiyin Piaochang Xianxiang Taidu De Diaocha (The Survey on Social Attitude towards Prostitution in Wuhan City).' *Zhongguo Jiankang Jiaoyu* (Chinese Health Education) 9: 39–41.
Liu Zhiqiang. 2005. 'Institution and Inequality: The Hukou System in China.' *Journal of Comparative Economics* 33: 133–57.
Liu Zuoxiang. 1998. *'Zhuanxing Shiqi De Zhongguo Shehui Cixu Jiaogou Jiqi Moshi Xuanze* (The Social Control Structure and the Choice of Pattern of the Chinese Society in the Era of Transmission).' *Falü Pinglun* (Law Review) 5: 37–9.
Lu Lin and Wang Xi. 2008. 'Drug Addiction in China.' *Annals of the New York Academy of Science* 1141: 304–17.
Office of China National Narcotics Control Commission. 25 June 2008. 'Significance and Content of the Anti-Drug Law.' Available at http://www.china.org.cn/e-news/news080625-3.htm (accessed 16 February 2016).
Peerenboom, Randall. 2004. 'Out of the Pan and Into the Fire: Well-Intentioned but Misguided Recommendations to Eliminate All Forms of Administrative Detention in China.' *Northwestern University Law Review* 98(3): 991–1104.
Pei Zhaobin. 2007. 'Zhi'an Guanli Chufafa Yu Xingfa De Xianjie Yu Chongtu (The Connection and Conflict of SAPL and Criminal Law).' *Gong'an Yanjiu* (Policing Studies) 10: 58–62.
Petersilia, Joan. 2001. 'When Prisoners Return to Communities: Political, Economic and Social Consequences.' *Federal Probation* 65: 3–8.
Ren Xin. 1999. 'Prostitution and Economic Modernization in China.' *Violence Against Women* 5(12): 1411–36.
Rojek, Dean G. 2001. 'Chinese Social Control: From Shaming and Reintegration to "Getting Rich Is Glorious".' In *Crime and Social Control in a Changing China*, edited by Jianhong Liu, Lening Zhang and Steven F. Messner, 89–104. Westport, Connecticut; London: Greenwood Press.
Rozelle, Scott, Huang Jikun and Zhang Linxiu. 2002. 'Employment, Emerging Labour Markets, and the Role of Education in Rural China.' *China Economic Review* 13: 313–28.
Shanghai Community Corrections Office (Shanghai Shequ Jiaozheng Bangongshi). 2012. 'Women Zai Qianxing – Shanghai Shequ Jiaozheng Shinian Gongzuo Jishi (We are Moving Ahead: A Silhouette of Ten Years' Community Correction Work in Shanghai).' (Internal Material), 75–6.
Shanghai Youth Daily. 26 June 2006. 'Wangshang Diaocha Xianshi Shanghai Shiming Dui Xiduzhe Tongqing Dayu Bishi (Complex Attitudes of Shanghai Residents towards Drug Users, 30% Sympathetic and 40% Discriminatory). Available at http://news.sina.com.cn/c/2006-06-26/085010253526.shtml (accessed 16 February 2016).
Shaw, Victor. 1998. 'Productive Labor and Thought Reform in Chinese Corrections: A Historical and Comparative Analysis.' *The Prison Journal* 78(2): 186–211.
Sun Buqin, Yugao Ye and Linjun Tai. 2001. '615 Li Hailuoyin Yilaizhe Fuxi Yuanyin Diaocha Yu Fenxi (Researching and Analysing Reasons of Relapse of 615 Heroin Abusers).' *Zhongguo Yaowu Yilaixing Zazhi* (Chinese Journal of Drug Dependence) 3: 214–16.
Tan Songhua. 2003. 'Nongcun Jiaoyu: Xianzhuang, Kunnan Yu Duice (Rural Education: Current Situation, Difficulties and Solutions).' *Beijing Daxue Jiaoyu Pinglun* (Peking University Education Review) 1: 99–103.
Tang Xiaotian. 2004. 'Shequ Jiaozheng Shidian Yu Jiaozheng Zhiliang De Tigao (The Pilot of Community Correction and the Improvement of Correctional Quality).' *Dangdai Faxue* (Contemporary Law Review) 18: 13–20.

Tang Xinghui. 2001. 'Nongming Xidu Burong Hushi (Drug Use by Rural Population Should Not Be Ignored).' *Zhongguo Yaowu Lanrong Fangzhi* (Chinese Journal of Drug Abuse Prevention and Treatment) 2: 25–6.

Tian Gen and Wang Lihui. 2005. 'Zhongguo Nongcun Jiaoyu De Xianzhuang Fenxi Ji Yingdui Cuoshi (The Analysis of Current Situation of Rural Education and Resolution).' *Gansu Nongye* (Gansu Agriculture) 12: 68.

Wang Chunguang. 2001. 'Xinshengdai Liudong Renkou De Shehui Rentong Yu Chengxiong Ronghe De Guanxi (The Relationship between Social Reorganization and Rural–Urban Assimilation of Floating Population in the New Generation).' *Shehuixue Yanjiu* (Sociology Research) 3: 63–76.

Wang Dazhong. 2004. 'Liudong Renkou Fanzui Wenti Toushi (Exploring the Criminal Phenomenon of Floating Population).' *Zhongguo Renmin Daxue Xuebao* (Journal of China' People's University) 5: 139–43.

Wang Dazhong, Cai Yanru, Zhang Xiaodong and Guo Bing. 2007. 'Beijingshi Liudong Renkou Fanzui Wenti Diaocha Baogao (The Survey Report on the Issue of Crime Committed by the Floating Population in Beijing).' *Zhongguo Renmin Gong'an Daxue* (Journal of Chinese People's Public Security University) 2: 9–15.

Wang Qi. 2007. 'Lun Woguo Shequ Jiaozheng De Zhixing Zhuti (The Enforcement Body of China's Community Correction).' *Zhongguo Sifa* (Justice of China) 2: 55–8.

Wang Shun'an. 2008. *Shequ Jiaozheng Yanjiu* (The Study of Community Corrections). Jinan: Shandong renmin chubanshe.

Wang Wuding. 1999. '*Wailai Liudong Renkou Guanli He Shehui Wending* (The Management of Floating Population and Social Security).' *Shanghai Gong'an Gaodeng Zhuanke Xuexiao Xuebao* (Journal of Shanghai Police College) 5: 2–6.

Windrow, Hayden and Guha, Anik. 2005. 'The Hukou System, Migrant Workers, and State Power in the People's Republic of China.' *Northwestern Journal of International Human Rights* 3: 1–18.

Wong, Daniel, Fu Keung, Chang Yingli and He Xuesong. 2007. 'Rural Migrant Workers in Urban China: Living a Marginalised Life.' *International Journal of Social Welfare* 16: 32–40.

Wu, Harry X. and Li Zhou. 1996. 'Rural-to-Urban Migration in China.' *Asian-Pacific Economic Literature* 10: 54–67.

Wu Xiaogang and Treiman, Daniel. 2004. 'The Household Registration System and Social Stratification in China, 1955–1996.' *Demography* 41(2): 363–84.

Wu Yuedong and Ma Yanli. 2011. 'Shequ Jiaozheng Zhidu Zai Nongcun Diqu De Jiangou (The Construction of Community Correction System in Rural Areas).' *Renmin Luntan* (People's Tribune) 2: 118–19.

Xia Xianliang and Wang Yingxin. 2002. 'Zhongguo Hukou Zhidu Gaige De Lilun Fenxi (The Theoretical Analysis of China's Hukou System).' *Chengshi Fazhan Yanjiu* (Urban Studies) 4: 15–23.

Xinjing Newspaper. 6 January 2014. 'Sifabu: Shequ Jiaozheng Bu Shi Laojiao Tidaiping (The Justice Bureau: The System of Community Corrections Is Not a Replacement for Re-Education Through Labour).' Available at http://news.xinhuanet.com/legal/2014-01/06/c_125959074.htm (accessed 16 February 2016).

Yang Fangquan. 2005. '*Shequ Jiaozheng Bentuhua Wenti De Sikao* (The Thinking of Localization of Community Correction).' *Zhongshan Daxue Xuebao Shehui Kexueban* (Journal of Sun Yatsen University) 2: 69–74, 125–26.

Yang Hui. 2010. 'Wailai Zaijin Yu Beijingji Xidu Renyuan Qingkuang Duizhao Fenxi (The Comparison Analysis between Drug Users With Beijing Hukou and Without Beijing Hukou).' *Zhongguo Yaowu Lanyong Fangzhi Zazhi* (Chinese Journal of Drug Abuse Prevention and Treatment) 4: 190–92.

Yang Lin and Li Pengcheng. 2007. 'Xiduzhe Huigui Shehui De Guocheng: Guishu Yu Rentong De Boduo (The Process of Drug Abusers' Reintegration into Society: The Deprivation of Belonging and Cognition).' *Xinlixue Tanxin* (Psychological Exploration) 2: 91–5.

Zhai, Keith. 28 December 2013. 'China's Labour Camp System Officially Abolished.' *South China Morning Post*. Available at http://www.scmp.com/news/china/article/1391659/china-formally-abolishes-re-education-labour-camps-eases-one-child-policy (accessed 16 February 2016).

Zhang Kai, Jiang Zuzhen and Zhang Xiaomin. 2009. 'The Study on Community Detoxification Model and Its Operational Mechanism (Shequ Jiedu Moshi Jiqi Yunzuo Jizhi Yanjiu).' *Henan Sifa Jingguan Zhiye Xueyuan Xuebao* (Journal of Henan Judicial Police Vocational College) 1: 31–4.

Zhang Shaoyan. 2001. 'Guanyu Laodong Jiaoyang Lifa De Jichu Wenti Sikao (The Thinking of Basic Issues of Legislating the Re-Education Through Labour).' *Faxue* (Legal Science) 3: 40–44, 64.

Zhang Shaoyan. 2003. 'Lun Laodong Jiaoyang Lifa De Jige Jichuxing Wenti – Jianli Woguo Qingzui Chufa Zhidu De Lilun Chuangxin (The Basic Issues of Legalizing Re-Education Through Labour – The Theoretical Innovation of Establishing Minor Punishments in China).' *Xiandai Faxue* (Modern Law Science) 2: 23–30.

Zhao Chengzheng, Liu Zhimin, Zhao Dong, Liu Yanhong, Liang Jiahui, Tang Yilang, Liu Zeyuan, Zheng Jiwang. 2004. 'Drug Abuse in China.' *Annals of the New York Academy of Science* 1025: 439–45.

Zou Keyuan. 2002. 'The "Re-Education Through Labour" System in China's Legal System.' *Criminal Law Forum* 12: 459–85.

4 Deprivation of liberty against one's will in mental health institutions in contemporary China

Zhiyuan Guo

Introduction

There are two situations in which a person with mental illness may be deprived of their liberty and treated against their will in a mental health facility. The first derives from a violent act committed by a mentally ill person to the extent that it would constitute a crime if done by someone who is mentally stable. Under such circumstances, this person can be committed to a psychiatric hospital for compulsory treatment. The second situation involves dangerousness, where it is determined that personal safety or the safety of others is compromised because of a mental disorder. In this circumstance, the mentally ill patient can be hospitalised and medicated without their consent or the consent of their guardians. Compulsory treatment (*qiangzhi yiliao*) and involuntary hospitalisation (*fei ziyuan zhuyuan zhiliao*) have been practiced for years in China. However, formal legislation was not established until the *Criminal Procedure Law (Xingshi Susong Fa)* (CPL) was amended in March 2012 and the first *Mental Health Law (Jingshen Weisheng Fa)* (MHL) was enacted in October 2012. This chapter will examine the recent legal reforms in relation to compulsory treatment and involuntary hospitalisation, comment on key issues from statutes and preliminary empirical findings, and put forward proposals for further reforms in these two areas. The first section provides a historical overview of the social understanding of mental health in China, followed by a brief introduction of relevant legal reforms. The second section focuses on the benefits and problems of the new compulsory treatment institutions, and also touches on some practical obstacles in implementing new legislation. The third section analyses the benefits and problems concerning involuntary hospitalisation and identifies some issues in need of improvement. The final section draws conclusions by comparing the legislation on compulsory treatment and the practice of involuntary hospitalisation.

Background: history and recent legal reforms on deprivation of liberty against one's will in mental health facilities in China

Historical development[1]

According to Ng (1990), mental disorders did not begin to be considered a legal matter in China until the seventeenth century.[2] At the time, relevant legislation addressed two main objectives: the isolation of 'the insane' from society and the punishment of violent acts committed by mentally ill people. The Qing government (1644–1912) started to adopt more interventionist measures in dealing with mentally ill individuals, including registration and confinement. Since then and over the centuries that followed, legal and institutional treatment of mentally ill people was dominated by two main approaches. The first related to social control and ensured that the behaviour of mentally ill people would not have a negative impact on social order. To this end, the first 'psychopathic hospitals' started to appear in China's major cities during the 1920s and 1930s. Their establishment was not merely aimed at restricting the liberty of murderers who were deemed insane; they also provided medical care and treatment (Hu et al. 2006), previously provided exclusively within the family. The second approach was concerned with the question of clemency in cases of homicide.

After the founding of the People's Republic of China (PRC) in 1949, psychiatric hospitals were gradually established in each province with the aim of improving social security and stability. Services were completely disrupted during the Cultural Revolution, as it was believed that mental illness was the result of the corrupt old political system and that it was society that needed to be cured rather than the individuals suffering from mental illnesses. Not surprisingly, the development of psychiatry during the Maoist era was heavily influenced by Soviet psychiatric theory, doctrine and practices. Munro (2000) argues that, as was the case with the Soviet Union, China started to use and abuse psychiatric treatment to deal with counter-revolutionaries, and political and religious dissenters. He claims that during the Cultural Revolution, the distinction between political crime and mental illness was abandoned, and dissenters were seen as being possessed by a 'counter-revolutionary' form of madness.

Mental health legislation gradually began to emerge as the result of a number of changes. These included the re-establishment of psychiatric services in 1978, the enactment of criminal and civil legislation which contained specific provisions regarding the treatment of mentally ill people[3] and the issuing of a number of other kinds of regulations on the treatment of those with mental illnesses.[4] However, mental health legislation and regulations were not comprehensive and generally lacked procedural safeguards for mentally ill individuals.

Except for the longstanding emphasis on the maintenance of social order, another feature in China's policy of dealing with mental illness is the heavy burden imposed on the family of individuals with mental health problems. Since the Qing dynasty, the *Great Qing Code* (*Da Qing Lü Li*) required that families report the existence of mentally ill family members to the authorities so that they could be kept under strict confinement. Even in contemporary China, families remain ultimately responsible for the care and monitoring of mentally ill family members; they are duty-bound to ensure that the 'afflicted' do not disrupt social order. Such over-reliance on families creates many problems though. On the one hand, people with severe mental illnesses are more often than not permanently confined at home by family members, or are abandoned and left to wander the streets. These people are sometimes referred to as 'loose cannons' and such neglect poses a potential threat to public safety and may cause tragedy (see for example, Bao 2010). On the other hand, the guardians (mainly family members) are often the main source of rights' violations, because of their own pecuniary interests or other types of gains.

Recent legal reforms

Over the past decade, mental health problems have become increasingly evident in Chinese society. According to statistics released by the China Centre for Disease Control and Prevention in 2009, more than 100 million people suffer from mental diseases of various types, and more than 16 million are seriously mentally ill (Hays 2011). According to the Ministry of Public Security, there are over 10,000 criminal cases committed by mentally ill individuals each year (Chen 2011). These findings have created tremendous pressure on the Chinese government, and mental health law reforms became a pressing agenda. Since traditionally China addressed mental health issues from a criminal perspective (using the *Criminal*

Procedure Law), the current framework of China's mental health legislation involves both mental health and criminal procedure law.

Codification of compulsory treatment

Under Article 18 of the *Criminal Law* 1997, defendants with mental illness do not bear criminal responsibility in certain cases; the same Article stipulates that ' . . . his [sic] family members or guardians shall be ordered to keep him under strict watch and control and arrange for his medical treatment. *When necessary, the government may compel him to receive medical treatment*' (Criminal Law 1997; emphasis added). This provision could be seen as the substantive legal cornerstone for compulsory institutional treatment. However, the *Criminal Law* 1997 does not provide any explicit definition or explanation for the word 'necessary', which is critical for the imposition of compulsory treatment. Under the CPL 1996, it was not clear who is entitled to impose the compulsory treatment on the mentally ill even though, in practice, it was generally police who made the final decision. The *People's Police Law* (*Renmin Jiancha Fa*) 1995 endowed police with the power of imposing temporary protective measures upon those with severe mental illness; this automatically granted police the power to initiate mental examination ex officio and to make the decision to commit a mentally ill person for compulsory treatment. Without participation of interested parties and their legal representatives, not to mention judicial review by courts and judicial supervision by procuratorates, these police practices of control and sometimes manipulation have been long criticised for lack of transparency and the possibility of infringing citizens' rights, including sending those considered dissenters to mental health hospitals.[5]

Empirical studies indicate that past compulsory treatment practices were problematic for three main reasons. First, they were not subject to judicial review, and police enjoyed complete discretionary power of determining who should qualify for compulsory treatment. Second, there were no explicit criteria to screen candidates for compulsory treatment. Police sometimes based their decisions on extra-legal considerations influenced by political considerations or very practical constraints – the availability of beds in mental health hospitals, for example. Third, there were no standards or procedures on release after compulsory treatment. Thus, mentally ill individuals were either detained for longer periods than needed, or were released when they were still mentally unstable; this posed danger to both personal safety and public security (Guo 2012).

Compulsory treatment involves not only the deprivation of liberty of mentally ill individuals, but also forced medical treatment in a psychiatric hospital. Consequently, it is directly related to the protection of citizens' fundamental rights, and, as such, it should require strict adherence to due process principles. For this reason, the amended CPL 2012 has established a new special procedure titled '*Procedures for Involuntary Medical Treatment of Mental Patients Legally Exempted from Criminal Liability*' (*Yifa Bu Fu Xingshi Zeren De Jingshen Bingren De Qiangzhi Yiliao Chenxu*). For the first time, this section sets out the scope, procedures and supervision mechanisms for compulsory psychiatric treatment in criminal cases.

In addition, following twenty-seven years of intense debate, on 26 October 2012, the National People's Congress Standing Committee released the *Mental Health Law*, China's first mental health legislation. The provisions on involuntary hospitalisation have received significant attention in China and abroad, largely because of well-known abuses by the medical establishment to detain or punish even the mentally healthy. However, a detailed discussion in the next section will demonstrate that, despite a moderate degree of progress, this legal development fails to address some of the existing problems.

Compulsory treatment: comments and analysis

Brief introduction to the legal framework on compulsory treatment

The *Criminal Procedure Law* 2012 in Part Five (Chapter Four, Articles 284–89) addresses procedures for the compulsory treatment of the criminally insane. This legislation has since been supplemented by twenty Articles from the Judicial Interpretations issued in 2013 by the Supreme People's Court (*Zui Gao Renmin Fayuan Guanyu Shiyong Zhonghua Renmin Gongheguo Xingshi Susong Fa De Jieshi*) (hereafter 'SPC Interpretations 2013'), twenty further Articles from the Supreme People's Procuratorate Regulations (*Renmin Jianchayuan Xingshi Susong Guize*) (hereafter 'SPP Regulations 2013') and also three Articles as a result of case-handling rules from the Ministry of Public Security 2013 (*Gong'an Jiguan Banli Xingshi Anjian Chengxu Guiding*) (hereafter 'MPS Rules 2013'). The comments below attempt to provide some insight into the relevant legislation, and specifically the interpretation of the compulsory treatment of mentally ill individuals.

Criteria for compulsory treatment

The CPL 2012, Article 284, for the first time specifies three criteria for the compulsory treatment of a mentally ill person: if he/she (a) has committed a violent crime, endangered public security or has caused death or injury to others; (b) was determined to be not guilty because of insanity after a mental health assessment in accordance with law; and (c) poses a continuing risk of endangering public security. If one (or more) of these conditions are met, the mentally ill individual may be compelled to receive medical treatment in a special psychiatric hospital called an *ankang* hospital. The hospital has changed its name to the Compulsory Treatment Centre (*qiangzhi yiliao suo*) as a result of enforcement of the 2012 CPL.[6] The SPP Regulations 2013 (Article 539) and SPC Interpretations 2013 (Article 524) add the requirement that the violent behaviour should already constitute a crime, which is actually an explanation of the first criterion. Chinese scholars tried to summarise these criteria in different terms (see for example Cheng and Chai 2013; Wang 2012), but it seems that the problem is not about how to label each criterion, but about how to implement them in practice, especially how to evaluate each of the criterion on a case-by-case basis.

Preliminary empirical results from a survey study in Beijing found that, of the three criteria, the 'continuing risk' criterion is always considered in combination with the occurrence of violence, largely because there are no available tools for police, prosecutors or judges to evaluate the potential risk of certain persons. It is widely held, at least among practitioners, that when a mentally ill individual has committed a violent act and caused death or injury to others, they therefore pose a continuing risk of endangering public security. This popular viewpoint suggests that an understanding of potential risk has been absorbed into the consideration of violence; as a result, the 'potential risk' criterion loses its value. This practice is reasonable in some sense, but there must be circumstances in which even if a mentally ill person committed a violent act and caused serious consequences, they may desist from harming others again in the future. For example, those who committed a crime because of transient mental illness (*yiguoxing jingshenbing* or *lütuxing jingshenbing*) that occurs only once in a lifetime usually pose no danger to self or others in the future; thus it is unnecessary to put this kind of patient under compulsory treatment.

Another problem recognised by some Chinese scholars is that the CPL 2012 merely requires the compulsory treatment of those who suffered from severe mental illness at the time of committing crime (Wang and Wang 2012). The law does not include those individuals whose mental illness breaks out during the criminal proceedings as the subject of compulsory treatment. Furthermore, the compulsory treatment required by the CPL 2012 is only for those mentally ill offenders who, as a result of criminal proceedings, are found not to bear criminal responsibilities. Offenders who suffer from diminished capacity are still held criminally responsible and, as a result, are subject to regular criminal proceedings. However, it is not unusual that these mentally ill suspects or defendants also need treatment because of the negative impact of their mental illness on their competency to stand trial.[7] Judicial interpretations state that during investigation, prosecution or trial, if the defendant or other parties suffer from mental illness, the relevant proceedings should adjourn until they regain their mental capacity (Guo 2010, 35), but it does not mention if compulsory treatment can be imposed upon such persons to 'restore' their competency.

Initiation of the compulsory treatment procedure

Perhaps the most significant progress with respect to the newly introduced compulsory treatment is the judicial review mechanism established by Article 285 of the CPL 2012. Putting the decision of compulsory treatment in the hands of the judiciary rather than administrative bodies is a key step towards ensuring that the decision is made neutrally and on the basis of legal standards (Daum 2013). Compulsory treatment is a measure involving the potential deprivation of a citizen's personal freedom and forcing them to take psychiatric medicine and treatment. As such, due process of the law, including the judicial review mechanism as one of the most important requirements, ought to be followed for measures that will affect the critical rights of an individual.

One of the criteria for compulsory treatment under the CPL 2012 is that a suspect or defendant should be legally evaluated as a mentally ill person not bearing criminal responsibility. Thus, the psychiatric evaluation process should precede a hearing regarding compulsory treatment. In practice, it is individual police officers who request or approve psychiatric evaluations in almost 80 per cent of all cases involving an insanity plea. In the remaining cases, it is the prosecutors or the judges who initiate a mental examination process, either on their own initiative or upon application by the defence. In spite of the fact that police are in the front line to deal with the mentally ill, the CPL 2012 provides that the court can initiate a compulsory treatment procedure either upon prosecutor's application or on its own initiative. The police can only submit its compulsory treatment opinion to the procuratorate and the latter can forward it; if the procuratorate agrees with the police's opinion, a compulsory treatment application is made to the court (CPL 2012, Article 285). This division of labour is to ensure the neutrality of decision-making, and avoid the possible abuse of power by administrative bodies.

Judicial and administrative interpretations tried to create more detailed rules for the initiation of compulsory treatment procedures, but they both failed to tackle some key issues. For example, the first paragraph of Article 532 of the SPC Interpretations 2013 offers courts little guidance on when to initiate a compulsory treatment hearing, saying only that if it appears the defendant

> might meet the requirements for compulsory treatment, [the court] shall follow the statutory procedures for carrying out a forensic medicine mental health examination. Where, having been examined, the defendant is found to be a mentally ill person not bearing criminal responsibility under law, the procedures for compulsory treatment should be used to carry out trial.

Here, the standards are not clarified. This same problem is evident in the Interpretations by the SPP and the MPS.

Some other legal interpretations are also found to be problematic. For example, the SPP Regulations 2013 also state that the procuratorate has thirty days to decide whether an application of compulsory treatment should be filed with the court. This period may be extended for an unspecified duration if the public security organ is requested to supplement evidence supporting its opinion, and the time used in a supplementary investigation will not be counted against the procuratorate's time for handling the case (SPP Regulations 2013, Article 544). This time limit seems too long considering the urgent need and the division of power. After all, it is the court rather than the procuratorate that makes the final decision. The task for the procuratorate is just to pass the application over to the court and there is no need for it to spend thirty days to make such a transitional decision.

In another example, the SPP Regulations provides in Article 545 that

> when the people's procuratorate found the public security organ should have initiated the compulsory treatment procedure but failed to do so, it may ask the public security organ to justify their nonfeasance in written form within seven days. Upon review, if the procuratorate does not agree to the public security organ's justification, it shall notify the latter to initiate the compulsory treatment procedure.

Since this oversight mechanism will cause a procedural back flow, for the sake of efficiency it seems better to let the procuratorate file the application directly.

Temporary restrictive measures for protection (linshixing baohu cuoshi)

Once a compulsory treatment procedure is initiated, and while waiting for the court to make the final decision, the mentally ill person might pose threats to their personal safety or the safety of others. For this reason, the CPL 2012 provides that 'prior to the people's courts making a compulsory treatment decision, the public security organs may adopt temporary restrictive measures to protect mentally ill persons exhibiting violent behaviour' (CPL 2012, Article 285, para. 3). These 'temporary restrictive measures for protection' are not intended to be compulsory treatment that requires a judicial determination, but to be very limited measures allowing the public security bodies to protect the public while awaiting a formal process.[8] Given that it could be regarded as a distinct type of detention, 'temporary restrictive measures for protection' should be undertaken with respect to statutory procedures. Therefore, the law is required to explicitly provide for its categories, contents, time limits, remedies and so on.

Actually, in its case-handling rules, the MPS seemingly recognises the potential abuse of these temporary restrictive measures or restraints, because it requires that such restraints be approved at county level or above (MPS Rules 2013, Article 333), be removed when there is no danger to society (Article 334),[9] and the means, methods and intensity of the restraints should not go beyond the needs of avoiding danger to the personal safety of the mentally ill person and public security (Article 334). These provisions, though extremely vague, indicate the public security body self-consciously imposing restrictions on temporary restrictive measures for protection.

The MPS Rules 2013 also make efforts to ensure these measures are truly temporary (Article 332).[10] However, the SPP interpretation gives the procuratorate up to thirty days to determine if an application for compulsory treatment should be filed with the court. During this period, together with a potential extended period (as explained earlier), the mentally ill person remains under the restraints and they are potentially deprived of liberty for a long time. While most are held in mental health facilities in the name of 'protective restrictive measures', in some provinces, due to lack of specialised institutions of detention, protective restrictive measures are rarely used and the mentally ill are held in detention centres responsible for the detention of criminal suspects and offenders.

Most importantly, the MPS Rules 2013 even provide that, if necessary, the suspect or defendant may be sent to a psychiatric hospital for treatment (Article 333). This pre-treatment, although sometimes necessary, makes it so that compulsory treatment can actually be provided solely at the will of public security forces. If not strictly limited and supervised, this will expand the public security powers so as to consume the rule and undermine the judicial character of the decision entirely.

The procuratorate has the power to supervise the imposition of temporary restraint measures not only by admonishing the public security organs to impose restrictive measures when it fails to do so, but also by demanding that they remove the restraints when it is inappropriate to exercise such measures. However, it remains to be seen whether such oversight is effective in practice.

Commitment hearing: judicial review of compulsory treatment

Article 286 of the CPL 2012 sets up a judicial review mechanism for the determination of the compulsory treatment of a mentally ill person,[11] and emphasises the principle that this decision involving grave interests of the subject of application should be made by a panel of judges through a hearing. The hearing is somewhat adversarial in that both the prosecutor and the subject of application or their legal representatives should be present and in contest with each other.[12] When the family wishes to care for the suspect themselves, they have to present supporting evidence and such evidence may be examined and debated in the courtroom (SPC Interpretations 2013, Article 530). However, the SPC Interpretations 2013 provide for an exception by authorising an indirect trial, that is, the subject of application or his legal representatives can choose a review of the relevant files instead (see Article 529). This is understandable considering the long-existing stigma attached to mentally ill people and their families in Chinese society.

Nevertheless, neither the CPL 2012 nor the judicial interpretations answer technical questions such as who should participate in the collegial panel. Experiences from foreign jurisdictions indicate that judges require consultation with psychiatrists when deciding on forced medication. So it is always necessary to include psychiatrists in the collegial panel or at least invite them as consultants. Data that I have collected as part of a preliminary survey on the issue reveal that in some provinces, psychiatrists are invited to act as people's assessors.

Another technical issue not covered by current law or interpretations is the meeting with the subject of application. Although the SPC Interpretations 2013 provide that 'When trying cases where the people's procuratorate has requested compulsory treatment, a meeting shall be had with the subject of the application' (Article 529), it is not clear when the meeting should take place – before or after the hearing, or both.

The vacuum of such operational guidelines has become an obstacle to the implementation of the new law. While some provinces have been drafting local implementing regulations, a national and unified set of guidelines is still missing.

Release to community

Compulsory treatment is a form of detention for the purpose of protection and medication, so it should be terminated when the treatment is no longer required. To ensure the mentally ill will not be unduly detained for an excessive amount of time, the CPL 2012 requires periodical evaluation by treatment establishments and a judicial review mechanism.[13] Judicial interpretations also indicate detailed procedures and release options (SPC Interpretations 2013, Article 542). That is to say, when reviewing the opinion submitted by the treatment establishment after a periodical evaluation, the court should handle the matter according to the following two distinct situations, and within one month. First, where the person under compulsory treatment is no longer dangerous and there is no need to continue compulsory treatment, a decision shall be made to remove compulsory treatment and the family of the person under compulsory treatment may be ordered to carefully watch over and treat the person. Second, where the person under compulsory treatment is still deemed to be dangerous and there is a need to continue compulsory treatment, a decision shall be made to continue compulsory treatment.

Within five days of making a decision, the people's courts shall deliver the decision to the compulsory treatment establishment, the person applying to remove compulsory treatment, the person under compulsory treatment, and the people's procuratorate. If the decision is to terminate compulsory treatment, the compulsory treatment establishment should be notified to cease compulsory treatment on the day they receive the decision.

Rights protection for the subject of compulsory treatment

The CPL 2012 also recognises the importance of protecting the rights of mentally ill individuals in the process of imposing and implementing compulsory treatment. Under current law and interpretations, three rights are granted to mentally ill people.

First, the law endows mentally ill individuals with the right to legal representation and legal aid. Article 528 of the SPC Interpretations 2013 echoes the provision of Article 286 of the CPL 2012 and states that

> [i]f the subject of the application or defendant has not appointed a litigation representative, a legal aid organization shall be contacted to appoint a lawyer to serve as his legal representative and to provide him with legal assistance. Under these provisions, the mentally ill person without criminal responsibility enjoys free counsel in compulsory treatment procedure.

However, as the law does not mention if the mentally ill person has the right to a legal aid lawyer in the proceedings before compulsory treatment procedure is initiated, CPL 2012 has granted a right to a legal aid lawyer to those mentally ill with diminished criminal responsibility (Article 34) from the investigation stage. In contrast, mentally ill individuals with more severe symptoms, thus assuming no criminal responsibility, have to wait until the compulsory treatment procedure begins. This could happen at any stage of the criminal proceedings. It would seem that a mentally ill person with diminished criminal responsibility enjoys unreasonably more protection than those found not to bear criminal responsibility. The right to a legal aid lawyer for an individual potentially the subject of compulsory treatment needs to be extended to the very beginning, that is, the stage of investigation.

Second, the CPL 2012 grants the person subject to compulsory treatment, a victim or their legal representatives, or their near relatives, the right to apply for reconsideration to the next highest level of court if they are not satisfied with the decision (Article 287). This right can be exercised once again if the reviewing court rejects the application for reconsideration (SPC Interpretations, Article 540). This is a reasonable provision because while the first application might be groundless, the second one may be relevant for the different situation caused by the lapse of time. However, if we compare this provision with Article 538 of the SPC Interpretations 2013 that provide for the remedy for prosecution's appeal, there is unequal treatment between the prosecution and the mentally ill. That is to say, when the person subject to compulsory treatment is not satisfied with the decision, they can only seek remedy by means of applying for reconsideration, and during the reconsideration, they are still under compulsory treatment (SPC Interpretations 2013, Article 536). However, when the prosecution appeals, the court will review the case via appellate proceeding rather than administrative review proceeding.

Thirdly, as mentioned above, the person subject to compulsory treatment and their family can apply for the removal of compulsory treatment, but the application can only have the effect of initiating the court's review. The court still needs to perform the review on the basis of the treatment establishment's diagnostic evaluation.

Supervision by the procuratorate

Except for the rights' protection for mentally ill people, the CPL 2012 and its corresponding interpretations also provide for procuratorate's supervision over imposition and implementation of compulsory treatment.

The SPP Regulations 2013 spell out the division of labour within the procuratorate in relation to compulsory treatment procedure. The public prosecution section (*gongsu bumen*) is in charge of filing the application for compulsory treatment with the court and appearing before court when a commitment hearing is conducted. It also supervises both the procedure and the outcome of the commitment hearing. The 'prisons and reformatories supervision section' (*jiansuo jiancha bumen*) is in charge of supervision of temporary restrictive measures for protection and the implementation of compulsory treatment (in an *ankang* Hospital or Compulsory Treatment Centre). In practice, however, since the task of supervising compulsory treatment is a completely new requirement, a new section has been created to fulfil this task in some provinces. Empirical data is still needed to illustrate how the procuratorate supervises compulsory treatment and to what extent the current law and interpretation addresses the problem in practice.

In conclusion, this brand new special procedure introduces a judicial review mechanism for compulsory treatment in cases involving defendants deemed to be mentally ill. Under the CPL 2012, the court can commit a mentally ill person to an *ankang* hospital for compulsory medical treatment. This occurs through a formal hearing when the mentally ill person meets the required legal criteria. At the same time, the CPL 2012 requires a periodic assessment and judicial approval for the release of mentally ill patients, and puts compulsory medication under the procuratorate's supervision. These provisions should not only prevent mentally ill offenders from arbitrary forced treatment, but also ensure that only those who are considered mentally stable and pose no danger to the public can be released back into the community. Generally speaking, although there is room for improvement, these provisions are basically in line with international standards (WHO 2005).[14] Of course, more detailed rules[15] should be created based on empirical understandings of practical needs in implementing the relevant law.[16]

Involuntary hospitalisation in the *Mental Health Law*

Policies governing involuntary admission constitute one of the most fundamental components of any nation's mental health care system. China's first *Mental Health Law*, released in October 2012, also lays out provisions on psychiatric commitment, providing for the principle of voluntary hospitalisation with 'dangerousness or risk of dangerousness' as a necessary component of forced civil commitment.

Principle of voluntariness for diagnoses and its exceptions

According to the World Health Organization, autonomy and informed consent should form the basis of the treatment and rehabilitation of people with mental disorders (WHO 2005). China's MHL 2012 echoes this international standard by stating that: 'Except where the law provides otherwise, an individual may not be medically evaluated to determine whether they have a mental disorder against his will' (Article 28). This Article actually announces a principle of voluntariness for diagnoses. The only exception to the voluntary diagnoses principle is that 'close family members may deliver a person suspected of having a mental disorder to a medical establishment for a mental disorder diagnosis' (Article 28). While ideally one's close family members would have the best interests of the mentally ill person in mind, this is not always the case and civil commitment can be a powerful weapon. China has already seen publicised cases of spouses delivering each other for treatment so as to claim their assets, and parents delivering their adult children for diagnosis when they disapprove of a romantic partner.[17] This exception makes it easier for family members to have each other held, at least temporarily (MHL 2012, Article 28, paragraph 3). In earlier drafts of the MHL, the period for diagnosis was limited to seventy-two hours, but the final text does not contain this requirement and only requires that diagnosis be performed without delay (MHL 2012, Article 29).

Principle of voluntariness for hospitalisation and the dangerousness exception

Traditionally, hospitals in China had the right to take patients from their homes and forcibly admit them merely at the request of the patients' relatives or police.[18] Voluntary hospitalisation and treatment of persons with mental illness was not the norm in the past. According to a national survey covering seventeen Chinese cities in 2002, the proportion of voluntary hospitalisation in mental health hospitals was only 18.5 per cent (Pan et al. 2003). Although this kind of practice can indeed help some patients receive much-needed treatment promptly, it also has the potential of doing harm. Therefore, the MHL 2012 extends the principle of voluntariness to hospitalisation (residential treatment) but still leaves some exceptions, providing that a person suffering from a mental disorder has the right to refuse residential therapy, except when '[h]e or she has already exhibited self-harming conduct or there is a danger of self-injury; or, he or she has already exhibited conduct that endangers the safety of others, or there is danger that he or she will endanger the safety of others' (MHL 2012, Article 30). These provisions emphasise voluntary hospitalisation and treatment as the first line of treatment; they require informed consent from the patient or the family member or guardian and they restrict the use of involuntary treatment by laying out a dangerousness or risk of dangerousness requirement.

More than that, the MHL 2012 also grants a mental health patient and their guardians the right to contest the decision of involuntary hospitalisation. When the patient has already exhibited self-harming conduct or there is danger of self-injury, the guardian has the power to agree or disagree to residential therapy. When the mental health patient has already exhibited conduct that endangers the safety of others, or there is danger that he or she will endanger the safety of others, or if the patient or their guardian disagrees with the decision of involuntary hospitalisation, either of them can apply for a second diagnosis or evaluation and even for an independent expert evaluation (MHL 2012, Article 32). The MHL also grants patients and their guardians the right to file lawsuits when they believe their rights have been infringed upon (MHL 2012, Article 82).

However, one of the main concerns regarding these safeguards is related to the lack of control over guardians. Almost all the safeguards take it for granted that guardians would act in the best interest of the patients. However, empirical evidence contained in the survey I have conducted reveals that this is not always the case. For example, what if the guardians have a conflict of interest? The MHL 2012 has not resolved this problem and it has even granted extensive rights to the guardians without subjecting them to appropriate control or oversight. When persons are found to be physically dangerous to themselves, their own objection to treatment is not considered, only that of the guardian. In the case that the guardian does not have best interests of the patient in mind, the person has no protection at all.

Absence of judicial review

It is a basic jurisprudential principle that all people are entitled to a full and impartial judicial hearing prior to a loss of liberty (Gostin 1987, 360). Especially in the area of involuntary civil commitment law, the presence of regular and on-going judicial review has served as a bulwark of protection against arbitrary state action (Perlin 1998). Therefore, to reduce the discretion of physicians and limit medical paternalism, many countries have enacted laws transferring the authority to order an involuntary admission from physicians to non-medical authorities (Dressing, and Salize 2004). In China, this shift has not yet manifested because the MHL 2012 still emphasises the dominant role of doctors by providing that 'the diagnosis of mental disorders shall be made by certified psychiatric physicians' (MHL 2012, Article 29). In cases where the patient or their guardian object to commitment, and the patient has been found dangerous to others, they may seek a second opinion from two more physicians, and if still unpersuaded, may themselves hire forensic evaluators, who are part of a small subset (about 2,000 nationally) of psychiatric physicians, for a final review (MHL 2012, Article 32). All these provisions suggest the diagnosis of mental disorders under the MHL 2012 is a medical, not legal, determination, in which the court does not play a role at all.[19]

Moreover, under the MHL 2012, involuntary residential treatment does not require a finding of a specific medical disorder, but only of a 'severe mental illness', defined broadly as causing 'serious deficits in abilities like social adjustment, an incomplete understanding of his own well-being or of objective reality, or an inability to handle his own affairs' (MHL 2012, Article 83). Thus, the determination of whether involuntary commitment is needed is part of the same purely medical diagnosis that must find a 'severe mental illness'. Simply put, there are fewer protections provided for unwilling mental patients under the MHL 2012. The MHL 2012 procedures, medical in nature and lacking the procedural protections of the courtroom, provide an easy way to confine a person indefinitely without court review. Many of the shortcomings of the MHL 2012 reflect a longstanding bias which prioritises the patient's requirement to receive treatment over the patient's rights and autonomy.

Generally speaking, China's MHL 2012 is not in line with international standards because it does not adhere to the WHO checklist for mental health legislation. Most notably, there is an absence of the existence of an independent authority to authorise all involuntary admissions. Related to this, the WHO checklist provides that the independent authority is to make a decision rapidly and that they engage in time-bound periodic reviews of admission (WHO 2005, 133).

Conclusions

As illustrated above, both the *Criminal Procedure Law* 2012 and the *Mental Health Law* 2012 set up procedural rules for the involuntary commitment of persons with mental illness. The release of this legislation shows that China is aware of its problems involving psychiatric treatment, which include both under-inclusion (the failure to give people the treatment they need) and over-inclusion (where people who should not be committed are committed to hospital), and is taking action at the highest levels to resolve them. However, a close look at these laws demonstrates a lack of unified strategy in dealing with the involuntary commitment of mentally ill individuals.

In both pieces of legislation, the confinement of a mentally ill individual is a form of preventative detention, based on providing treatment in an environment where the patient cannot harm others. Under the CPL 2012, having already committed a dangerous crime is a prerequisite to a patient's commitment and must be proven in court. The treatment of persons found not to bear criminal responsibility under the law in a Ministry of Public Security-run psychiatric facility is not technically a punishment, but is aimed at ensuring that another offence does not occur. The MHL 2012, however, does not require either an act of violence or a court proceeding of any kind before commitment – only a vague risk of dangerousness to self or others, as verified by a psychiatric doctor. This suggests that while the CPL 2012 has introduced a judicial review mechanism to determine whether compulsory commitment is necessary, the MHL 2012 still places the power to hospitalise a person with a mental disorder in the hands of psychiatric hospitals and guardians, neither of whom can always make the decision in the best interest of the patient. It is also paradoxical that a person with mental illness may enjoy more protection when he or she commits a crime-like violent act than if he or she just poses danger to self or others.

Given that involuntary commitment, whether compulsory treatment or involuntary hospitalisation, is a deprivation of liberty, alternative measures should be offered to reflect the principle of proportionality. Considering the shortage of beds in *ankang* hospitals across the country, a form of psychiatric probation could be implemented, allowing outpatient treatment for patients who are able to regain control of their actions while taking medicine, with maintaining a drug regimen a condition of the release. Compulsory medication is also an infringement on liberty, but a patient found to require compulsory treatment under criminal law, or their legal representative, might be given the choice of this less restrictive option. The MHL 2012 already mobilises social forces to participate in the care of mentally ill people in their area, and this could include the supervision of those released under compulsory treatment orders. At the very least, this would allow persons under compulsory treatment orders to consult with attorneys and other physicians more easily. The greatest obstacle to a community-based compulsory medication model may be the lack of professionals who can work in the community to ensure that outpatients take their medicines every day. Very few medical students want to be psychiatric experts, due to the longstanding stigma attached to both mentally ill people and mental health professionals. Therefore, the better protection for those with mental illness depends ultimately upon the change of public attitudes towards psychiatric patients.

Notes

1 For more details see Nesossi (23 January 2013).
2 Ng (1990) offers one of the most comprehensive monographs on the legal treatment of mentally ill people in imperial China.

3 This legislation includes the *Criminal Law* (*Xing Fa*) 1979, the *Criminal Procedure Law* 1979, the *Civil Procedure Law* (*Mingshi Susong Fa*) 1982, the *General Rules of Civil Law* (*Minfa Tongze*) 1987 and the *Security Administrative Punishment Regulation* (*Zhi'an Guanli Chufa Tiaoli*) 1987.
4 Examples of these are the *Provisional Regulations on Psychiatric Evaluation of Mental Illness* (*Jingshenjibing Sifa Jianding Zanxing Guiding*) 1989 and the *Procedural Rules on Forensic Analysis* (*Sifa Jianding Chengxu Tongze*), issued on 7 August 2007 by the Ministry of Justice.
5 For example, Macartney and Whitwell (2010) report on Xu Lindong, a villager of the Henan province, who was confined in the Zhumadian Municipal Psychiatric Hospital after having filed a series of complains against the local government. Transferred to the Luohe City Psychiatric Hospital, Xu was held against his will for a total of six and a half years, put under physical restraints forty-eight times, and given electric shocks on fifty-four occasions during his confinement. Having tried several times to escape, and twice attempted suicide, Xu was released because of pressure resulting from media coverage of his case.
6 The psychiatric service system of China is institutionally complex. It is uncertain how many administrative systems (*xitong*) have their own psychiatric facilities, but these great numbers of mental health services are provided by only four departments. The largest mental health service is governed by the Ministry of Health and its local bureaus. Nationally, these public psychiatric hospitals are accessible to urban and rural citizens who have health insurance covering their medical costs. The second largest service is managed by local departments of the Ministry of Civil Affairs. These facilities mainly serve those who are unemployed or homeless and those whose families are otherwise too poor to pay for their care. The third largest service is within the military. Military hospitals primarily serve military personnel and their families. However, in recent years, a number of these hospitals have begun providing care on a fee-for-service basis to local citizens. Finally, there is a service managed by the provincial or municipal departments of public security, called *ankang* hospitals. These hospitals provide care for mentally ill criminal offenders (Yang et al. 2010). Surprisingly, not all the *ankang* are under direct control of public security organs.
7 The problem of competency to stand trial has not yet received sufficient attention in China (Guo 2010).
8 According to preliminary empirical research data that I have collected, 'temporary restrictive measures for protection' is no different from compulsory treatment in practice, because doctors assume that those with severe symptoms of mental illness cannot be controlled without taking psychiatric medicine.
9 The second paragraph of Article 334 in the MPS Rules 213 provides that the public security shall remove temporary protective measures to restrain those mentally ill persons who do not pose a danger to society, if restraining measures can be removed without creating a danger to society.
10 The MPS Rules 2013 Article 332 provides that the public security organ must submit an opinion on compulsory treatment to the procuratorate within only seven days of finding the treatment necessary.
11 It is noteworthy that a commitment hearing can also be held in appellate procedure; where if a people's court in the course of hearing the second-instance trial of a criminal case discovers that a defendant might meet the requirements for compulsory treatment, it may handle the case according to the compulsory treatment procedures; it may also decide to return the case to the original trial court for a new judgment (SPC Interpretations 2013, Article 534).
12 See second paragraph of Article 286 of the CPL 2012; see also SPP Regulations 2013 Article 549.
13 According to the 2012 *Criminal Procedure Law,* when a compulsory treatment establishment submits an opinion (after periodical evaluation) to have compulsory treatment removed or when the person subjected to compulsory treatment and their close family apply for removal of compulsory treatment, the people's court shall form a collegiate panel to perform a review.
14 According to the WHO (2005) checklist, laws governing the police's role in mental health admissions should include the following: 1) place restrictions on the activities of the police to ensure that persons with mental disorders are protected against unlawful arrest and detention, and are directed towards the appropriate health care services; 2) allow family members, carers or health professionals to obtain police assistance in situations where a patient is highly aggressive or is showing out-of-control behaviour; 3) require that persons arrested for criminal acts, and in police custody, be promptly assessed for mental disorder if there is suspicion of mental disorder; 4) make provision for the police to assist in taking a person to a mental health facility who has been involuntarily admitted to the facility; and 5) make provision for the police to find an involuntarily committed person who has absconded and return him/her to the mental health facility (WHO 2005, 146–7).

15 Local implementation rules have been issued only in some provinces, but comprehensive rules at the national level are still needed to unify the practice across the country.
16 Since 2013, the author has been working on a research project involving survey data in collaboration with the China Law Center at Yale University.
17 For example, Chen Dan, an engineer living in Beijing, was estranged from her family as they disapproved of her boyfriend. She was brought to the hospital by her parents; the mental institution held her for seventy-two hours for observation before ultimately releasing her (Liu 8 July 2015).
18 In China, a basic form of involuntary admission at the request of police is called 'medical protection hospitalisation'. Such hospitalisation requires a specific and confirmed mental disorder diagnosed according to China's diagnostic system (CCMD–3) or diagnostic criteria adopted internationally (ICD-10).
19 There still lingers a longstanding stigma against mental illness, with the popular assumption being that mentally ill persons pose a threat to the social order (Park et al. 2005). As a result, the legislation leans more toward ensuring of public safety than the guaranteeing of patients' rights.

References

Chen Weidong. 2011. 'Goujian Zhongguo Tese Xingshi Tebie Chengxu (Constructing Special Criminal Procedures with Chinese Characteristics).' *Zhongguo Faxue* (Chinese Legal Science) 6: 32–42.
Cheng Weidong and Chai Yufeng. 2013. 'Jingshengbing Huanzhe Qiangzhi Yiliao De Xingzhi Jieding Ji Chengxu Jiegou (Analysis of Nature and Procedure on Compulsory Treatment for Mentally Ill).' *Anhui Daxue Xuebao* (Anhui University Journal) 1: 124–36.
Bao Congying. 2010. *A Thorny Road Out of the Asylum*. CRIENGLISH.com. Available at http://english.cri.cn/8706/2010/12/19/2041s610942.htm (accessed 16 February 2016).
Daum, Jeremy. 20 May 2013. 'Still Crazy After All These Years.' Available at http://chinalawtranslate.com/still-crazy-after-all-these-years/?lang=en (accessed 16 February 2016).
Dressing H. and Salize, H.J. 2004. 'Epidemiology of Involuntary Placement of Mentally Ill People Across the European Union.' *The British Journal of Psychiatry* 184: 163–8.
Gostin, Lawrence. 1987. 'Human Rights in Mental Health: A Proposal for Five International Standards Based upon The Japanese Experience.' *International Journal of Law and Psychiatry* 10(4): 353–68.
Guo Zhiyuan. 2010. 'Approaching Visible Justice: Procedural Safeguards for Mental Examinations in China's Capital Cases.' *Hastings International and Comparative Law Review* 33: 21–54.
Guo Zhiyuan. 2012. 'Xingshi Susong Zhong Jingshenbing Jianding De Chengxu Baozhang Shizheng Diaoyan Baogao (Empirical Survey Report on Procedural Safeguards for Mental Examinations in Criminal Proceedings).' *Zhengju Kexue* (Evidence Science) 6: 721–36.
Hays, Jeffrey. 2011. 'Mental Health in China: History, Freud, Lack of Care and High Numbers.' *Facts and Details*. Available at http://factsanddetails.com/china/cat13/sub83/item1720.html (accessed 16 February 2016).
Hu Jinian, Higgins, James and Higgins, Louise. 2006. 'Development and Limits to Development of Mental Health Services in China.' *Criminal Behaviour and Mental Health* 6: 69–76.
Liu Yang. 8 July 2015. 'Chen Dan in the Online Publishing of False Information.' *Beijing News*.
Munro, Robin. 2000. 'Judicial Psychiatry in China and Its Political Abuses.' *Columbia Journal of Asian Law* 14(1): 3–125.
Macartney, Jane and Whitwell, Tom. 27 April 2010. 'Xu Lindong, Sent to Asylum for Writing a Petition, Is Freed After Six Years.' Available at http://www.thetimes.co.uk/tto/news/world/asia/article2492392.ece (accessed 16 February 2016).
Nesossi, Elisa. 23 January 2013. 'The 2012 Mental Health Law 精神卫生法 – An Interview with Guo Zhiyuan 郭志媛.' Available at http://www.thechinastory.org/2013/01/the-2012-mental-health-law-精神卫生法-an-interview-with-guo-zhiyuan-郭志媛/ (accessed 16 February 2016).
Ng, Vivien. 1990. *Madness in Late Imperial China: From Illness to Deviance*. Norman, OK: University of Oklahoma Press.
Pan Z., Xie B. and Zheng Z. 2003. 'A Survey on Psychiatric Hospital Admission and Relative Factors in China.' *Journal of Clinical Psychological Medicine* 13(5): 270–2.

Park L., Xiao, Z., Worth J. and Park, J.M. 2005. 'Mental Health Care in China: Recent Changes and Future Challenges.' *Harvard Health Policy Review* 6(2): 35–45.
Perlin, Michael. 1998. *Mental Disability Law: Civil and Criminal*. New York: Lexis Law Publishing.
Yang Shao, Bin Xie, Del Vecchio Good, Mary Jo and Good, Byron J. 2010. 'Current Legislation on Admission of Mentally Ill Patients in China.' *International Journal of Law Psychiatry* 33(1): 52–7.
Wang Haiyan and Wang Yinglong. 2012. 'Woguo Xingshi Qiangzhi Yiliao Chengxu Yanjiu (Research on China's Compulsory Treatment Procedure).' *Jianghuai Luntan* (Jianghuai Forum) 5.
Wang Jiancheng. 2012. 'Lun Qiangzhi Yiliao Chengxu De Lifa Goujian He Sifa Wanshan (On Legislative and Judicial Reforms on Compulsory Treatment).' *Zhongguo Xingshifa Zazhi* (Criminal Justice Journal of China) 4.
World Health Organization. 2005. *WHO Resource Book on Mental Health, Human Rights and Legislation*. Geneva: World Health Organization.

Part II
Criminal justice reforms and deprivation of liberty

5 Residential surveillance
Evolution of a Janus-faced measure

Joshua Rosenzweig

Introduction

In the field of criminal procedure, coercive measures (*qiangzhi cuoshi*) serve three main functions: prohibiting suspects from posing additional harm to society, preventing them from obstructing the processes of criminal investigation or adjudication and ensuring their availability to face questioning or stand trial (Li Jianming 2012, 16). Because the degree of social harm and other circumstances can vary widely across individual cases, the law makes a variety of coercive measures available to law enforcement officials, each featuring a different degree of coercion in the level of restriction imposed on individual rights and the conditions under which such restrictions are experienced.

In Chinese criminal procedure, the measure known as 'residential surveillance' (*jianshi juzhu*) was initially intended to serve as a relatively lenient, non-custodial coercive measure applicable in a relatively limited set of situations. Over time, it has undergone substantial legislative elaborations aimed at (1) standardising its application and enforcement and (2) encouraging its use to reduce reliance on pre-trial detention. In the course of this effort, residential surveillance has been dissociated from its earliest intentions as a largely interchangeable alternative to release on guarantee pending further investigation and become established in its own right as a distinct measure.

Numerous factors, ranging from the broader patterns of socio-economic change in China to the context in which crime-fighting activity is carried out and evaluated, have conditioned the ways that residential surveillance has been implemented in practice over the decades. During this time, a number of problematic tendencies have emerged in relation to the enforcement of residential surveillance, and these have led many legal experts and practitioners to advocate its abolition. Ultimately, however, residential surveillance has been retained in subsequent revisions of the *Criminal Procedure Law* (*Xingshi Susong Fa*) (CPL) for its largely theoretical potential to reduce custodial detention and its more proven utility as a law enforcement tool.

The most recent CPL revision process in 2011–12 has resulted in residential surveillance taking two quite distinct forms, each with rather contradictory rationales for existence. On the one hand, the ordinary form of residential surveillance is still justified as a means of reducing pre-trial detention; on the other, an exceptional, 'non-residential' form has become formalised as a special detention measure for dealing with offenders considered by the authorities to be especially serious threats to the socio-political order. Though a public consultation process enabled a broader set of voices to raise concerns about aspects of this latter use of residential surveillance, the public debate tended to remain focused on relatively narrow issues without addressing more fundamental problems associated with the particular practice of 'designated-location' residential surveillance.

Consequently, the CPL 2012 has opted to retain residential surveillance in this dual and contradictory form that emphasises its role as an alternative to custodial detention while simultaneously legalising many of the measure's more problematic aspects. Failure to properly acknowledge the contradictions inherent in residential surveillance is likely to ensure both that it remains difficult to apply in its 'ordinary' form and that the enforcement of its exceptional form continues to endanger the core individual rights of criminal suspects subjected to it.

Residential surveillance: early intentions and articulations

Looking back to the earliest legislative articulations of the practice of residential surveillance, it is clear that it was originally intended as a non-custodial alternative to arrest (*daibu*) to be used in relatively limited circumstances. After establishing that arrest is to be used in cases involving counter-revolutionary or other offences punishable by imprisonment or death, Article 2 of the *Regulations on Arrest and Detention* (*Daibu Juliu Tiaoli*) 1954 listed residential surveillance and 'release on guarantee pending further investigation' (*qubao houshen*) as exceptional measures to be used against an individual who met the conditions for arrest but who could not be incarcerated due to serious illness or because she was either pregnant or nursing an infant. No other statutory guidance was provided regarding precisely what distinguished these two non-custodial measures, but it seems reasonable to conclude that residential surveillance was mainly contemplated for use in situations where a guarantor could not be secured (Zuo 2012a, 58).

In principle, at least, non-custodial coercive measures were given certain priority by the drafters of the CPL 1979, perhaps out of a sincere intention to restrict and regulate detention following the institutional chaos and legal nihilism of the Cultural Revolution. Consequently, law enforcement and judicial agents were authorised to use residential surveillance under one of the following five conditions: (1) when an offence was relatively minor and did not warrant punishment by imprisonment or death and there was no need for arrest; (2) when the main facts of the case had been ascertained and punishment by imprisonment was indicated but non-custodial measures would be sufficient to prevent further harm to society; (3) when arrest was necessary but the individual suffered from an acute, highly infectious, or otherwise serious illness; (4) when arrest was necessary but the individual was a woman who was either pregnant or nursing an infant; or (5) when arrest was indicated following the use of criminal detention but there was insufficient evidence to obtain approval from the procuratorate (CPL 1979, Articles 38, 40 and 44; Hao 1982, 32).

Though the conditions for use of non-custodial measures such as residential surveillance were expanded under the CPL 1979, the legislation continued to treat residential surveillance and release on guarantee pending further investigation as largely indistinguishable from each other by failing to define when one measure should be used as opposed to the other. However, the new law did provide a rather rudimentary definition of how residential surveillance was to be implemented. According to Article 38(2), residential surveillance meant prohibiting a suspect or defendant from leaving a 'designated area' (*zhiding quyu*). The measure was to be enforced by the local public security organ; however, this responsibility could also be delegated to the people's commune or work unit to which the individual was connected.

Problematic enforcement practices

By many accounts, the vague definition of residential surveillance in terms of its targets and enforcement made it subject to a number of abuses during the 1980s and 1990s. First, there was the problem of residential surveillance being used against persons for whom no coercive measures should have been used, such as witnesses or other persons with knowledge of the case but who were not suspects (Hao 1982, 32). Police were known to use residential surveillance as a way of pressuring individuals to settle debts or hand over illegal proceeds (Cui 1996, 104). Residential surveillance was also sometimes used within factories or enterprises to deal with disciplinary matters that did not rise to the level of criminal offence (Hong 1983, 23). On the other hand, observers also noted improper use of residential surveillance in situations where custodial detention or arrest was called for – for example, where keeping the suspect under residential surveillance was insufficient to prevent further threat to society (Hao 1982, 32).

Even more prevalent and troubling problems arose from the lack of statutory specificity regarding the meaning of the 'designated area' in which residential surveillance was to be enforced. In practice, this area could be set quite restrictively to be a room in a guesthouse, a space inside the local police station or work unit, or even a detention centre (Hao 1982, 33; Hong 1983, 23; Cui 1996, 104–5). As the boundaries of the designated area became narrower and in the absence of rules governing how residential surveillance should be enforced, critics worried that the measure risked turning into a form of complete isolation and deprivation of personal liberty.

Looking at residential surveillance from the perspective of law enforcement, one also notes that the relevant provisions of the CPL 1979 offered little in the way of sanctions for those who evaded the restrictions of residential surveillance. Escape from a detention facility was punishable under the *Criminal Law* by up to five years' imprisonment (*Criminal Law* (*Xing Fa*) 1979, Article 161), but the law was silent about any punishment for escape from residential surveillance. This created two incentives that discouraged use of residential surveillance as a replacement for custodial detention. Investigators felt more certain about the ability of arrest and detention to ensure that suspects were available to the judicial process and could not pose any threat to society. When residential surveillance was used, those in charge of enforcement had an incentive to place targets under isolation by employing stringent conditions like 24-hour monitoring and restrictions on meeting with friends and relatives (Dai 1988). This potential for residential surveillance to devolve into 'disguised detention' (*bianxiang juliu*) was identified early on. Critics blamed a general lack of understanding and professional training among police, together with residual 'leftist' thinking that placed too little emphasis on respect for constitutionally guaranteed rights and an operational preference for 'isolated investigation' (*geli shencha*) (Hong 1983, 23). The risk was further compounded by the ability of police to delegate enforcement responsibility to others (such as work units) and exacerbated by the absence of any statutory limit on how long the measure could be imposed – giving residential surveillance the potential to become a form of 'life imprisonment' (Cui 1996, 105).

In 1984, the Supreme People's Court (SPC) was confronted with the problem of residential-surveillance-as-detention when it was asked by the Henan High People's Court to rule on the question of whether a defendant's penal sentence could be reduced for pre-trial time spent under residential surveillance. The SPC noted that Chinese law only allowed defendants to receive credit for 'time served' in custodial detention – in other words, excluding time spent under the less restrictive measure of residential surveillance. However, the court also observed that residential surveillance had been carried out improperly in the specific case in question because authorities had placed the defendant inside a detention house. The SPC ruled that, given such 'disguised detention', the defendant was in fact entitled to a reduction of sentence, but it also instructed the lower court to inform the public security organ in question to pay attention to proper implementation of the law in future (Supreme People's Court of the PRC 1984).

The matter of unlawful implementation of residential surveillance came up again in 1991, when the SPC was asked by the Fujian High People's Court for its opinion on whether an individual held under residential surveillance in a manner tantamount to detention could file an administrative lawsuit under the *Administrative Procedure Law* (APL) (*Xingzheng Susong Fa*) 1989. The APL excludes measures taken during criminal investigation from matters that could be pursued through administrative litigation, but one view within the lower court maintained that, in order to reduce unlawful implementation of residential surveillance, such cases ought to be treated as administrative actions subject to prompt review by the court. Though admirable for its desire to use judicial review to ensure the procedural rights of individual suspects, this position clearly lacked solid footing in both statute and practice at the time. Consequently, the SPC again specifically ruled out any administrative litigation in such cases, limiting the suspect's options to the filing of a 'complaint' (*fanying*) with the superior public security organ (Supreme People's Court of the PRC 1991).

Reforming residential surveillance

In the discussions that preceded revision of the CPL in 1996, there were many who recommended abolition of residential surveillance on grounds that its utility as a coercive measure had been outflanked by the flawed manner in which it was implemented. Police seldom used it, and when they did it typically entailed either 'disguised detention' (which risked violating the rights of suspects and defendants) or else surveillance in name only (which rendered it pointless) (Song 1992, 141). In spite of these problems, however, residential surveillance was ultimately retained in the 1996 revision because it was felt that there remained a need for an intermediate non-custodial measure with more stringent restrictions than release on guarantee (Cui 1996, 104–8). New provisions were added to the CPL 1996 to elaborate on the circumstances in which residential surveillance could be applied (Article 51), set clearer rules governing its implementation (Article 57), and establish explicit limits on the duration of its enforcement (Article 58).

After the 1996 revisions, it became clearer that, relative to release on guarantee pending further investigation, residential surveillance would involve tighter restrictions approaching a kind of 'soft detention' (*ruanjin*) (Zuo 2012a, 59). New limits were placed on the target's ability to meet with other people during the period of residential surveillance (CPL 1996, Article 57).[1] Compared to the more expansive 'designated area', which could in practice extend to the city or county of residence, the new statute obliged a person placed under residential surveillance to remain within their 'domicile' (*zhuchu*) unless given permission to leave and stated that 'those without a fixed domicile' could be confined to a 'designated residence' (*zhiding de jusuo*) (CPL 1996, Article 57). In recognition of the more substantial degree of restriction, the 1996 CPL also established a shorter time limit for residential surveillance (six months) relative to release on guarantee pending further investigation (one year) (Article 58).

But because the 1996 law provided no definition of what was meant by 'fixed domicile', it was not absolutely clear when residential surveillance could be enforced in a designated residence. Initially, at least, this enabled routine abuse of residential surveillance as 'disguised detention' to continue unabated until procedural regulations issued in 1998 by the Ministry of Public Security (MPS) took steps to remedy that lacuna (Ma and Feng 2007, 156). Under those provisions, a residence qualified as 'fixed' if it was (1) 'legal' (*hefa*) and (2) located in the jurisdiction (prefecture- or county-level) of the public security organ investigating the case (MPS *Procedural Regulations* 1998, Article 98). The MPS regulations also placed limits in principle on the locations available for use as 'designated residences', explicitly prohibiting public security organs from establishing dedicated facilities or using detention centres or public security 'work locations' for the purposes of implementing residential surveillance (Article 98).

Adaptation and practice of residential surveillance

The attempt to formalise conditions for a new type of 'non-residential' residential surveillance appears to have been motivated in large part by a desire to do three things simultaneously: adapt to new socio-economic conditions, make residential surveillance more operationally attractive as a non-custodial coercive measure and curb abuse of residential surveillance as 'disguised detention'. After two decades of socio-economic reform, increasing rural–urban and intra-urban population mobility made it more likely that a person would live someplace other than the location officially listed as their place of household registration. Especially in economically developed parts of China such as the coastal provinces, migrants came to make up a substantial majority of those suspected of criminal offences (Cheng and Lai 2010, 44–5). This was a population that tended to have limited access to suitable guarantors that would allow for non-custodial release pending further investigation, so without the ability to designate a residence for the purposes of residential surveillance they would be in danger of being effectively excluded from access to non-custodial coercive measures entirely – posing a dilemma in terms of equality before the law.

Likewise, the loosening of state control over society placed a heavier burden on police. De-collectivisation of agriculture and the rise in numbers of the urban self-employed (*getihu*), contract workers, and laid-off and unemployed people made it increasingly impossible for work units, enterprises or mass organisations to take effective responsibility for monitoring criminal suspects as had been envisioned under the CPL 1979 (Chen 2007, 83). Meanwhile, the fiscal decentralisation begun in the 1980s left many police units facing budget shortfalls well into the following decade, which in turn created incentives to use residential surveillance in illegal or inappropriate ways as a means of raising funds to cover essential operating costs (Tanner and Green 2007). For example, 'designated-location' residential surveillance could be used as leverage to press for the payment of fines by those penalised for prostitution or traffic-related offences. It could also be used to exert pressure in tax-related cases, cases involving illicit gains or even corruption cases, with the idea being that release and even the dropping of charges would be conditioned on payment (Chen 2003, 41).

The limited empirical evidence that has been published gives strong indications that after the 1996 revision of the CPL, residential surveillance was used mainly in cases involving the migrant population but that its overall usage remained infrequent relative to other coercive measures. In their survey of locations in Sichuan, Ma Jinghua and Feng Lu (2007) found that residential surveillance was overwhelmingly used as a substitute for release on guarantee in cases involving migrant suspects, in line with the measure's intent. But they found that most instances of 'ordinary' residential surveillance amounted to *de facto* release, with no real monitoring, while the few instances of designated-location residential surveillance they cite are of an extremely short duration – days, compared to the maximum six months available under law (Ma and Feng 2007). In a much larger sample based on records from 1999 to 2000 in a single district in Loudi, Hunan, Chen (2003) found that of 603 suspects put under residential surveillance, only 15 were monitored in their residence, versus 588 who were placed in a 'designated residence', which happened to be a public-order lockup, in violation of the law. More significantly, only 180 of the total 603 people placed under residential surveillance ultimately had their cases transferred for arrest or prosecution, while most of the rest saw their cases 'transformed' into administrative punishments (Chen 2003).

Further reform of residential surveillance

Not long after the first revisions to the CPL in 1996, China adopted a number of new normative standards that created pressure for additional procedural reforms. In October 1998, China signed the *International Covenant on Civil and Political Rights*, which, upon ratification, would have many ramifications for criminal procedure. Five months later, the National People's Congress (NPC) amended China's constitution to declare that the PRC 'practices ruling the country in accordance with the law and building a socialist country of law'. In his valedictory work report to the 16th Party Congress in October 2002, former General Secretary Jiang Zemin declared 'respect and protection of human rights' to be a component of 'socialist democracy' and specifically mentioned reform of procedure law as a key element of legal reform, one necessary to 'safeguard the legal rights and interests of citizens' (Jiang 8 November 2002).

In October 2003, the NPC Standing Committee included further revision of the CPL in its five-year legislative plan. Legal scholars seized the new atmosphere and commitment to further procedural reform and produced a number of comprehensive revision proposals they hoped might serve as grist for the legislative mill. In consideration of the many practical problems surrounding residential surveillance, most of these proposals advocated its elimination altogether (see for example, Fan 2004, 323; Xu 2005, 362; Tian and Chen 2007, 14). If residential surveillance had to be retained, scholars proposed a number of new provisions designed to limit its use only to specified offences (Fan 2004, 323) or protect the lawful rights and interests of individual targets – for example by requiring notification of relatives, shortening the duration, ensuring communication with lawyers and family members, and providing channels to challenge the decision to impose residential surveillance itself (Chen 2006, 365–71).

An initial consensus on establishing a number of rights-based amendments to the CPL was met with vigorous opposition from law enforcement institutions (Ke 11 February 2007), resulting in the abandonment of a draft revision proposal in 2007. Work on a new and more extensive set of amendments re-commenced in late 2008 under the leadership and guidance of the Central Political–Legal Committee. On 24 August 2011, a new draft proposal to amend the CPL (hereafter 'CPL Draft Proposal 2011') was put before the NPC Standing Committee and, shortly thereafter, published at the commencement of a one-month period in which members of the public could offer comments and submit recommendations through the NPC website (*Renda wang* 30 August 2011).

Members of the public submitted nearly 81,000 comments during the month-long period of public consultation from 30 August to 30 September, with more than half of all comments sent in during the first week. Among the many controversies surrounding the proposed amendments to the CPL, changes to the provisions regarding residential surveillance and other coercive measures became a topic of heated debate within Chinese public opinion, and concerns were raised about the law's potential to legitimise 'secret arrest' (Rosenzweig 2013).

The draft legislation proposed a number of changes that seemed aimed at some of the long-standing problems associated with residential surveillance. Clearer distinctions were made between the criteria for release on guarantee pending further investigation and residential surveillance. Notably, the use of residential surveillance was made contingent on meeting the stricter standards for formal arrest, though investigators could also employ it in lieu of release on guarantee if a guarantor could not be found (CPL Draft Proposal 2011, Article 29). Investigators were given new discretion to impose residential surveillance on grounds of 'special circumstances' or 'investigative necessity,' though these formulations were left undefined (2011 CPL Draft Proposal, Article 29). Perhaps most significantly, explicit conditions were set out to govern the use of the 'designated residence' form of the measure. In addition to those 'without fixed abode', a location could be designated for residential surveillance under the following circumstances: (1) in 'cases involving crimes of endangering state security, terrorist activity, or major bribery'; (2) when enforcement of the ordinary form of residential surveillance could 'potentially hinder the investigation'; and (3) upon permission from a superior procuratorate or public security organ (CPL Draft Proposal 2011, Article 30).

When using the designated-abode form of residential surveillance, investigators would be required to notify a suspect's relatives within twenty-four hours of the reason and location where the residential surveillance was being carried out, except 'when it is impossible to give notice' or when (1) the case involves crimes of endangering state security or terrorist activity and (2) 'when notification has the potential to interfere with the investigation' (CPL Draft Proposal 2011, Article 30).

The proposed amendments also included other provisions designed to protect the rights of individuals placed under 'non-residential' residential surveillance. Those subject to the measure were given the right to retain a defence lawyer, though separate provisions allowed police to prohibit meetings between a suspect and his lawyer if the case involved state security or terrorist offences (CPL Draft Proposal 2011, Articles 7 and 30). Procuratorates were empowered with oversight over decisions and enforcement related to designated residence residential surveillance, though the draft legislation left it unclear how exactly that oversight would be carried out (CPL Draft Proposal 2011, Article 30). On the other hand, police were given broader power to limit suspects' ability to meet with others and would be authorised to use electronic surveillance technology to help enforce the restrictions on movement called for under residential surveillance (CPL Draft Proposal 2011, Article 33).

Residential surveillance and the 'secret arrest' debate

In the public debate that took place during the consultation period, the provisions concerning notification for residential surveillance and other coercive measures generated considerable concern. Overall, there was a sense that the provisions would create a dual-track system of coercive measures in which rights and protections guaranteed to suspects in most criminal cases could be substantially restricted in cases involving allegations of state security offences, terrorism or serious corruption. The flexible definition of some of these criminal offences – for example the provision in Article 105(2) concerning 'inciting subversion' (Rosenzweig 2012) – contributed to concern that investigators might take advantage of the new provisions to carry out arbitrary and incommunicado detentions. These dangers associated with withholding notification were particularly acute for residential surveillance because of its maximum six-month duration, effectively allowing investigators to 'disappear' a suspect for an extended period of time without any effective remedy or check. With a few exceptions, however, criticisms were aimed at a more general concern about 'secret arrest' (*mimi jubu*), rather than specific coercive measures, and there was relatively little public discussion of the practice of residential surveillance beyond the notification provisions.

Critics warned of 'rampant secret arrest' and decried what they viewed as an expansion of police power at the expense of individual rights (see for example, Wang 30 August 2011). A number of legal experts countered by pointing out that the changes being proposed to the CPL would actually limit – not expand – police ability to detain suspects without notification, because under the CPL 1996 investigators had been under no obligation to provide any notification of residential surveillance to a suspect's relatives (Yang and Zha 31 August 2011). Chen Weidong, the Renmin University Law Professor whose 2005 model code had effectively eliminated residential surveillance, showed signs of exasperation with critics as he rejected their fears about the potential for the new measures to be abused. 'You have to believe that the investigators handling such cases are all doing their jobs and are [acting] responsibly toward the cases,' he told an interviewer. 'How could they abuse power on behalf of terrorists and those who endanger state security?' (Yan 1 September 2011). The seriousness of these offences that 'seriously endanger the interests of the entire nation and threaten the lives and security of an unspecified majority of people' ultimately justified any deprivation of rights, which, Chen asserted, 'will not affect the rights of the broad popular masses (*renmin qunzhong*) or ordinary people (*laobaixing*) because they generally won't be involved in such offences' (Yan 2011).

Scepticism persisted, however, about such attempts to segment the application of procedural rights. As a *Southern Metropolis Daily* editorial explained:

> The reason that the 'victim public' opposes [these provisions in the CPL] is because they fear that, given the label of 'suspects' without reason, they may become victims of law enforcement. It's not that they lack deep understanding; it's just that they realized long ago how law enforcement personnel have created miscarriages of justice and comported themselves over these many years. (*Southern Metropolis Daily* 2 September 2011)

In an attempt to address concerns about 'secret arrest', changes were made to a new draft of the proposed amendments to the CPL, which the NPC Standing Committee considered in a second reading on 26 December 2011. With respect to residential surveillance, a rather weak provision was included requiring authorities to notify family members immediately 'once the conditions of interfering with the investigation have disappeared' (Peng 25 January 2012). Pressure to address concerns of 'secret arrest' did not let up, however, and when draft amendments were finally submitted to the plenary session of the 11th NPC on 8 March 2012, the notification exclusion for residential surveillance had been eliminated from the legislation.

'Non-residential' residential surveillance under the Criminal Procedure Law 2012

Though critics of 'secret arrest' could claim a limited victory, exclusive focus on the issue of notification had obscured a number of specific problems associated with the practice of residential surveillance. Even after being stripped of most of the notification exceptions, the provisions of the CPL 2012 concerning residential surveillance remained extremely problematic, especially in the 'non-residential' or 'designated-location' form. According to Wang Mingwen, one of several NPC delegates who tried unsuccessfully to eliminate 'designated residence' residential surveillance entirely, the lack of regulations governing such spaces 'could very well render pointless all of the hard work on the prohibition of torture and the exclusion of illegal evidence' (cited in Ye 29 March 2012). Such fears were particularly appropriate since the CPL itself would have less bearing on the way residential surveillance would be implemented in practice than the accompanying institutional regulations issued by the MPS and Supreme People's Procuratorate (SPP) in advance of the law coming into force on 1 January 2013.[2]

As noted above, the CPL 2012 authorises designation of a location for residential surveillance either when the suspect lacks a 'fixed residence' or when each of the following conditions are met: (1) the case involves offences involving endangering state security, terrorism, or 'extremely serious bribery'; (2) enforcement of the residential form of residential surveillance has the potential to 'impede the investigation'; and (3) permission is granted by a superior-level procuratorate or public security organ (CPL 2012, Article 73).

Both the MPS and SPP regulations define 'fixed residence' as a 'legal' (*hefa*) residence (*zhuchu* or *jusuo*) in the city or county where the case is being handled (2013 MPS Procedural Regulations, Article 108; 2013 SPP Procedural Regulations, Article 10). There is, however, no clear standard for what constitutes 'legality' of a residence in the context of criminal procedure, leaving the matter open to a degree of interpretation. According to the definition of 'domicile' under civil law, legal residence might be defined as the place of household registration.[3] Many Chinese reside in locations different from their places of household registration, however. Chinese civil law provisions also contain the concept of 'habitual residence', which requires a period of continuous residence of one year or more.[4] But there is also the problem of determining whether a rental unit can be considered a 'fixed' residence or how to handle individuals who reside in shared rentals or dormitories (Wu and Liu 25 June 2013).

With respect to the other set of conditions governing use of 'designated residence' residential surveillance, both the MPS and SPP have attempted to define for the first time the meaning of the phrase 'impede the investigation'. Taken together, these two sets of regulations lay out six main areas of concern: (1) the potential to destroy or fabricate evidence; (2) the potential to interfere with witness testimony or coordinate statements; (3) the potential to lead an accomplice to evade arrest or obstruct the investigation; (4) the potential for escape, self-mutilation, or suicide; (5) the potential for the suspect or defendant to pose a risk to witnesses or accusers; and (6) the matter of whether a family member or co-worker (*qi suozai danwei de renyuan*) has been implicated in the crime (2013 MPS Procedural Regulations, Article 107; 2013 SPP Procedural Regulations, Article 110).

The implementation regulations have also attempted to establish new conditions for 'designated residence'. The 1998 MPS regulations had stated only that 'detention centres, administrative detention facilities, holding cells, or other work spaces in the public security organ' could not be designated as residences for the purposes of residential surveillance and special facilities could not be constructed for the purpose (1998 MPS Procedural Regulations, Article 98). In addition to retaining these basic prohibitions, both the MPS and SPP regulations also set positive obligations for the selection of 'designated residences', requiring them to (1) possess conditions for ordinary living and rest; (2) accommodate monitoring and management; and (3) ensure security (2013 MPS Procedural Regulations, Article 108; 2013 SPP Procedural Regulations, Article 110). Despite being required to provide conditions for 'ordinary living and rest', however, this standard is left undefined and there is no corresponding obligation upon law enforcement authorities to ensure that individuals under residential surveillance enjoy these basic human activities to any particular extent.

Another significant change in the CPL 2012 concerning residential surveillance was the provision crediting time spent under residential surveillance in a 'designated location' against any future sentence (CPL 2012, Article 74). For fixed-term imprisonment or penal servitude (*juyi*), the credit amounted to a reduction of one day for every two days spent under residential surveillance, whereas a sentence of public surveillance (*guanzhi*) was reduced on a one-to-one basis (cf. Criminal Law 1997 Articles 41, 44 and 47). In one respect, this is a clear recognition of the difference between 'ordinary' and 'non-residential' residential surveillance and a tacit acknowledgment of the latter's quasi-custodial nature. But some have questioned whether such credits should automatically be applied in all cases, given the two different types of criminal suspects covered by the measure: those suspected of state security offences, terrorism, or corruption, on the one hand, and those suspected of 'ordinary' offences who lack a 'fixed residence' on the other. While the former category may experience 'non-residential' residential surveillance as a measure akin to custodial detention, Professor Zuo Weimin (2012b) is sceptical that many suspects in the latter category would be subjected to the same degree of stringency. This, he has argued, creates the potential for substantive inequality in punishment based solely on the presence or absence of a suitable residence for the purposes of residential surveillance (Zuo 2012b, 33–8).

When placing a suspect or defendant under residential surveillance in a designated residence, investigators are required to notify the individual's family within twenty-four hours, but the law does not prescribe any particular form or content of such notification (MPS Procedural Regulations 2013, Article 108). The SPP regulations specify that such a notice includes the 'reason' for the residential surveillance, but the MPS regulations require only the completion of a written notification (SPP Procedural Regulations 2013, Article 114; MPS Procedural Regulations 2013, Article 109). This is a notable departure from the corresponding provision in the first draft of the CPL amendments, which specified that notice should include the cause and location of enforcement (CPL Draft Proposal 2011, Article 30). Though some tried to argue that notifications would most likely include the reason and location of the 'designated residence' (Chen and Gao 4 April 2012), since the revised CPL took effect public security organs seem to have interpreted the law's silence on the matter as licence to withhold such information (see for example, The Dui Hua Foundation 8 January 2013).

One area of notable improvement in the revisions to the CPL has been the extension of the criminal defence lawyer's role into the investigative stage and provisions to facilitate meetings between suspects and their lawyers (see, however, Rosenzweig et al. 2013, 490–503). However, failure to provide information about the whereabouts of a criminal suspect placed under residential surveillance outside of their home has the potential to negate that suspect's right to access defence counsel. Investigators are obligated to inform suspects of their right to appoint a defence lawyer, but lawyers are unlikely to gain easy access to a person under 'non-residential' residential surveillance because Article 37(4) of the CPL 2012 gives investigators discretion to withhold approval of lawyer-client meetings in cases involving state security offences, terrorism or extremely serious corruption – the same categories that serve to define who may be held under this exceptional form of residential surveillance in the first place. According to the MPS regulations, such approval should only be denied on grounds that the meeting would 'impede the investigation' (defined as above) or if there were a potential to 'leak state secrets' (MPS Procedural Regulations 2013, Article 49). The latter category is notoriously flexible when applied to state security investigations; even when approval is obtained, the delay involved can be significant.

The experience

The relatively unregulated nature of the 'designated residence' increases the potential that this exceptional form of residential surveillance becomes an extreme form of *de facto* custodial detention beyond what is ordinarily experienced in a detention centre, with the isolated nature of the custody creating a perfect environment for physical and psychological abuse. This concern is confirmed by the experiences of individuals who were subjected to this form of residential surveillance under the provisions of the CPL 1996, along with the experiences of others whose 'disappearance' under police custody substantially resembled residential surveillance despite police failure to complete the measure's formal procedural requirements (for the latter category, see Gao 8 February 2009; Ng 14 September 2011). Their experiences suggest that Chinese police have used 'non-residential' residential surveillance not only as an adjunct to criminal investigation but as a form of direct punishment and intimidation as well.

When democracy activist He Depu was placed under residential surveillance in a designated location in November 2002, domestic security police from Beijing stripped him of his clothing and forced him into an unheated, windowless room. There, he was required to remain on a wooden bed and given only a thin rayon quilt to keep warm. Rotating teams of guards forced him to remain lying on the bed and insisted that his hands and feet be visible at all times. He was not allowed to shave, cut his hair or nails, or shower. His guards abused him verbally and physically, stretching his limbs out when he failed to keep his hands and feet visible. Forced to remain in this fixed position for hours on end, He developed painful, bloody lesions but was not allowed to see a doctor or change his bed covering. Exhausted by his 85-day ordeal under residential surveillance, He found himself looking forward to those moments when he was taken out for interrogation, because then he was able to sit on a stool. According to He, who would go on to spend eight years imprisoned on charges of 'inciting subversion', the brutality of the regime he endured under residential surveillance was far worse than anything he experienced in Beijing's detention centre or prisons (He and Jia 23 September 2011).

Artist Ai Weiwei was kept in two separate 'designated residences' during an 81-day period under residential surveillance in 2011. Despite having been told that he was being held on tax charges, police also interrogated him about alleged ties to the so-called 'Jasmine Revolution' movement that had occurred that spring. Two paramilitary guards watched his every move around the clock – including as he slept, showered and used the toilet – from inside a small, padded room with artificial lights glaring twenty-four hours a day (Bradsher 12 August 2011; Wong 27 May 2012). In another case, Guangzhou-based rights lawyer Liu Shihui, another early casualty of the 2011 crackdown, spent 108 days under residential surveillance on suspicion of 'inciting subversion', during which time he was interrogated day and night for five straight days without sleep until he collapsed from exhaustion (Siweiluozi Blog 22 August 2011). Around the same time, investigators held Shanghai rights lawyer Li Tiantian under residential surveillance for 95 days, forcing her to submit to endless and humiliating questions regarding intimate details of her sexual relationships and threatening her with physical violence if she did not answer truthfully (Li Tiantian 5 April 2012; Lam 30 May 2011).

Round-the-clock surveillance, continuous interrogations and other sleep deprivation, beatings, denial of personal hygiene, threats and humiliation, use of restraints such as handcuffs for days on end, being forced to sit or kneel in stress positions or confined to bed for extended periods of time are featured in the accounts of those who have been subjected to 'designated-location' residential surveillance or otherwise 'disappeared' by police in connection with alleged political offences. The inhuman and degrading treatment experienced by these individuals during residential surveillance may be atypical, a consequence of their having been suspected of threatening the political order. Yet it is precisely this class of offenders – along with other groups deemed to be among the most serious threats to the existing socio-political order – that has been singled out for use of a measure that enables such deprivations of rights and dignity. This suggests that this particular coercive measure functions to create psychological and physical pressure intended to 'soften up' detainees and make them more pliant for interrogation and willing to produce confessions, truthful or otherwise.

Concluding thoughts

How did a measure originally intended as a lenient alternative to custodial detention develop such a problematic alternative identity? The extension of residential surveillance into non-residential spaces under the 1996 CPL was initially intended to make the measure more flexible and practicable in the context of China's changing socio-economic environment. At the same time, there was an effort made by both legislators and the institutions charged with enforcement to regulate the measure by prohibiting the use of certain types of locations and imposing obligations on both the enforcers and subjects of residential surveillance. These new rules may have had an impact on the availability of residential surveillance in the first place, but they did little to constrain the behaviour of those who enforced the 'designated residence' type of residential surveillance when it *was* applied, leaving them with considerable discretion as far as how life was arranged inside these spaces.

Under a criminal justice system that privileged efficiency and results over procedures and rights, a police apparatus that exercised power with few restraints and little accountability, and a growing sense of socio-political instability that made a priority of 'stability preservation', certain uses of residential surveillance became institutionalised in practice for their instrumental value in, among other things, separating an individual from their network of contacts and using the fear associated with such dislocation to condition the behaviour of both suspects and those associated with them. A system of implicit rules, unauthorised practices, and outright fictions began to surround these usages of residential surveillance. Despite growing recognition that use of this kind of residential surveillance was problematic from the perspective of rights protection, the utilitarian value of this measure and the practices that went along with it ensured that it could not be completely abolished. The apparent 'solution' has been to use legal reform to, on the one hand, legitimate these implicit rules and unauthorised practices by placing them under the law while, on the other hand, also trying to limit their application in order to better justify the costs of such practices in terms of individual rights suspended.

As a result, residential surveillance has effectively developed into two completely distinct measures with rather different rationales for existence. On the one hand, there remains the idea of residential surveillance as an alternative to the custodial measures of criminal detention and arrest. Over time, the effort to distinguish residential surveillance from release on guarantee has positioned the measure as the more stringent of the two non-custodial measures, and there is still a clear sense that its existence – at least in its ordinary, residential form – is justified on grounds of the need to help reduce China's extremely high use of pre-trial detention. But, at the same time, 'designated residence' residential surveillance has developed into an extraordinary, highly flexible form of *de facto* extended detention employed not because of any lenience relative to arrest but, instead, because its relative *severity* facilitates the handling of certain highly sensitive cases.[5]

In other words, the non-residential form of residential surveillance has become, for all intents and purposes, a separate coercive measure. Failure to acknowledge this dual nature openly in the context of the CPL is deeply troubling, because the practice of non-residential residential surveillance poses serious risks to core civil rights nominally protected under China's constitution: the right of personal freedom, the right to legal defence, and the rights to make appeals and allegations of wrongdoing. Considering these risks, it is not unreasonable to conclude that this form of residential surveillance is at least as severe a measure as the custodial measures of criminal detention or arrest and, therefore, deserves special scrutiny (Sun 2013). As Professor Sun Yuhua has argued: 'We may want to expand the application of residential surveillance to reduce the use of detention and arrest, but if residential surveillance itself is, because of a few crucial flaws, less able to protect human rights than detention or arrest, then what is the point of expanding its use?' (Sun 2013, 152).

To mitigate the risks to individual rights, Sun (2013) contends that the non-residential form of residential surveillance ought to be acknowledged as a separate custodial measure and a range of procedural protections should be put in place. These include requiring decisions to be made or approved by a 'neutral' body (following the decision-making model for arrest, for example), a system of pre-trial hearings to determine appropriateness or remedy illegality, and the designation of suitable locations by the judicial administration organ, rather than public security. Moreover, access to defence counsel should be ensured, the duration of the measure should be reduced and compensation for unlawful use should be made available.

Looking at the matter more through the prism of effectiveness and fairness, rather than constitutional rights, Professor Zuo Weimin (2012b) comes to many of the same conclusions about the 'designated residence' form of residential surveillance. Though Zuo (2012b) maintains that decisions about its suitability within China's criminal justice system must be based on observation of how the measure is actually applied, he is critical of the legislative flexibility and omissions that can encourage abuse and inefficiencies. Considering the relatively unregulated nature of the locations chosen for the 'designated residence' form of residential surveillance, it is not unreasonable to have concerns about disguised detention, problematic interrogations or torture. He recommends that a system of quasi-judicial oversight should be established in which approval over decisions be given to the procuratorate (or the courts, in procuratorial investigations), suspects and their defence counsel have ample opportunity to make their opinions heard during the decision-making process, and imposition of 'non-residential' residential surveillance is subject to ongoing, periodic review (Zuo 2012b).

It is worth noting that many of these reform proposals would be welcome remedies to flawed implementation of other coercive measures, which points to the fact that many of the problems of 'designated residence' residential surveillance originate in the ways that coercive measures are used in pursuit of goals other than the three general aims proposed in the introduction. Many attempts to justify the practice of 'designated residence' residential surveillance are based on an idealised version of how the measure ought to be enforced (see for example, Sha 2013). In reality, though, residential surveillance (and, perhaps to a lesser extent, other coercive measures) has been used not as a means of preventing suspects from posing harm to society or obstructing criminal investigation, but rather as a tool of criminal investigation or even as a form of summary punishment.

Though one of the official principles guiding the most recent revision to the CPL was the idea of seeking balance between crime-fighting and protection of human rights, it is this imperative to find balance that has enabled these instrumental uses of coercive measures like residential surveillance to enter the law itself. If China's criminal procedure legislation were instead guided by a notion of procedural justice aimed solely at restricting and normalising the exercise of state power to ensure that rights are not violated in the course of the state's exercise of its legitimate power to control crime, then the prospects for the non-residential form of residential surveillance would be put in doubt or at least subjected to a very different set of considerations in determining its merits. Since such a shift would entail new thinking about not only criminal justice but also fundamental political and constitutional issues, the prospects for addressing the more problematic aspects of residential surveillance will await a combination of focused attention on the measure's flaws in theory and practice and continued public pressure to do more to establish procedures and mechanisms to limit the exercise of state power in the interest of protecting private rights.

Notes

1 See also *Ministry of Public Security Procedural Regulations for the Handling of Criminal Cases by Public Security Organs* (*Gong'an Jiguan Banli Xingshi Anjian Chengxu Guiding*), implemented 14 May 1998 (hereafter 'MPS Procedural Regulations 1998'), Article 97.
2 *Ministry of Public Security Procedural Regulations for the Handling of Criminal Cases by Public Security Organs* (*Gong'an Jiguan Banli Xingshi Anjian Chengxu Guiding*), implemented 1 January 2013, (hereafter 'MPS Procedural Regulations 2013'); *Supreme People's Procuratorate (Provisional)*

Criminal Procedure Rules for People's Procuratorates (Renmin Jianchayuan Xingshi Susong Guize (Shixing)), implemented 1 January 2013 (hereafter 'SPP Procedural Regulations 2013').

3 Supreme People's Court of the PRC, Opinion of the Supreme People's Court on Several Questions Concerning Application of the Civil Procedure Law of the PRC (Zuigao Renmin Fayuan Guanyu Shiyong Zhonghua Renmin Gongheguo Minshi Susongfa Ruogan Wenti De Yijian), issued 14 July 1992, Article 4.

4 Supreme People's Court of the PRC, (Provisional) Opinion of the Supreme People's Court on Several Questions Concerning Implementation of the General Principles of Civil Law of the PRC (Zuigao Renmin Fayuan Guanyu Guanche Zhixing Zhonghua Renmin Gongheguo Minfa Tongze Ruogan Wenti De Yijian (Shixing)), issued 26 January 1988, Article 9.

5 For a slightly different articulation of this point, see Bian 23 March 2012.

References

Bian Jianlin. 23 March 2012. 'Jianshi Juzhu Ruguo Zhixing Buhao, Liangdian Keneng Quan Da Baitiao (If Residential Surveillance Is not Implemented Well, Its Highlights Will Remain Unfulfilled).' Sina.com. Available at http://news.sina.com.cn/pl/2012-03-23/172424164542_2.shtml (accessed 16 February 2016).

Bradsher, Keith. 12 August 2011. 'Conditions of Chinese Artist Ai Weiwei's Detention Emerge.' The New York Times. Available at http://www.nytimes.com/2011/08/13/world/asia/13artist.html (accessed 16 February 2016).

Chen Guangzhong, ed. 2006. Zhonghua Renmin Gongheguo Xingshi Susongfa Zai Xiugai Zhuanjia Jianyigao Yu Lunzheng (Annotated Expert Draft for Re-amendment to the Criminal Procedure Law of the People's Republic of China). Beijing: Zhongguo fazhi chubanshe.

Chen Jianxin. 2003. 'Dui Jianshi Juzhu Cuoshi Shishi Xianzhuang De Diaocha Yu Sikao (Investigation and Thoughts on the Present State of Implementation of Residential Surveillance).' Renda Yanjiu (National People's Congress Research) 133: 40–2.

Chen Jingfang. 2007. 'Jianshi Juzhu Qiangzhi Cuoshi Ying Yu Feichu (Residential Surveillance Ought to Be Abolished).' Renmin Sifa (People's Judicature) 17: 83–6.

Chen Weidong and Gao Tong. 4 April 2012. 'Cong Liu Ge Fangmian Chongsu Jianshi Juzhu Zhidu (Reshaping Residential Surveillance from Six Aspects).' Jiancha Ribao (Procuratorate Daily). Available at http://newspaper.jcrb.com/html/2012-04/04/content_96681.htm (accessed 16 February 2016).

Cheng Rongbin and Lai Yuzhong. 2010. 'Lun Feichu Jianshi Juzhu De Liyou (Reasons to Abolish Residential Surveillance).' Shandong Jingcha Xueyuan Xuebao (Journal of the Shandong Police Academy) 109 (January): 44–8.

Cui Min. 1996. Zhongguo Xingshi Susongfa De Xin Fazhan: Xingshi Susongfa Xiugai Yantao De Quanmian Huigu (New Developments in China's Criminal Procedure Law: Complete Account of the Discussions about Revision of the Criminal Procedure Law). Beijing: Zhongguo renmin gong'an daxue chubanshe.

Dai Tao. 1988. 'Zhixing Jianshi Juzhu Zhong Xuyao Jiejue De Jige Wenti (Several Issues Needing to Be Resolved in the Implementation of Residential Surveillance).' Faxue (Jurisprudence) 6: 39.

Fan Chongyi, ed. 2004. Xingshi Susongfa Xiugai Zhuanti Yanjiu Baogao (Research Report on the Subject of Revising the Criminal Procedure Law). Beijing: Zhongguo renmin gong'an daxue chubanshe.

Gao Zhisheng. 8 February 2009. 'Dark Night, Dark Hood, and Kidnapping by Dark Mafia—My Account of More than 50 Days of Torture in 2007.' Human Rights in China. Available at http://www.hrichina.org/sites/default/files/oldsite/PDFs/PressReleases/2009.02.08_Gao_Zhisheng_account_ENG.pdf (accessed 16 February 2016).

Hao Chiyong. 1982. 'Zhengque Yunyong "Jianshi Juzhu" Zhe Yi Qiangzhi Cuoshi (Proper Usage of "Residential Surveillance").' Faxue (Jurisprudence) 11: 32–3.

He Depu and Jia Jianying. 23 September 2011. 'Guanyu Zhonghua Renmin Gongheguo Xingshi Susongfa Xiuzheng'an (Cao'an) De Xianshen Shuofa (Personal Views on the [Draft] Amendments to the Criminal Procedure Law of the People's Republic of China).' Canyu.org. Available at http://www.canyu.org/n31317c6.aspx (accessed 16 February 2016).

Hong Qiusheng. 1983. 'Qiantan Jianshi Juzhu (Brief Discussion of Residential Surveillance).' *Renmin Sifa* (People's Judicature) 3: 23.
Jiang Zemin. 8 November 2002. 'Quanmian Jianshe Xiaokang Shehui, Kaichuang Zhongguo Tese Shehuizhuyi Shiye Xin Jumian—Zai Zhongguo Gongchandang Dishiliuci Quanguo Daibiao Dahui Shang De Baogao (Comprehensively Build a Moderately Well-Off Society, Open New Fronts for Socialism with Chinese Characteristics: Report to the 16th National Congress of the Chinese Communist Party).' *Xinhuanet.com*. Available at http://news.xinhuanet.com/newscenter/2002-11/17/content_632278.htm (accessed 16 February 2016).
Ke Liangdong. 11 February 2007. 'Xiugai Xingshi Susongfa Bixu Zhongshi De Wenti (Issues That Need Emphasis for Revision of the Criminal Procedure Law).' *Fazhi Ribao* (Legal Daily).
Lam, Oiwan. 30 May 2011. 'China: Detained Rights Lawyer Interrogated about Sex Life.' *Global Voices Online*. Available at http://globalvoicesonline.org/2011/05/30/china-detained-rights-lawyer-interrogated-about-sex-life (accessed 16 February 2016).
Li Jianming. 2012. 'Shiyong Jianshi Juzhu Cuoshi De Hefaxing Yu Gongzhengxing' (Legality and Fairness in the Application of Residential Surveillance).' *Faxue Luntan* (Legal Forum) 27(3): 14–22.
Li Tiantian. 5 April 2012. 'Muqian Zhongguo Fazhi Da Daotui, Weiquan Lüshi You Qieshen De Tihui (Rights Defense Lawyers Have Personal Experience of China's Current Backsliding on Rule of Law).' *Human Rights in China*. Available at http://www.hrichina.org/en/content/5966 (accessed 16 February 2016).
Ma Jinghua and Feng Lu. 2007. 'Jianshi Juzhu: Gongneng Yu Shiyong' (Residential Surveillance: Functions and Application). In *Zhongguo Xingshi Susong Yunxing Jizhi Shizheng Yanjiu* (Empirical Research into Operational Mechanisms of Chinese Criminal Procedure), edited by Zuo Weimin, 151–63. Beijing: Falü chubanshe.
Ng Tze-wei. 14 September 2011. 'Making People Vanish.' *South China Morning Post*.
Peng Dongyu. 25 January 2012. 'Xingshi Susongfa Xiuzheng'an Cao'an Wancheng Er'shen (Second Reading of Criminal Procedure Law Draft Amendment Completed).' *Zhongguo Renda* (China's People's Congress). Available at http://www.npc.gov.cn/npc/zgrdzz/2012-02/10/content_1687790.htm (accessed 16 February 2016).
Renda wang. 30 August 2011. 'Xingshi Susong Fa Xiuzheng'an (Cao'an) Tiaowen Ji Cao'an Shuoming ((Draft) Amendments to the Criminal Procedure Law, with Commentary).' Available at http://www.npc.gov.cn/npc/xinwen/lfgz/2011-08/30/content_1668503.htm (accessed 16 February 2016).
Rosenzweig, Joshua. 2012. 'The Sky Is Falling: Inciting Subversion and the Defense of Liu Xiaobo.' In *Liu Xiaobo, Charter 08, and the Challenges of Political Reform in China*, edited by Jean-Philippe Béja, Hualing Fu and Eva Pils, 31–59. Hong Kong: Hong Kong University Press.
Rosenzweig, Joshua. 2013. 'Disappearing Justice: Public Opinion, Secret Arrest and Criminal Procedure Reform in China.' *The China Journal* 70: 73–97.
Rosenzweig, Joshua D., Sapio, Flora, Jiang Jue, Teng Biao and Pils, Eva. 2013. 'Comments on the 2012 Revision of the Chinese Criminal Procedure Law.' In *Comparative Perspectives on Criminal Justice in China*, edited by Mike McConville and Eva Pils, 455–503. Cheltenham, UK: Edward Elgar.
Sha Ningbo. 2013. 'Zhiding Jianshi Juzhu Zai Zhencha Jieduan De Shijian Tanjiu (An Inquiry into the Practice of Residential Surveillance in a Designated Location During the Investigation Phase).' *Fazhi Yu Shehui* (Legal System and Society) 5: 251–52.
Siweiluozi Blog. 22 August 2011. 'I've Only Begun to Scratch the Surface: Liu Shihui Reveals Details of 108-Day Detention.' Available at http://www.siweiluozi.net/2011/08/ive-only-begun-to-scratch-surface-liu.html (accessed 16 February 2016).
Song Qiang. 1992. 'Lun Woguo Xingshi Qiangzhi Cuoshi Xin Tixi' (On a New System of Coercive Measures for China). In *Xingshi Susongfa De Xiugai Yu Wanshan* (Reform and Improvement of the Criminal Procedure Law), edited by Zhongguo Faxuehui Susongfa Yanjiuhui, 136–45. Beijing: Zhongguo zhengfa daxue chubanshe.
Southern Metropolis Daily. 2 September 2011. 'Xingsufa Daxiu, Gongzhong Buan Yu Youju Xu Dedao Shujie (Revision of the Criminal Procedure Law: The Public's Unease and Concern Must Be Alleviated).'

Sun Yuhua. 2013. 'Zhiding Jusuo Jianshi Juzhu De Hexianxing Shenshi' (Reviewing the Constitutionality of Designated-Residence Residential Surveillance). *Faxue* (Jurisprudence) 6: 146–53.
Supreme People's Court of the PRC. 18 December 1984. Zuigao Renmin Fayuan Guanyu Yifa Jianshi Juzhu Qijian Kefou Zhedi Xingqi Wenti De Pifu (Response from the Supreme People's Court Regarding Whether Time Spent in Residential Surveillance May Reduce the Penal Sentence in Accordance with the Law). Available at http://www.chinalawedu.com/news/1200/23079/23081/23127/2006/3/zh12542282717360022970-0.htm (accessed 16 February 2016).
Supreme People's Court of the PRC. 24 May 1991. Zuigao Renmin Fayuan Xingzheng Shenpanting Guanyu Dui Gong'an Jiguan Caiqu Jianshi Juzhu Xingwei Bufu Tiqi Susong Fayuan Yingfou Shouli Wenti De Dianhua Dafu (Telephone Reply from the Supreme People's Court Administrative Division Regarding Whether Courts Should Accept Litigation Challenging Use of Residential Surveillance by Public Security Organs). Available at http://china.findlaw.cn/fagui/cxf/23/24448.html (accessed 16 February 2016).
Tanner, Murray Scot and Green, Eric. 2007. 'Principals and Secret Agents: Central Versus Local Control over Policing and Obstacles to "Rule of Law" in China.' *China Quarterly* 191 (September): 644–70.
The Dui Hua Foundation. 8 January 2013. 'China Ushers in Non-Residential Residential Surveillance.' *Dui Hua Human Rights Journal*. Available at http://www.duihuahrjournal.org/2013/01/china-ushers-in-non-residential.html (accessed 16 February 2016).
Tian Wenchang and Chen Ruihua, eds. 2007. *Zhonghua Renmin Gongheguo Xing Shi Su Song Fa Zai Xiugai Lüshi Jianyigao Yu Lunzheng* (Annotated Lawyers' Draft for Re-Amendment of the Criminal Procedure Law of the People's Republic of China). Beijing: Falü chubanshe.
Wang Heyan. 30 August 2011. 'Xingsufa Xiuding Zhengqiu Yijian: Bufen Tiaokuan Daotui Yinfa Danyou (Criminal Procedure Law Revision Seeks Opinions: Regression in Some Provisions Causes Concern).' *Caxing.com*. Available at http://china.caixin.com/2011-08-30/100296591.html (accessed 16 February 2016).
Wong, Edward. 27 May 2012. 'First a Black Hood, Then 81 Captive Days for an Artist in China.' *The New York Times* A10.
Wu Shichun and Liu Jiyan. 25 June 2013. 'Lun Jianshi Juzhu Zhidu Zhong De Zhixing Changsuo (On the Location of Implementation for Residential Surveillance).' *Chongqing Fayuan Wang* (Chongqing Court Online). Available at http://cqfy.chinacourt.org/article/detail/2013/06/id/1017241.shtml (accessed 16 February 2016).
Xu Jingcun, ed. 2005. *Zhongguo Xingshi Susongfa (Di Er Xiuzheng'an) Xuezhe Nizhigao Ji Lifa Liyou: Tiaowen, Shiyi Yu Lunzheng* (Scholarly Proposal and Legislative Reasoning for China's Criminal Procedure Law [Second Amendment]). Beijing: Falü chubanshe.
Yan Mu. 1 September 2011. '"Mimi Jubu" Chuyu Ban'an Baomi Kaolü ("Secret Arrest" Done in the Interest of Preserving Case-Handling Secrecy).' *Diyi Caijing Ribao* (China Business News). Available at http://www.yicai.com/news/2011/09/1055458.html (accessed 16 February 2016).
Yang Weihan and Zha Wenye. 31 August 2011. 'Xingsufa Xiuding Neirong Youliyu Fanzui Xianyiren Renquan Baohu (Revised Criminal Procedure Law Benefits Protection of Criminal Suspects' Human Rights).' *Xinhuanet.com*. Available at http://news.xinhuanet.com/legal/2011-08/31/c_121940680.htm (accessed 16 February 2016).
Ye Zhusheng. 29 March 2012. 'Xingsufa Xiuding, Shiheng De Boyi (Revision of the Criminal Procedure Law: An Imbalanced Competition).' *Nanfengchuang* (South Reviews). Available at http://www.nfcmag.com/article/3401.html (accessed 16 February 2016).
Zuo Weimin. 2012a. 'Fansi Jianshi Juzhu: Cuoluan De Lifa Yu Gan'ga De Shijian' (Reflections on Residential Surveillance: Confused Legislation and Awkward Practice). *Xuexi Yu Tansuo* (Study and Exploration) 8: 58–63.
Zuo Weimin. 2012b. 'Zhiding Jianshi Juzhu De Zhiduxing Sikao (Institutional Considerations Regarding Residential Surveillance in a Designated Location).' *Fashang Yanjiu* (Journal of South Central Institute of Political Science and Law) 3: 33–8.

6 China's pre-trial detention centres
Challenges and opportunities for reform

Lei Cheng and Elisa Nesossi

Introduction

In the People's Republic of China (PRC), pre-trial detention centres (*kanshousuo*)[1] detain criminal suspects prior to their trial, offenders whose remaining sentence is three months or less and criminal offenders sentenced to death and awaiting execution (Regulations of the Criminal Detention Centres of the People's Republic of China, Article 2).[2] They are established at the county level or above, administered by the Bureau for the Management of Prison and Criminal Detention Centres of the Ministry of Public Security (MPS)[3] and supervised by the people's procuratorate at various administrative levels. While the MPS provides overall coordination,[4] local police forces and detention police departments operate local detention centres all across the country. Provincial governments finance local police forces and therefore also determine the budget and human resources of these institutions. In addition to the *Criminal Procedure Law* (CPL) 2012, the *kanshousuo* are regulated by the State Council *Regulations of the Criminal Detention Centres* (*Zhonghua Renmin Gongheguo Kanshousuo Tiaoli*) 1990 (hereafter *Regulations* 1990) and by a number of specific rules, regulations and measures concerning different areas of work.

While the total number of pre-trial detention centres is not publicly available, Chinese scholars estimate that today there are about 2,700 such institutions across the country and approximately one million pre-trial detainees. The majority of people who undergo criminal proceedings in China – nearly 90 per cent, according to Chinese scholars' estimates (Chen Weidong 2005, 2) – are subject to a period of detention within *kanshousuo*. As we observe in this chapter, the extensive use of pre-trial detention is due to the following conditions: the way in which criminal proceedings are structured; the strong link between authorities responsible for detention and investigation; and the flaws in the system of pre-trial measures alternative to detention –'taking a guarantee and awaiting trial' (*qubao houshen*)[5] and residential surveillance (*jianshi juzhu*) (see Chapter 5 in this volume).[6] This chapter outlines these problems and assesses some of the challenges to the process of legislative reform.

Notwithstanding the central role of *kanshousuo* in the overall functioning of the criminal justice system in contemporary China, for decades these institutions have been neglected by both public and academic debates on reform (Nesossi 2008; Cheng 2014). Their internal practices and legislation have been surrounded by secrecy and their institutional setting considered politically sensitive because it is strictly intertwined with key functions and objectives of the MPS. Indeed, while their primary role is that of detaining criminal suspects and defendants prior to and during the trial, their functions have also been strongly linked to practices of criminal investigation and associated with wider social and political objectives of fighting crime and maintaining social stability (*weihu shehui wending*) (Nesossi 2014; Cheng 2014).

The year 2009 represented a turning point in the official and public approach towards pre-trial detention. The 'hide and seek' (*duo mao mao*) accident in Yunnan Province, where a detainee died in detention having been beaten by his fellow cellmates, together with numerous other reports about cases of unnatural death (*fei zhengchang siwang*) in several detention centres around the country, brought the spotlight to bear on various problems concerning the administration of pre-trial detention centres. As discussed in Chapter 7 in this volume, for the first time since the establishment of the PRC, the abuses, poor living conditions and the lack of respect of detainees' rights came under close scrutiny and generated both a public outcry in Chinese media and a call for legislative and institutional reforms in scholarly and official circles.

Notwithstanding the numerous debates that have unfolded since, at the time of writing, the legal and administrative structure of pre-trial detention centres have remained unchanged. Thus, today these institutions continue to be governed by the MPS according to the now-obsolete *Regulations* 1990. There are, however, reforms in the pipeline.

Below we discuss proposals for reform of pre-trial detention centres' institutional powers and legislation that have been debated in particular since 2009. After a brief historical overview, we examine challenges and opportunities for reforms in this area of the criminal justice system. We also comment on the draft of the *Criminal Detention Centres Law* (*Kanshousuo Fa*) currently under scrutiny by the National People's Congress (NPC).

Pre-trial detention centres prior to 2009

Before 1990

In China, pre-trial detention institutions have a relatively brief history associated primarily with modern and contemporary times. Pre-trial detention centres did not exist in imperial China. Historical records report that under the Qing Emperor Yongzheng (1678–1735), for the first time prisoners started to be organised between internal prison wards (*nei jian*) and external wards (*wai jian*). While sentenced inmates were locked in inner and more secluded sections, juveniles and criminal suspects waiting for trial were detained in the external wards (Cheng 2014, 24). Pre-trial detention centres were introduced into China only at the end of the Qing dynasty via Japan when, in 1906, emperor Guangxu (1871–1908) ordered the establishment of pre-trial detention centres to detain criminal suspects awaiting trial (Zhongguo renmin daxue 1979, 152). In November that year and during the following year, the imperial legislative department (*fawu bu*) issued legislation imposing the establishment of pre-trial detention institutions attached to courts (Liu 2010; Wang 2007). Similar legislation was also issued locally with the aim of standardising the establishment and administration of such institutions as well as, in some localities, the living conditions of pre-trial detainees (Cheng 2014, 27).

In 1913, the distinction between two different institutions of detention – prisons and detention centres for the detention of persons awaiting or undergoing trial, offenders sentenced to light sentence, and civil defendants – was formalised through the promulgation of two sets of rules concerning respectively pre-trial detention centres (28 January 1913) and prisons (1 December 1913) (Dikötter 2002).[7] New rules on pre-trial detention centres and county prisons were passed in May 1919 (Commission on Extraterritoriality 1926; Dikötter 2002, 3). Following the establishment of the Chinese Soviet Republic in November 1931, the Chinese Communist Party (CCP) opened a number of detention centres[8] under the control of the Committees for the Elimination of Counter-Revolutionaries (*sufan weiyuanhui*).[9] These were detaining criminal suspects awaiting trial, including suspects of counter-revolutionary crimes and general criminal cases. From 1929 up to 1934, the Central Executive Committee of Chinese Soviet Republic (*Zhongyan Zhixing Weiyuanhui*) created two different kinds of *kanshousuo*. First, it established institutions at the provincial, county and district level which detained criminal suspects awaiting trial and offenders sentenced to short-term imprisonment (offenders sentenced to long-term imprisonment were detained within reform through labour institutions (*laodong ganghua yuan*)). Secondly, on the basis of the *Statute of the Chinese Soviet Republic Provisions Governing Punishment Counter-Revolution* (*Zhonghua Suwei Gongheguo Zhengzhi Fan Geming Tiaoli*) 1934, it imposed the creation of detention centres responsible for the treatment of counter-revolutionary offenders (Zhang 2005, 18–19; English translations by Butler 1983 and Griffin 2015).

Soon after the founding of the PRC in 1949, all the laws and regulations that had governed China during the Nationalist period were dismantled and new laws and regulations promulgated instead. To regulate places of detention, in 1950 the Ministry of Justice (MoJ) and the MPS issued the *Decisions on the Armed Protection of Prisons, Reform through Labour Team and Detention Centres (Guanyu Ge Ji Jianyu, Laogai Dui He Kanshousuo Wuzhuang Jiehu De Jueding)* and, later that year, the *Instructions for the Transferring of Prisons, Detention Centres and Reform through Labour Team to the Ministry of Public Security (Guanyu Jianyu, Kanshousuo He Laodong Gaizao Dui Yizhuan Gui Gong'An Bumen Lingdao De Zhishi)*. In different ways, these directives were aimed at centralising and regularising the control over places of detention. Accordingly, prisons, detention centres and reform through labour teams were transferred from the administration of the MoJ to the MPS.

Pursuant to the 1954 PRC *Regulations for Reform Through Labour* (*Laodong Gaizao Tiaoli*), detention centres were a 'part of the people's democratic dictatorship' (Article 2) whose function was 'to assume the responsibility for understanding the conditions of criminals awaiting sentence'. Inmates were given 'thought reform' (Article 4) and 'reform through labour' under the supervision of the 'public security' and were compelled to reform attitudes (Article 1). Mistreatment and corporal punishment were 'strictly prohibited' (Article 5). Under the *Regulations for Reform Through Labour* 1954, four main institutions were responsible for carrying out reform through labour: prisons and reform through labour camps were responsible for the detention of convicted detainees; detention centres were responsible for unconvicted detainees; and institutions for the detention of juvenile delinquents were responsible for the re-education of juvenile offenders (Article 3). Until 1990, The *Regulations for Reform Through Labour* 1954 remained the main document of reference in regulating detention centres.

Pre-trial proceedings on detention and arrest were defined by the *Regulations on Arrest and Detention (Daibu Juliu Tiaoli)* 1954.[10] The *Regulations* distinguish 'detention' (*juyi* or *juliu*) and 'confinement in custody' (*jiya*). Detention preceded the decision of arrest and was to be used by public security organs against a suspect without the prior approval of the procuratorate. The time limit for detention was 72 hours and the place of detention was unspecified. Confinement in custody followed arrest – subject to the approval of the procuratorate or a decision by the people's court – and continued from the time the defendant was investigated and tried up the time of execution of the sentence. Upon admission, criminal suspects were to be subjected to a health examination. People with 'mental illness or acute or malignant contagious diseases, serious illness endangering the life of the offender while in custody, pregnant or childbirth six months or less before the time of commitment' (*Regulations for Reform Through Labour* 1954, Article 37) might not be detained.[11] Family members were to be informed of the reasons for arrest and the place of confinement, except in situations where this was seen as an obstacle to the investigation or there was no way to give notification (*Regulations for Reform through Labour* 1954, Article 4).

On the whole, up until 1979, the history of detention centres, of their administration and legalisation, has been closely and explicitly interwoven with political objectives. In March 1958, the representative of the MPS during the first National Conference on Pre-Trial Work proclaimed that the principle promoted for the detention work was 'combining class struggle and humanism'. Seven years later, during the Second National Conference on Pre-Trial Work, the MPS reiterated that the principle to be followed in pre-trial work was a 'resolute combination of class struggle and revolutionary humanism'. In July 1979, during the Third National Conference, the MPS promoted 'a combination of closely guarding [sic] on detainees and thought education' as its working principle and issued the *Criminal Detention Centres Working System* (*Kanshousuo Gongzuo Tiaoli*)[12] – an internal document to be used to direct the administration of criminal detention centres (Zhang 2005, 9).

The year 1983 was marked by two main events of great significance to the institutional and legislative history of pre-trial detention centres. In 1983, the administration of reform through labour camps (*laodong gaizao*) (today's prisons) passed under the jurisdiction of the MoJ (restored in 1979), while pre-trial detention centres, like institutions for administrative detention, remained under the control of the MPS. This signalled the key role that pre-trial detention centres would have had in facilitating pre-trial investigation by public security authorities on the basis of the then recently enacted CPL 1979. Furthermore, the start of the first 'Strike Hard' (*yanda*) campaign caused a dramatic increase of the detained population and a progressive deterioration of the conditions of places of detention,[13] which forced the MPS to design a more specific regulatory system.

Taking the *Criminal Detention Centres Working System* 1979 as its point of reference, the MPS prepared the draft proposal of new regulations. In 1986, the MPS endorsed the proposal to the State Council, which approved it and inserted it into its legislative plan. In March 1988, after a process of consultation with local police authorities, members of the Supreme People's Court (SPC), the Supreme People's Procuratorate (SPP), the Ministry of State Security, the MoJ, the Ministry of Personnel and the Ministry of Finance, the MPS sent the final legislative proposal to the State Council, that approved it two years later (Yun 2000).

1990–2009

The *Regulations* 1990 is the first legislative document specifically promulgated to regulate the PRC's pre-trial detention centres. It comprises 52 Articles organised in 11 Sections, including the initial General Provisions (Articles 1–8) and final Supplementary Provisions (Articles 45–52). The other nine Sections respectively include: detention procedures (Articles 9–15); professional duties of the detention centres' police (Articles 16–18); procedures for interrogation and escort of criminal suspect (Articles 19–21); detainees' living and hygienic conditions (Articles 22–27); meetings and correspondence (Articles 28–32); education and prizes (Articles 33–37); procedures upon release (Articles 38–40); supervision by the people's procuratorate (Articles 41–42); and other miscellaneous regulations (Articles 43–46).

During the 1990s, following the enactment of the *Regulations* 1990 and the *Methods of Implementation of the Regulations on Criminal Detention Centres (for Trial Implementation)* (*Kanshousuo Tiaoli De Shishi Banfa*) 1991,[14] the MPS issued more than 100 rules and notices aimed at regulating and standardising the system of administration and supervision of criminal detention centres. The SPP also issued a significant number of relevant rules and 'guidances' (*zhiding*) to regulate related procuratorial work (Wang et al. 2014).

Notwithstanding the declared purpose of being custodial institutions, pre-trial detention centres have always also served as places for investigating criminal cases. Since 1955, the process of detention and investigation have been closely combined (*zhen ya he yi tihua*), with the same team of police officers being asked to both interrogate and guard detainees. At the stage of preliminary inquiry (*yushen*), police officers with professional interrogation skills were responsible for interviewing suspects detained in pre-trial detention centres in order to prepare and compile the case evidence (CPL 1979, Article 3 and Section 2; CPL 1996, Article 90; 1979 MPS Rules on Preliminary Inquiry Work 1979). While this arrangement was meant to facilitate the process of evidence collection, it caused significant problems with the administration of pre-trial justice and the protection of detainees' rights. Since detention served the primary purpose of crime investigation, detention officers were prone to authorising practices that could be regarded as dubious from a legal and rights perspective but that, from a crime control perspective, could facilitate results. Measures include prolonged interrogation and removal of detainees from detention centres for interrogation, extraction of confession through torture and other illegal means, and limited access of detainees to lawyers and the outside world (Cheng 2014; Xu 2006,19).

In July 1997, the administration of detention centres underwent a major change when the MPS abolished the preliminary inquiry procedure by police officers in most provinces and consolidated pre-trial investigation and inquiry into one departmental unit (*zhenshen yi tihua*) (Bao 1998; Yun 2005). This means that since 1998 detention centre police were no longer responsible for collecting evidence and, at least in theory, became a relatively independent team in charge only of the management of detention. However, given the past close working relations between the guarding and investigation teams and the continued control by the public security over detention centres, the MPS still required – albeit informally – detention authorities to act as 'data tank of crime information' (*fanzui xinxi ku*) (Cheng 2014, 106) and 'second war location for cracking down on crime' (*daji xingshi fanzui di er zhanchang*) (Chen and Cheng 2004, 2; Wang 2001, 21).[15]

In 2008, strengthening supervision of police stations (*paichusuo*) and detention centres and improving their legislative framework were listed among the priorities of criminal justice reform (Zhao 2010). In July 2008, the State Council issued regulations that formally defined the responsibility of the Bureau for the Management of Prison and Criminal Detention Centres over the management of pre-trial detention centres, pre-arrest detention centres (*juliusuo*), detention for education centres (*shourong jiaoyu suo*), forced drug detoxification centres (*qiangzhi geli jiedusuo*), drug recovery centres (*jiedu fukang zhongxin*) and mental health hospitals (*ankang yiyuan*) (Zhao 2010). Since then, most of the provinces, cities and local public security authorities have fully abolished their investigation department (*yushen bumen*) in detention and established specialised departments responsible for the professional direction of institutions of detention (*jianguan bumen*). These changes have impacted profoundly on the management of pre-trial detention centres by facilitating the separation between their detention and investigative functions (Cheng 2014).

The post-'hide and seek' era (2009–2014)

Notwithstanding the changes mentioned in the previous section, prior to 2009, pre-trial detention centres had been relatively understudied and little was known about this aspect of the Chinese criminal justice system. They had suffered from weak public scrutiny from Chinese policymakers and had generally been unfamiliar to both the scholarly community and the public. Two main issues have contributed to bring them into the spotlight: first, the 'hide and seek' accident and the numerous other deaths in custody reported in Chinese media between 2009 and 2010 (*China Daily* 20 April 2009); and, secondly, the 2012 revision of the CPL1996 and the related debates.

The 'hide and seek' effect

Poorly funded and managed, and regulated by largely obsolete legislation, pre-trial detention centres were already facing numerous challenges at the time when the 'hide and seek' accident occurred in a pre-trial detention centre in Yunnan Province in 2009. In February of that year, media reportage on the accident involving the death of a youth called Li Qiaoming in the Jinning detention centre projected the problems of criminal detention centres into the spotlight (Liu and Zhang 21 February 2009; Luo 27 February 2009). Indeed, between 2009 and 2010, the Chinese national media reported more than ten other 'unnatural deaths', raising public indignation and fuelling intense debates (*China Daily* 20 April 2009). These accounts reported very difficult living conditions within detention centres, widespread violence and flawed management systems.

Public reports triggered discussions not only among the general public and legal scholars, but also among many of the public security authorities responsible for the administration of detention centres. The latter started to openly express their malcontent, admit their close links with the authorities responsible for crime investigation and acknowledge that pre-trial detention centres had always been a fairly marginalised institution within the entire system of criminal justice administration, fully subordinated to crime investigation authorities (Cheng 2014, 96).

The need to reform the system became formally recognised through official speeches by the then Minister of Public Security, Zhou Yongkang. Zhou asserted the importance of public scrutiny over pre-trial detention centres and the public security authorities. In his view, public scrutiny would have had positive implications on people's perception about the government and the Party, and, as a result, would have had a positive impact on the maintenance of social stability (Xinhua 21 August 2012; Nesossi 2014). The link between the issue of social instability and public discontent about governmental performance in the management of detention became prominent just at the time when the need for social stability was identified by authorities as the Party's most important political imperative (Nesossi 2014; Trevaskes et al. 2014). This assumed connection between social instability and adequate administration of detention centres precipitated the development of legislative and administrative reforms to pre-trial detention as a political priority (Cheng 2014, 97).

The reform agenda promoted by the MPS emphasised issues such as effective management of budget and technical resources. It also stressed principles like transparency and accountability to be realised through adequate monitoring and supervision by the procuratorate and the wider public (Nesossi 2014).

In April 2009, the MPS and the SPP launched a five-month campaign to scrutinise the conditions of all the national criminal detention centres, aiming to strengthen internal and external supervision over them and improve the procedures for reporting accidents (Sui 17 April 2009). In May, the MPS published *Ten Regulations on Watching Against and Combating Bullying in Detention Centres* and the *Notice on Centralizing the Management of Women Detainees in Detention Centres* (*Kanshousuo Jizhongguanya Nuxing Zai Yarenyuan Tongzhi*). A few months later, the MPS and the Ministry of Health promulgated the *Notice on Strengthening and Promoting the Public Security and Supervisory Organs that Work on Medical Treatment and Health in Detention Centres* (*Guanyu Jiaqiang Kanshousuo Gonggong Weisheng Fuwu De Tongzhi*). On 20 July 2009, the MPS issued the *Opinion on Strengthening and Improving Pre-Trial Detention Centres' Work* (*Gong'an Bu Guanyu Jin Yi Bu Gaijin Gong'an Jiguan Gongzuo De Yijian*) and launched a series of related initiatives of reform. Two years later, the MPS issued the *Notice on Pushing on Innovation of Pre-Trial Detention Centres' Management* (*Gong'an Bu Jiansuo Guanliju Guanyu Tuijin Kanshousuo Guanli Jizhi Chuanxin De Tongzhi*) requiring: the establishment of a detainee risk evaluation system to support differentiated security measures; the introduction of a psychological intervention system; the improvement of the procedures for the rights notification procedure to make detainees aware of their rights during detention; the revision of the detainee daily schedule to guarantee eight hours of rest time, two hours for outdoor activity, and more free time for entertainment, self-learning and broadcasting music; the creation of hotline telephone and online appointment system for lawyers; and finally, the strengthening of the system of supervision, including the opening of pre-trial detention centres to external monitoring (Ministry of Public Security 16 August 2011; Cheng 2014, 43; Nesossi 2014, 234–8).

To encourage detention authorities to adequately perform their required tasks, issues of security and the quality of work in pre-trial detention centres started to feature among the performance indicators used to evaluate Party and government officials at different levels, as well as detention officers (Cheng 2014, 98–100). In this way, the quality of work in pre-trial detention centres (or lack thereof) could affect their career development and promotion. Moreover, according to the principle of 'establishing responsibility' (*zeren zhuiqiu zhidu*) for incidents and 'unnatural death' in custody, individual officers and their superiors began to be held responsible for any of such accidents occurring in places of detention (Cheng 2014, 100–1).

Furthermore, since 2009, there have been numerous changes concerning human and financial resources of places of detention. This has meant an increase in the number of personnel allocated to detention institutions, a better and more regulated allocation of detention guards according to the size of the detention facility and the number of detainees, and an increase of funding from the Ministry of Finance (the amount of funding from public security still remains secret) (Cheng 2014, 103–5).

The 2012 revision of the Criminal Procedure Law

In the years 2009–2012, at the time when social stability was the key political imperative informing all criminal justice politics (Trevaskes at al. 2014), combating the extraction of confession of torture (*xingxun bigong*) and reforming the CPL 1996 were among the key topics debated by criminal justice scholars. Exposés of miscarriages of justice and deaths in custody demonstrated that detention authorities had often acquiesced to practices aimed at cracking a case (*po'an*) with direct consequences to the enjoyment of detainees' rights to a fair trial. These cases led Chinese academics and lawyers to openly challenge the pervasiveness of pre-trial detention, the widespread abuses perpetrated against criminal suspects and defendants, their difficulty in accessing lawyers and the weaknesses in the existing system in relation to alternatives to detention (bail, for example). Scholars began advocating for specific changes to the management of the detention centres and their legislative framework, inserting their arguments into wider debates concerning procedural justice and human rights (Nesossi 2012).

Thus, conforming to the spirit of promoting procedural guarantees and the respect of the rights of detainees, public security authorities responsible for detention were called to change their approach towards issues of detention and detainees. In this respect, Zhao Chunguang from the MPS claimed:

> Detention authorities must comply strictly with the policy of respecting and protecting human rights, always keeping in mind the principles of 'education, reform and rescue' of detainees. They must change some old views that privilege only security at the expenses of human rights protection. Nobody can infringe against detainees' rights. As detention police officers, if we infringe against the rights of detainees, we can become criminal

suspects as well. So, to conclude, we have the right to manage them, but we do not have the right to infringe against their rights (cited in Cheng 2014, 98).

In this spirit, torture prevention mechanisms were put in place in pre-trial detention centres, including routine physical examinations of detainees, 24x7 CCTV monitoring and recording systems, physically separated interrogation rooms[16] and measures to prohibit interrogation practices which would impact on the routine schedule of meals and rest. In some detention centres, authorities experimented with new systems for informing detainees of their rights and attempted to strengthen the supervisory role of the on-site procuratorate (Nesossi 2012; see also Chapter 7 in this volume).

The final revision of the CPL in 2012 gave further momentum to the reformist debates as it introduced provisions guaranteeing improved access to lawyers and the prohibition of extraction of confession through torture. To facilitate detainees' access to lawyers, Article 37 of the amended Law specifies that meetings between a defence lawyer and a criminal suspect or defendant in custody have to be arranged within forty-eight hours from the time they are requested and should be unmonitored (even though the meaning of 'unmonitored' is left unspecified). Moreover, in order to discourage instances of torture happening prior to the admission into detention centres or in other interrogation places, the CPL 2012 requires the police to transfer suspects to pre-trial detention centres as soon as possible after their apprehension, but no later than twenty-four hours; and once the suspects are transferred into the pre-trial detention centres, they are to be questioned only in the designated rooms (CPL 2012, Articles 83, 91 and 116).

An important issue resulting from the 2012 revision of the CPL that impacts on detention during pre-trial proceedings is the threshold imposed on arrest. The revised Article 79(1) provides that an individual may be arrested when he or she poses a risk to society manifested in any of a number of acts. These include committing a new crime involving endangering national security, public security or social order; destroying or forging evidence, for instance, interfering with the testimony of a witness or making a false confession in collusion; retaliating against a victim, an informant or accuser; or attempting to commit suicide or escape. Given the vagueness of these terms, a large number of actions by individuals can easily be construed as an arrestable offence. According to Cheng (2014), this has the potential to lead to an increase in the number of arrests and of detainees held in pre-trial detention centres.

MPS or MOJ? Regulations or law?

The two most controversial issues regarding the reforms of pre-trial detention centres concern the legislation governing pre-trial institutions and the organs responsible for their administration. The issue of control and administration of pre-trial detention centres, in particular, has proved extremely contentious, as it touches on the core interests and the powers of the very influential security authorities. As discussed in the previous section, the crux of the problem concerns the overlapping of functions between the authorities responsible for crime investigation and those responsible for detention, with the latter still being subordinate to the former. Since the early days, detention centres have been used as 'information centres' for ascertaining the facts about criminal activities, a function that public security authorities are reluctant to relinquish.

While legal scholars have been involved in the relevant debates, their views are far from homogenous. Since the early 2000s, some have argued that the authority to administer pre-trial detention centres should be transferred altogether from the MPS to the MoJ. This would guarantee a net separation between detention and investigation practices to ensure better protection of detainees' rights and to bring China's detention practices in line with relevant international standards and practices (Huang 26 March 2009). Others have supported the view that detention of individuals prior to the arrest in 'pre-trial pre-arrest institutions' (*juliusuo*) could be maintained under the control of the MPS, while the detention of criminal suspects following arrest and of sentenced offenders should operate through the prison system and administered by the MoJ (Cheng 2014, 111). Some scholars also support the view that pre-trial detention centres could be controlled by a third party, that is, an external body coordinated by the people's government and the system of the people's congress at various levels. Such an arrangement would guarantee complete institutional independence and better allocation of funding. In fact, scholars argue that in view of the significant local discrepancies in terms of human, financial, medical and logistic resources, the administration of detention centres by the central governmental authorities would secure increased uniformity all throughout the country (Cheng 2014, 182).

In comparison to institutional reforms, legislative changes appear difficult but politically less contentious and, as such, more openly discussed among legal scholars and officials. Two main views have emerged. Some have been calling for a revision of the existing *Regulations* 1990. They argue that a substantial rejuvenation of their language would bring them in line with more recent legislative documents including the *Legislation Law* (*Lifa Fa*) 2000,[17] the *Prison Law* (*Jianyu Fa*) 1994 (as amended in 2012) and the CPL 2012. From an institutional perspective, this position would favour the MPS' control over pre-trial detention institutions (Cheng 2014, 59). Others have suggested the issuing of a new law by the NPC Standing Committee (Jiang 24 February 2010; Chen 14 March 2011). This would indicate a substantial reform to the way pre-trial detention centres are regulated and administered. It would in fact promote a shift from a document that regulates the administrative aspect of detention and that is purely authority-centred, to a law that focuses on the protection of the rights of detainees and regulates the administration of detention accordingly (Cheng 2014).

The draft of the pre-trial detention centre law

The first official step towards legislative reform was taken in March 2000. At the time, the Bureau for the Management of Prison and Criminal Detention Centres established a small working group (*gongzuo xiaozu*) responsible for the amendment of the *Regulations* 1990. The group requested written suggestions from various departments in the public security, including the SPC, the SPP, the National Committee for Development and Reform, the Ministry of Finance, the Ministry of Health and the People's Armed Police. Through a series of consultations, the small working group recommended the amendment of 29 Articles of the *Regulations* 1990 and an expansion of the text of the Regulations to include 100 Articles.

In 2008, the central government included reforms to the pre-trial detention legislation into its reform priorities (Cheng 2010). The following year, in the aftermath of the 'hide and seek' accident, scholars started to criticise more openly the *Regulations* 1990 and to advocate for the enactment of a *Criminal Detention Centres Law* in line with the obligations imposed by international standards and with the requirements of the *Legislation Law* 2000 (Cheng 2014). In March 2009, the NPC Double Meeting (*lianghui*) expressed support for the issuing of a new law and in 2011 the NPC sent a motion to the MPS and the State Council calling for the promulgation of a national level law (Chen 15 February 2012).

With the MPS concentrating primarily on changes to the management of detention centres and on issues impacting upon the recurrence of deaths in custody, reforms to the legislation were considered less urgent. Thus, progress in this area was slow. It was only after December 2013 that the MPS began to consult with the relevant departments (the central Political-Legal Committee, the SPC, the SPP, the MoJ, the People's Armed Police, the Ministry of Finance, the State Committee for Development and Reforms, the State Committee for Family Planning and the Chinese Legal Studies Association) to produce a final draft of the legislation.

In 2014, the Legislative Working Committee of the NPC inserted the issuing of a *Criminal Detention Centres Law* in its five-year legislative plan, proposing five main objectives. Firstly, the new Law would bring pre-trial detention centre legislation in line with the revised CPL, to 'maintain a unified legal system' (*weihu fazhi tongyi*). Secondly, it would clarify the role and the relationship among the different authorities responsible for the administration of criminal proceedings, including detention and investigation. Thirdly, the new Law would promote the respect and protection of criminal suspects' human and legal rights (*hefa quanli*). Fourthly, it would define in legal terms established practices and concepts related to detention. And, lastly, it would regulate and strengthen existing management practices in detention centres.

The draft Law, which, at the time of writing, is still under discussion, clarifies the institutional nature and the responsibility of pre-trial detention authorities. In this respect, it provides that pre-trial detention centres are state institutions for the criminal detention of unconvicted criminal suspects and defendants, prisoners whose remaining prison term is less than three months, and those sentenced to death awaiting execution. It also clarifies that these institutions are responsible for the smooth running of criminal proceedings, the prevention of crime and the respect and protection of human rights. These provisions suggest that it is the responsibility of detention centres to ensure that all detainees are safe, that they cannot flee and that they will participate in criminal proceedings in accordance with the law. In addition, it also suggests that authorities have the responsibility of ensuring that detention is carried out according to clear legal standards and that the rights of detainees are protected.

While pursuant to the draft, the MPS remains the key administering authority and the people's procuratorate the main organ responsible for supervision of the police powers; the new law is also aimed at ensuring that investigative authorities, the procuratorate, the judiciary and the defence lawyers all exercise their procedural functions according to the CPL 2012. Even though it is not clearly spelled out in the draft legislation, commentators are hoping that, at least in principle, these reforms will involve a clearer distinction of functions between the authorities responsible for detention and those carrying out investigation.

The draft also provides for increased institutional transparency; it promotes and strengthens the system of supervision by the procuratorate and favours mechanisms for 'social supervision' (*shehui jiandu*). However, it does not define clearly the meaning of the concept of 'social supervision' and, in particular, it does not offer guarantees for the functional independence of members of the society responsible for supervision. In addition, it does not spell out the relationship between social supervision and the existing system of procuratorial supervision.

Respect of the rights of detainees features as one of the primary objectives of the legislation. Thus, one of the main concepts informing practices of detention is the administration (*guanli*) and education (*jiaoyu*) of detainees in a 'civilised' (*wenming*) manner. Specifically, this implies the positive obligation of the management of detention centres to provide decent and safe living conditions to detainees and to guarantee their fair treatment. In principle, such an approach might urge authorities to be alerted to the possible ill-treatment of detainees and to take appropriate action whenever this occurs.

Healthy living conditions also require that, prior to the admission into detention centres, each detainee is to undergo a health examination. The purpose of this provision appears to be twofold. First, it is a way to ensure that detainees have not been mistreated prior to admission into detention facilities during interrogation in police stations, and eventually to establish the causes of eventual physical scars or other signs of violence. Secondly, a health examination reveals whether detainees' physical conditions make them suitable for detention – the draft makes clear that very sick detainees and pregnant women[18] cannot be detained and should be subject to measures that are an alternative to detention. Other Articles in the draft Law provide for the treatment of sick detainees, food allocation, rest timing, adequate hygiene conditions in detention areas and prohibit forced labour.[19] Specific procedures are established to deal with instances of death in custody, that is, to understand their causes and establish who is responsible.

In view of the numerous instances of illegally prolonged pre-trial detentions that have been disclosed since the early 2000s, the Law regulates detention time limits and explicitly prohibits prolonged pre-trial detention (*chaoqi jiya*). It provides the procuratorate with the authority to amend instances of wrong or prolonged detention; however, it does not clearly specify the various avenues through which the procuratorate can actually take action in this respect.

Importantly, the draft Law defines conditions under which the questioning of detainees should take place. It provides that questioning should be conducted by at least two interrogators within a designated room of the pre-trial detention centre, who should also be informed by detention authorities about meals and resting time. In average cases, interrogators *may* audio record or audio-video record the entire interrogation process; however, audio or audio-video recording is compulsory only during interrogation of criminal suspects who may be sentenced to fixed term imprisonment, the death penalty or are involved in very serious cases. While recording has been considered an important tool to discourage illegal interrogation practices, the Law does not contain provisions concerning the treatment of such recording in relation to preserving, copying, tampering, modifying, erasing or publishing such material.

According to the draft, investigation authorities are still permitted to request interrogation to be carried out external to pre-trial detention centres, and in these cases, physical examination of the criminal suspects is required at the time of re-admission into detention. If scars or any signs of physical violence are found on their bodies, doctors are requested to establish and record their causes; records should be signed by doctors, detention authorities and the criminal suspects or defendants themselves. While these provisions represent positive developments in discouraging practices of extraction of confession through torture, they are still problematic from a number of angles. First, they implicitly assume a close working relationship between detention and investigative authorities, without clarifying whether and on what grounds detention authorities may or may not authorise the removal of detainees from detention centres for interrogation purposes. Secondly, apart from the written recording of the physical conditions of criminal suspects and defendants upon re-admission into detention centres, they do not provide for any other support or treatment for detainees who have been subject to violence during interrogation. Practices of psychological violence are not taken into account. Thirdly, the provisions are not specific about the number of times of requests for removal from interrogation can be made, or on the length of removal times, or on the disclosure of the location of interrogation. Lastly, while the Law provides detainees with avenues to complain and it requires detention authorities to act promptly on such issues, it is not explicit about the avenues through which the suspect can complain about mistreatment outside detention areas. In addition, it does not specify what actions need to be taken by the authorities once complaints are filed and it does not explicitly prohibit repercussions against the complainant.

While detainees should be informed of their rights, it remains unclear what specific rights they should be informed about and whether they should be also informed about possible available mechanisms to claim for their rights if these are violated. The section on 'meritorious services' – which explains good acts that can be performed by detainees – remains problematic as well, as it links sentencing and rewarding of detainees to acts of revealing clues about criminal activities, once again strengthening the link between detention and investigation.

The draft Law also provides that interrogation of juveniles should be carried out in the presence of their legal representatives, a family member, school authority or a member of relevant local organisations. However, it would be advisable that the Law spelled out that minors should not be held in detention centres unless it is unavoidable, and in cases where it is unavoidable, there should be more specific guarantees concerning interrogation procedures.

The Law provides for segregation of juveniles from adult offenders as well as of women and other categories of particularly vulnerable (new arrivals or sex offenders, for example) or dangerous detainees according to an established risk assessment mechanism (*fengxian pingu zhidu*). Given the circumstances that persons who are sentenced to death are transferred shortly before their execution to a detention centre, the draft Law should also pay special attention to their treatment. A special regime for prisoners who are awaiting execution is not included in the draft.

The draft Law provides detainees with access to their legal representatives, requesting detention authorities to arrange such meeting no later than forty-eight hours after the lawyers have made their requests to the detention authorities. Detention authorities must pass requests by detainees to see a lawyer to the authorities responsible for handling the case within twenty-four hours. When involving state security-related cases, acts of terrorism and other particularly serious criminal circumstances, such meetings should be approved by the investigative authorities. Meetings should be unmonitored (*bu bei jianting*) and should take place in the lawyer's meeting room (*lüshi huijian shi*). Notwithstanding these minimal guarantees, this part of the draft appears vague and problematic since it does not provide for details regarding the procedures by which detainees can request meetings with their legal representatives and how to complain if such meetings are denied. While it refers to 'meeting rules' (*huijian guiding*) that lawyers need to respect, it does not explain their content, leaving the interpretation of this expression to the discretion of the detention authorities. Moreover, while the draft requests the establishment of legal aid stations in places of detention, it is silent in relation to their work or the procedures for their functioning, the mechanisms through which detainees can access them or their relationship with the detention authorities and the procuratorate. Instead of directly contacting their lawyers to request a meeting, detainees have to forward their meeting requests through the pre-trial detention centres' police. Arguably, this approach runs the risk of making detainees wary of initiating such meetings.

The draft Law conveys the impression that in criminal proceedings the investigative stage (*zhencha jieduan*) is still a delicate one and that the investigative authorities are eager to maintain overarching control over it. This manifests in provisions that prevent detainees from having any direct contact between themselves and the outside world. Contact with their families, or diplomatic representatives in cases of foreign detainees, still needs to be authorised by the authorities responsible for the case and, if approved, supervised by such authorities.

Today, one of the problematic issues concerning the administration of pre-trial detention centres in the PRC is overcrowding and the lack of personal space for detainees in common cells. The draft Law, however, is silent in this respect. Indeed, to prevent overcrowding the Law should grant each detainee a minimum personal space quota (international standards request a minimum of a square meter per capita) and entitle detention centres managers to refuse admission of detainees above the formal capacity of the institution.

Finally, to ensure the protection of detainees' rights and the adequate management of detention facilities, the draft Law should provide for a detailed allocation of funding. The MPS and the Ministry of Finance *Notice on Further Strengthening the Financial Work of Pre-trial Detention Centres* (*Gong'an Guanyu Jin Yi Bu Jiaqiang Kanshousuo Jinfei Baozhang Gongzuo De Tongzhi*) 2009 provides that finances should be divided into three main categories. Funds ought to be allocated for the construction and maintenance of the detention centres, for the administration of detainees and for public use (*gong yong*). The specific channels through which such funding is allocated ought to also be established. Such distribution would need to be reflected in the Law so that detention centre expenditure would count towards a jurisdictions' annual governmental budget. This would impose less pressure on the individual pre-trial detention centres in the management of their finances and secure appropriate allocation for the management of detainees.

Conclusion

This chapter highlights both the opportunities and challenges to the process of reforming institutions administered by public security authorities that are deeply involved in the operationalisation of criminal justice politics, including fighting crime and maintaining social stability. It demonstrates how debates about legislative and institutional reforms may open windows of analysis into power relations, interests and values within institutions and society and how these relate to changes of the exercise of authority. Indeed, pre-trial detention in China is but one among the most evident examples where detention practices remain strictly interwoven with the development of penological ideas, political agendas and justice values. In this respect, the case of Chinese pre-trial detention centres brings to light the challenges faced in the process of disentangling practices of detention from those of investigation. This process would result from, as well as help to determine, a shift from a fighting crime mentality to a policing mindset that more fully respects the right to a fair trial, including rights protected in the pre-trial investigation process.

The chapter shows that scandals – the 'hide and seek' accident, for example – may contribute to the triggering of debates about reforms and the development of new sensibilities towards issues of criminality and detention. They may create social expectations for change and calls for reforms. Scandals are precipitous of change, but alone they are not sufficient factors that may lead to substantive legislative and institutional changes. This is especially the case in China today where institutional interests are at stake, as demonstrated by the debates surrounding the control over detention centres and over practices of detention and investigations.

In this context, a new legislative document such as the draft *Criminal Detention Centre Law* discussed in the body of this chapter would have the potential to contribute to standardising such changes to institutional sensibilities, values and practice. The insertion of human rights protection in the draft is but one a clear example. Having said that, and notwithstanding the various voices from legal academia favouring the issuing of this legislative document in line with international human rights standards and calling for a transparent and consultative process, the current proposed legislation remains significantly MPS-oriented, driven by managerial standards and by law enforcement imperatives rather than being aimed at genuinely protecting the rights of detainees. If enacted in this spirit of protecting institutional interests rather than individuals' rights, the legislation might add little to the current *Regulations* 1990 and will demoralise groups of scholars and lawyers who, over recent decades, have invested their energies in scrutinising different detention practices and legislation and in proposing possible ways forward.

Notes

1 The Chinese term *kanshousuo* may be translated as 'pre-trial detention centre', 'criminal detention centre' or 'criminal pre-trial detention centre'. These translations point to at least two key features of the institution: first, its role in detaining criminal suspects during pre-trial proceedings (although, as the chapter demonstrates, criminal defendants undergoing trial and offenders may be also detained in such institutions); secondly, its distinction from administrative institutions of detention. Unless specified, in this chapter, we interchangeably use the Chinese term *kanshousuo* or its English translations 'pre-trial detention centre' and 'criminal detention centre'.
2 See also Article 15 of the *Prison Law* (*Jianyu Fa*) 1994 (as amended in 2012); Articles 83, 91 and 253 of the *Criminal Procedure Law* (*Xingshi Susong Fa*) 2012.
3 The MPS is organised in a number of functional bureaus to cover such areas as domestic public security, criminal investigation, intelligence, cyber-crime, public order administration, border control, exit and entry administration, fire control, public information network security supervision, penitentiary administration (excluding prisons), traffic control, legal affairs, international cooperation, logistics and finance, drug control, science and technology, counter-terrorism and info-communications. Railway, navigation, civil aviation, forestry and anti-smuggling public security departments are under the dual leadership of their superior administration and the MPS.
4 According to Article 5 of the *Regulations* 1990, state security bureaus may also administer *kanshousuo* at different levels, including provincial, autonomous region and municipalities directly under the central government. Detention centres at higher levels may also be established and administered by the authorities responsible for the railways, traffic, forestry and aviation.
5 The system of 'taking a guarantee and awaiting trial' displays some similarities with the bail system in common law countries and is regulated by the CPL 2012 (Articles 64–72, 77, 79, 96–97, 165 and 254). On the differences between bail and the Chinese measure of 'taking a guarantee and awaiting trial', see Sun (2007, 127–33), Song and Luo (2007, 25–30) and Nesossi (2012, 57).
6 Residential surveillance is regulated by the CPL 2012 (Articles 64, 69, 72–79, 89, 96, 97 and 165).
7 The rules on prison remained in force with a few modifications and various additions until 1949 (Dikötter 2002, 67).
8 Du (2004, 24) reports that in areas established by Communists in pre-1949 China, there were nearly 150 criminal detention centres, 30 labour reform camps and 40 prisons where in total more than 70,000 prisoners were detained.
9 The Committee for the Elimination of Counter-Revolutionaries was formed in November 1927 as the coordinating organ for the elimination of the counter-revolutionary forces. According to Dutton (2005, 38), its method of action was based on a 'form of rough populist revolutionary justice' whereby the members of the Committee were 'the investigators, prosecutors, judges, juries and goal-keepers' (see also Griffin 2015).
10 A partial translation of the *Regulations on Arrest and Detention* 1954 and related material is offered in Cohen (1968, 360–68).
11 There is a slight discrepancy between Article 37 of the *Regulations for Reform Through Labour* 1954 and Article 2 of the *Regulations on Arrest and Detention* 1954. While the former required criminal suspects in those circumstances 'to be sent to a hospital, assigned to a guardian, or put in another appropriate place', the latter Regulations required for the adoption of the measures of 'taking a guarantee and awaiting trial' or residential surveillance.
12 In 1962, the MPS released an earlier draft in trial form.
13 According to the data reported by the People's Procuratorial Yearbook, during the years 1979–85 the number of people arrested and detained notably increased. Wong's (1997, 33–4) analysis of the data identified two main peaks: the years 1981–82 and the beginning of 1983.
14 The *Methods of Implementation* 1991 supplement the *Regulations* 1990. The two documents are very similar and the *Methods of Implementation* 1991 It includes 63 Articles organised in 11 Sections.
15 See also *Notice on Pre–Trial Detention Centres Continuing Discovering Crimes*, Notice No. 14 of 2004 (*Gong'an Bu Jiansuo Guanli Ju Guanyu Gong'an Jianguan Bumen Shenru Kaizhang Zhenwa Fanzui Gongzuo You Guan Wenti De Tongzhi*).
16 In these interrogation rooms, police officers shall be separated by iron fence from the detainees and cannot reach or touch them during questioning. Such room design is defined by the *Pre–Trial Detention Centres Construction and Design Rules* (*Kanshousuo Jianzhu Jiansheji Guifan*) 2000 jointly issued by MPS and Ministry of Construction.

17 See in particular Articles 8 and 9 of the *Legislation Law* 2000, which provide that 'only laws passed by the NPC or NPCSC may regulate coercive measures' (Article 8) and that

> the National People's Congress or its Standing Committee has the power to make a decision to authorize the State Council to formulate, according to actual needs, administrative regulations first on part of those affairs, except for the affairs concerning criminal offences and their punishment, mandatory measures and penalties involving deprivation of citizens of their political rights or restriction of the freedom of their person, and the judicial system (Article 9).

18 Women whose babies are less than one week old are allowed to take their newborns in to detention places to allow for feeding.

19 The Law provides that detainees may choose whether to work within detention centres and, in this case, that they should be remunerated accordingly.

References

Bao Suixian.1998. 'Gen Kuai, Gen Yan, Gen Shi. Zhongguo Gong'an Gaige Bei Wanlu (Faster, More Severe and More Concrete. China's Public Security Reform Memorandum).' *Renmin Gong'an* (People's Police) 20: 12–17.

Butler, William E., ed. 1983. *The Legal System of the Chinese Soviet Republic, 1931–1934*. Dobbs Ferry, N.Y: Transnational Publishers.

Chen Qiao. 14 March 2011. 'Daibiao Jianyi Zhiding Kanshousuo Fa Bimian Liqi Siwang Shijian (Representative Proposed the Enactment of a Detention Centre Law to Avoid Mysterious Deaths in Detention).' *Jinghua Shibao* (Jinghua City Paper). Available at http://news.sina.com.cn/o/2011-03-14/060122109263.shtml (accessed 16 February 2016).

Chen Weidong. 2005. *Mofan Xingshi Susong Fadian* (*Model Code of Criminal Procedure*). Beijing: Zhongguo renmin daxue chubanshe.

Chen Weidong. 15 February 2012. 'Xingshi Susong Fa Xiugai Hou Ying Jinkuai Zhiding Kanshousuo Fa (After the Amendment of the Criminal Procedure Law We Must Proceed Very Quickly with the Enactment of the Detention Centres Law).' *Fazhi Ribao* (Legal Daily). Available at http://epaper.legaldaily.com.cn/fzrb/content/20120215/Articel12002GN.htm (accessed 16 February 2016).

Chen Weidong and Cheng Lei. 2004. 'Dui Jingcha Xingshi Zhifa Shixian Zhong Ruogan Wenti De Shizheng Fenxi' (Several Problems Concerning Police Enforcing Practice of Criminal Law Taking a Positive Analysis Approach).' *Zhongguo Renmin Gong'an Daxue Xuebao* (Journal of Chinese People's Public Security University) 107(1): 1–9.

Cheng Lei 2010. 'Kanshousuo Falü Guifan De Xiugai Yu Wanshan (Revision and Improvement of the Legislation Regulating Detention Centres).' In *Shenhua Xingshi Sifa Gaige De Lilun Yu Shixian* (*Theory and Practice of Deepening Criminal Justice Reforms*), edited by Jianlin Bian, 71. Beijing: Zhongguo renmin gong'an daxue chubanshe.

Cheng Lei. 2014. *Kanshousuo Lifa Wenti Yanjiu* (*On the Legislation about Detention House*). Beijing: Zhongguo fazhi chubanshe.

China Daily. 20 April 2009. 'State Cleans House over Detentions.' Available at http://www.chinadaily.com.cn (accessed 16 February 2016).

Liu Ziqian and Zhang Wenling. 21 February 2009. 'Yunnan Jingfang Tongbao Duo Mao Mao Shijian. Cheng Li Wan Youxi Fasheng Yiwai (Yunnan Police Notify about the Accident of Hide and Seek. A Guy Called Li Had an Accident while Playing).' Available at *Zhongguo Qingnian Bao* (China's Youth Daily). http://news.sina.com.cn/c/2009-02-21/032717258307.shtml (accessed 16 February 2016).

Cohen, Jerome A. 1968. *The Criminal Process in the People's Republic of China, 1949–63: An Introduction*. Cambridge, MA: Harvard University Press.

Commission on Extraterritoriality. 1926. *Report of the Commission on Extra-territoriality in China*. London: H.M. Stationery Office.

Dikötter, Frank. 2002. *Crime, Punishment and the Prison in Modern China*. London: Hurst & Company.

Du, James. 2004. *Punishment and Reform. An Introduction to the Reform-Through-Labour System in the People's Republic of China*. Hong Kong: Lo Tat Cultural Publishing Co.

Dutton, Michael. 2005. *Policing Chinese Politics: A History*. Durham, NC: Duke University Press.
Griffin, Patricia E. 2015. *The Chinese Communist Treatment of Counterrevolutionaries, 1924–1949*. Princeton, New Jersey: Princeton University Press.
Huang Xiuli. 26 March 2009. 'Kanshousuo Gaige, 26 Nian Hou Ke Zai Chongqi. Zhuanfang Zhongguo Fanzui Xuehui Fu Mishu Zhang, Zhongguo Zhengfa Daxue Jiaoshou Wang Shun'an (The Reform of Criminal Detention Centres to Restart After 26 Years. Interview with Wang Shun'an, Vice-Deputy Secretary General of China Crime Academic Society and Professor at the Chinese University of Politics and Law).' *Nanfang Zhoumo* (Southern Weekend), 2.
Jiang Anjie. 24 February 2010. ' "Kanshousuo Tiaoli": "Da Xiu" Haishi "Lifa" ('Detention Centres Regulations': 'Great Amendment' or 'New Law'?).' *Fazhi Ribao* (Legal Daily), 9.
Liu Yuewu. 2010. 'Zhongguo Jindai Kanshousuo Zhidu Xingcheng Kao (On Creating the Detention Centre System in Modern China).' *Yunnan Shehui Kexue* (*Social Sciences in Yunnan*) 3: 136–40.
Luo Jieqi. 27 February 2009. 'Guanfang Tongbao "Duo Mao Mao" Shijian Diaocha Jieguo' (Officials Notify about the Results of the 'Hide and Seek' Accident).' *Caijing*. Available at http://www.caijing.com.cn/2009-02-27/110075141.html (accessed 16 February 2016).
Ministry of Public Security Bureau of Management of Prisons and Detention Centres. 16 August 2011. 'Gong'an Bu Jianguanju Shouci Tongguo Meiti Quanmian Xitong Gongbu Jinnian Lai Quanguo Gong'an Jianguan Gongzuo Fazhan Quanmiao (The Bureau of Management of Prisons and Detention Centres of the Ministry of Public Security for the First Time Presented through the Media a Full Description of the Development in the Work of the National MPS Bureau of Management of Prisons and Detention Centres During the Last Few Years).' Available at http://www.mps.gov.cn/n16/n1252/n1777/n2497/2897196.html (accessed 16 February 2016).
Nesossi, Elisa. 2008. 'Reforming Criminal Justice in the People's Republic of China. The Black Hole of Pre-Trial Detention.' *Journal of Comparative Law* 3(2): 305–15.
Nesossi, Elisa. 2012. *China's Pre-Trial Justice: Criminal Justice, Human Rights and Legal Reforms in Contemporary China*. London: Wildy, Simmonds and Hill.
Nesossi, Elisa. 2014. 'Detention, Stability and "Social Management Innovation".' In *The Politics of Law and Stability in China*, edited by Susan Trevaskes, Elisa Nesossi, Flora Sapio and Sarah Biddulph, 219–43. Cheltenham: Edward Elgar.
Song Yinghui and Luo Haiming, eds. 2007. *Qubao Houshen Shiyong Zhong De Wenti Yu Duice Yanjiu* (A Study of the Problems on the Use of 'Taking a Guarantee and Awaiting Trial and Related Solutions). Beijing: Zhongguo renmin gong'an daxue chubanshe.
Sui Xiaofei. 17 April 2009. 'Quanguo Kanshousuo Jianguan Zhifa Zhuanxiang Jiancha Huodong Jiang Yu 4 Yue 20 Ri Qidong (The National Specialised Inspection Activities on Management of Law Enforcercement in Detentioned Centres Will Be Launched on 20 April). *Xinhua Wang*. Available at http://news.xinhuanet.com/legal/2009-04/17/content_11197463.htm (accessed 16 February 2016).
Sun Lianzhong. 2007. *Xingshi Qiangzhi Cuoshi Yanjiu* (Study of the Criminal Coercive Measures). Beijing: Zhishi changquan chubanshe.
Trevaskes, Susan, Nesossi, Elisa, Sapio, Flora and Biddulph, Sarah, eds. 2014. *The Politics of Law and Stability in China*. Cheltenham: Edward Elgar.
Wang Bo. 2001. 'Yushen Zhidu Yu Zhencha Yi Tihua (A Combination Between the Pre-Trial System and Investigation).' *Beijing Renmin Jingcha Xueyuan Xuebao* (Journal of Beijing People's Police College) 2: 18–21.
Wang Qingqi. 2007. *Ge Sheng Shenpanting Pandu* (Verdicts from Each Province Trial Chamber). Beijing: Beijing daxue chubanshe.
Wang Yu, Zhao Fujie and Liu Weiming. 2014. *Kanshousuo Jiancha Xue* (A Study on the Procuratorate in Detention Centres). Tianjin: Tianjin shehui kexueyuan chubanshe.
Wong Kam. 1997. *Sheltering for Examination (Shoushen) in the People's Republic of China: Law, Policy and Practices*. School of Law, University of Maryland: Occasional Paper/Reprints Series in Contemporary Asian Studies.
Xinhua. 21 August 2012. 'Zhou Yongkang Zai Beijing Tianjin Zhengfa Jiguan Kaocha Zhi Qiangdiao Shenru Tuijin Zhifa Guifanhua Jianshe Zujin Yange Gongzhen Wenming Lianjie Zhifa

(Zhou Yongkang While Visiting the Political-Legal Authorities in Beijing and Tianjin Emphasised the Promotion of Standardization in Law Enforcement and the Promotion of Strict and Fair Law Enforcement).' *Xinhuawang*. Available at http://politics.people.com.cn/n/2012/0821/c1024-1879 7076.html (accessed 16 February 2016).

Xu Bin. 2006. *Wo Guo Xingzhen Yushen Wenti Yanjiu* (Study of the Problems of China's Pre-Trial Investigation). Unpublished PhD Thesis.

Yun Shancheng. 2000. 'Xiugai "Zhonghua Renmin Gongheguo Kanshousuo Tiaoli" Zhi Wo Jian (Personal Opinions on the Revision of the "People's Republic of China Regulations on Criminal Detention Centres").' *Hubei Gong'an Gaodeng Zhuanke Xuexiao Bao* (Journal of Hubei Police College) 3: 27–30.

Yun Shancheng. 2005. 'Wo Guo Xingshi Susong Fa Zhong "Yushen" Wenti Yanjiu (A Research on the Problem of Preliminary Investigation in the Criminal Procedure Law of the PRC).' *Guizhou Jingguan Zhiye Xueyuan Xuebao* (Journal of Guizhou Police Officer Vocational College) 17: 72–5.

Zhang Xuehua, ed. 2005. *Xiandai Gong'an Kanshousuo Lingdao Shiwu Quanshu* (The Complete Book of Concrete Issues of Contemporary Criminal Detention Centres for Public Security Leaders). Tianjin: Tianjin dianzi chubanshe.

Zhao Chunguan. 2010. 'Zhongguo Tese Shehui Zhuyi Gong'an Jianguan Yanjiu (Study of Socialist Public Security Management with Chinese Characteristics).' *Makesi Zhuyi Yu Xianshi* (Marxism and Reality) 5: 64–7.

Zhongguo Renmin Daxue Falü Xi Fazhi Shi Jiaoyanshi. 1979. *Zhongguo Jindai Fazhi Shi Ziliao Xuanbian (Di Yi Fence)* (Collection of Material on Chinese Modern Legal History). Beijing: Zhongguo renmin daxue.

7 Addressing the 'hide and seek' scandal
Restoring the legitimacy of *kanshousuo*

Nicola Macbean

Introduction

The death of Li Qiaoming in a detention centre (*kanshousuo*) in Yunnan came to epitomise the problems in China's criminal detention centres.

> On 30 January 2009 24-year old Li Qiaoming was taken into custody in Jinning county, Yunnan province, for felling trees without authorization. He was hospitalized on 8th February and died four days later of severe brain injuries. Jinning police said Li had died while playing 'hide-and-seek' with other inmates. Pushed by one inmate, Li, they claimed, had bumped into a wall as he fell. After the Kunming press reported the case Internet users began to question the cause of Li's death (Xinhua 20 February 2009).

Officials, scholars and lawyers began to cite the case, now referred to as the 'hide and seek' (*duo mao mao*) incident, to support the need for *kanshousuo* reform.[1] This chapter introduces some of the policy recommendations that were advanced and considers how the response to the 'hide and seek' scandal casts light on attitudes to the deprivation of liberty in China and the role of the *kanshousuo* in the criminal process. Taking place in a period of debate over criminal procedure reforms, the scandal informed discussions of a revised law which was eventually approved by the National People's Congress (NPC), in March 2012. A consideration of the response to the 'hide and seek' case assists us to tentatively 'evaluate' China's overall approach to detention and the extent to which the criminal process is founded on respect for human rights (Ashworth 1998).[2]

The *kanshousuo* incarcerates suspects awaiting trial, convicted offenders with less than three months left to serve (*Criminal Procedure Law* (CPL) 2012, Article 253)[3] and prisoners facing execution. A largely neglected subject of interest to Chinese and international scholars, the *kanshousuo* is part of the criminal justice system. With the abolition of the administrative punishment of re-education through labour (Xinhua 28 December 2013), the *kanshousuo*'s status as the largest detention facility under police control is likely to come under more scrutiny. The increase in the numbers of foreigners being detained in China will also ensure greater attention from diplomats and the international media to this key institution in the criminal justice system.

Under fire from the public and the media, the Yunnan authorities promptly announced the convening of a 'truth-finding committee' to investigate Li Qiaoming's death. A fifteen-member panel comprising five netizens, three reporters, four public security and prosecutors' staff, two company employees and a college student was invited to the Jinning detention centre to investigate what had happened (Xinhua 20 February 2009). However, despite promises of openness, their report was inconclusive (Reuters 25 February 2009) and it was the procuratorate that eventually determined that fellow prisoners had beaten Li to death. Four officials were held responsible and punished (*China Daily* 27 February 2009).

Much of the public discussion of the 'hide and seek' case took place online and similar cases soon came to light (see for example, *China Daily* 27 February 2010, and the case of Wang Yahui who allegedly died after drinking a glass of hot water) and aroused further concern. The Chinese government's pragmatic efforts to build a legal system after the chaos of the Cultural Revolution have helped to ascribe meaning to the idea of law, and ideas about justice and human rights have begun to take hold among the Chinese public. Myriad influences from public legal education (*pufa*), promoted by the government itself, to the *weiquan* ('rights-defence') movement and its amplification by *Weibo*, China's version of Twitter, have resulted in a citizenry that is increasingly rights aware.

Public anger over the 'hide and seek' case was in danger of calling into question the extent of police powers to detain people. The case had parallels with the Sun Zhigang incident. Public outcry and a petition against the 'unconstitutional' custody and repatriation (*shourong qiansong*) centre, where the student Sun had been beaten to death in 2003, resulted in this form of administrative detention being dismantled (Hand 2006). Scandal has been a powerful driver of recent reforms to China's legal system (Fu 2009) and reformers were quick to put forward measures that would help to tackle abuses in *kanshousuo*. The government's need to restore public confidence in *kanshousuo* provided reformist officials and legal scholars with the policy space they needed to promote reforms. Although police control of *kanshousuo* has long hindered empirical research, the widespread reporting of Li's death in the media provided scholars and lawyers with greater latitude to raise their concerns.

This chapter describes a number of initiatives that have been proposed to strengthen due process in the decision to detain, improve treatment in detention, and increase oversight and access to a lawyer for those in *kanshousuo*. Many of these policy proposals were the outcome of cooperative research projects, including comparative studies of overseas practice and international law. While several of these recommendations received the support of officials at the local level, the failure, thus far, of most measures to be adopted nationally is illustrative of the challenges facing reform of China's criminal processes.

The globalisation of justice

As criminal justice systems become less self-contained, they are influenced by the practices in other countries and international treaties. A globalised citizenry increasingly expects that minimum standards of treatment, compliant with notions of a fair trial, will prevail when its citizens are in conflict with the law overseas. Nevertheless, there is political resistance to the trend towards convergence in practice and control of the criminal justice system remains a powerful marker of sovereignty for many countries. Although many Chinese citizens are increasingly attracted to the notion of universal values, their government has demonstrated growing ambivalence to global norms of justice.

The adoption of criminal laws in 1979 signified the start of legal reforms following the chaos of China's Cultural Revolution. China's adoption of a 'thin' rule of law has, as Peerenboom (2007) suggests, been pragmatic and supportive of the transition from poverty to a middle-income country. The Chinese Government's formal commitment to rule by law (*yifa zhiguo*) was reiterated most recently in the *Decision concerning Some Major Questions in Comprehensively Promoting Governing the Country According to Law* (*Zhonggong Zhongyang Guanyu Quanmian Tuijin Yifa Zhiguo Ruogan Zhongda Wenti De Jueding*) (hereafter 'the *Decision*') following the 4th plenary session of the 18th Chinese Communist Party

Central Committee in October 2014 (unofficial English translation at *China Copyright and Media* 2014), the first such meeting to focus exclusively on the legal system. The *Decision* sets out a vision of the law as a tool for the modernisation of governance. The document exhorts those responsible for implementing the *Decision* to improve judicial fairness, the credibility of the judiciary and eliminate interference from special interests.

Official support for human rights in China nevertheless remains ambivalent. The country was an early adopter of the *United Nations Convention Against Torture* 1984 in 1988, but has failed to ratify the *International Covenant on Civil and Political Rights* 1976 (ICCPR), which it signed in 1998. The state's obligations to protect human rights were acknowledged in the 2004 revision of the Constitution and in 2009 the country published its first National Human Rights Action Plan (2009–2010). The Government is clearly cognisant of the need to prevent the most egregious human rights' violations and the requirement, in the recent *Decision*, to prevent miscarriages of justice is indicative of these concerns. However, it is hard to reconcile the requirement, underlined in the *Decision*, that legal institutions and personnel remain subject to the leadership of the Party and the goal of building socialism with Chinese characteristics with the independent institutions which international practice recommends as essential pillars of human rights' protection.

Pre-trial detention and human rights

In the pre-modern period, confinement, as part of the judicial process, was not necessarily associated with punishment (Dikötter 2002). Dikötter (2002) describes how in imperial China and France suspects awaiting trial, as well as witnesses, could be detained for several months during the criminal investigation and trial. We can still observe tensions in the judicial process between the right to liberty and the use of pre-trial detention. International law has attempted to strike a balance between the demands of the criminal process and the rights of the individual.

Article 9 of the ICCPR sets out the principle that the detention or arrest of a person must be lawful and that the use of pre-trial detention should be the exception. The initial decision to detain or arrest someone is normally taken by the police and justified by the need to collect evidence as part of a criminal investigation. Any detention beyond the immediate need to compel a person to attend a police interview should be taken by a judicial authority (Article 9.3). In European jurisprudence, suspicion that the person arrested has committed an offence is not sufficient to justify continued detention unless there are other grounds, namely, the risk of absconding, tampering with the evidence, collusion or re-offending (Cape et al. 2010). The public interest justification for refusing an application to release will become harder once the evidence in a case has been collected and there should therefore, be regular opportunities to review the decision to detain pre-trial (Cape et al. 2010). A meaningful right to release individuals pre-trial implies a real right to obtain bail with growing recognition that this must also be available to those without the resources to pay a surety.

Pre-trial detention is likely to interfere with a person's right to a fair trial. Research in Europe demonstrates that those who are kept in detention pre-trial are often denied other rights of effective criminal defence (Cape et al. 2010). They frequently lack the conditions to prepare their defence and may face obstructions in finding, instructing and consulting with their lawyer. Ensuring due process in the pre-trial context has become essential if decision-making is to have legitimacy (Galligan 1994) and access to a lawyer is now regarded as crucial if procedural protections are not hollow promises. Pre-trial detention is likely to impact disproportionately on the poorest. Unable to access legal advice or assistance without legal aid or to provide financial guarantees, the poor are disadvantaged in police interviews and less likely to be granted bail. Lengthy pre-trial detention can also deprive families of the breadwinner and may bring unwelcome costs in the form of travel, provisions, lawyers' fees and bribes (Open Society Justice Initiative 2012).

Pre-trial detention also places suspects at increased risk of ill treatment and even torture. The risk of torture is most acute when victims are excluded from any contact with the outside world such as their family, doctor and lawyer (Rodley 1999). Since pre-trial periods can be long, there is an emerging consensus that any period in police detention should be kept to an absolute minimum, particularly since police stations and other police-run detention facilities are not normally adapted to being able to provide pre-trial detainees with the activities and other privileges to which the general prison population is entitled (United Nations 9 August 2013). To protect those deprived of their liberty, international law has an absolute prohibition against torture and requires that anyone deprived of their liberty should be 'treated with humanity and with respect for the inherent dignity of the human person' (ICCPR Article 10). As part of an international effort to prevent the use of torture, the *Optional Protocol to the Convention Against Torture* entered into force in 2006. State parties to the protocol are required to establish independent expert monitoring bodies to conduct regular inspections of all places where persons are deprived of their liberty, including pre-trial detention, and to accept periodic inspection visits by the Subcommittee on the prevention of torture.

Pre-trial detention in China

The main purpose of the *kanshousuo* is to detain individuals in the pre-trial criminal process. The institution has its roots in the gaols of imperial China; these held suspects awaiting trial and convicted criminals sentenced to penal servitude or on their journey to exile, or prisoners awaiting execution (Dikötter 2002). The Chinese term *kanshousuo* will be used in this chapter to clearly distinguish it from the other detention facilities, many of which are part of an 'administrative' system rather than the criminal process, while some operate outside any legal framework (Sapio 2010). China employs varied and extensive measures to maintain and restore social control in response to behaviour it sees as 'deviant, problematic, worrying, threatening, troublesome and undesirable' (Cohen 1985, 1–2, quoted in Pakes 2004, 1). Although Article 37 of the Chinese Constitution 1982 (as amended) establishes the citizen's right to liberty and that the only lawful restriction on such freedom can occur when a citizen is arrested by the police, with procuratorate or court approval, deprivation of liberty also takes place outside the criminal process. The lack of justiciable rights (Balme and Dowdle 2009) has largely rendered constitutional guarantees regarding the deprivation of liberty meaningless.

The police are the principal gatekeepers to the processes and institutions that manage offending behaviour, but the Party's own Central Discipline Inspection Committee separately oversees the *shuanggui* system of detaining, investigating and punishing Party members, primarily for corruption (Sapio 2010). An early decision in addressing deviant behaviour is the determination of whether the alleged offence reaches a threshold of criminality and will, therefore, be subject to the strictures of criminal procedure law. Relatively minor offending behaviour will be dealt with administratively, including the imposition of short-term administrative detention.

Kanshousuo are controlled by the Ministry of Public Security (MPS) and administered by local level public security bureaus (hereafter referred to as 'the police'). Although the courts and procuratorate also have the power to issue warrants compelling the appearance of an accused person, it is the police who are responsible for the initial stages of investigation into most criminal cases, except corruption. The CPL 2012 sets out the powers to detain (*juliu*) and execute arrests (*zhixing daibu*) (Article 3). An initial period of confinement normally takes place in a *juliusuo*, also under police control, or local police station before the police are required to transfer detainees, within twenty-four hours, to a *kanshousuo* (CPL 2012, Article 83). While some *juliusuo* are located in close proximity to the *kanshousuo*, prior to the 2012 CPL revisions there were reports of lengthy periods of detention in *juliusuo* or other locations, and allegations of ill treatment and torture.

Following an initial investigation period the police may recommend that the suspect be formally arrested (*daibu*). The CPL 2012 sets out time limits by which the police should submit a request to the procuratorate for examination and approval of arrest. The initial three-day deadline can, under special circumstances, be extended to thirty days and the procuratorate then have seven days to officially approve arrest after receiving the application from the police (CPL 2012, Article 89). The police have been criticised for making routine use of their exceptional power to detain for up to thirty days (McConville et al. 2011). Procuratorate approval of the police recommendation to arrest was long considered a formality. In 2010, as part of an effort to strengthen procuratorate oversight, the Supreme People's Procuratorate (SPP) and the MPS issued a joint regulation stipulating that under certain circumstances prosecutors are required to question suspects before approving arrest. These circumstances include cases involving juveniles, but also cases where the prosecutors may have doubts regarding the evidence or there are indications of a coerced confession. Commenting on the new regulations, Xu Yongjun from Haidian procuratorate, Beijing, said that, Haidian prosecutes about 5,000 cases each year, but prosecutors question suspects in only 50 per cent of the cases: 'we don't have enough people, and prosecutors have only seven days to decide whether or not to approve the arrest' (Zhang 16 September 2010). McConville et al. (2011) observe that some prosecutors fail to distinguish between the approval of arrest and the decision to initiate a prosecution.

Following arrest, a suspect may continue to be held for further investigation and interrogations by the police before the case is transferred to the procuratorate with a police recommendation on whether there should be a prosecution. While time limits for this investigation period are set out in the CPL 2012, they provide numerous opportunities, where new facts emerge, for the clock to be restarted; extended detention is recognised to be a common feature of Chinese criminal justice in both serious and non-serious cases (McConville et al. 2011). There is no presumption in favour of bail for criminal detainees. The law allows applications for bail to be considered by the police, procuratorate and court, but the rates have historically been extremely low. Lawyers complain of the ambiguities in the law and their low success rate in applications for bail; migrants and other poor suspects have very little chance of being granted bail given low levels of awareness and the need for the family to pay a surety (McConville et al. 2011).

China has made several undertakings to respect international law regarding the treatment of persons deprived of their liberty. As a state party to the *Convention Against Torture*, China is obliged to ensure the absolute prohibition of torture in its jurisdiction and take all measures to prevent cruel, inhuman or degrading treatment or punishment. As a signatory to the ICCPR, it should also aim to comply with the treaty's provisions pending ratification. China's second *National Human Rights Action Plan 2012–2015* (State Council Information Office 2012) makes specific promises to improve the protection of detainees' rights including preventing unnecessary detention, supervising detention time limits, improved oversight and investigations into deaths in custody. In its report for the *Universal Periodic Review by the UN Human Rights Council* (United Nations 2013), China outlined a number of measures it had taken to strengthen the safeguarding of detainees' rights, including the promulgation of regulations on detention (*juliusuo tiaoli*).

Decisions to detain

The power of the Chinese state to detain large numbers of people and the routine incarceration of suspects awaiting trial has not been widely called into question. Critics, however, argue that the CPL does not adequately regulate the use of detention, rather: 'Arrest and detention are the same thing. The time after arrest is the same as the time in detention. The requirements for handling the case are the same as the requirement for detention' (Dan 2012). In recent years legal scholars and reformist officials have been looking more closely at the decision-making procedures relating to pre-trial detention. Although there is support among many lawyers and legal scholars for bringing detainees periodically before an independent judicial power to review the continued lawfulness of detention, the required legal and institutional reforms are inconceivable in the current political environment. In an attempt to introduce some review of compulsory measures, reformers lobbied during the CPL 2012 revision process for strengthening the role of the procuratorate to examine the necessity of arrest and detention; this resulted in the introduction of new review powers for prosecutors (CPL 2012, Article 93).

This new provision goes hand in hand with more detailed provisions for granting bail (*qubao houshen*, 'seeking a guarantor while awaiting trial'). Nothing in the new provisions establishes a right to bail, but the inclusion of additional conditions that can be imposed on someone released from detention is intended to help mitigate the perceived risks posed by pre-trial release. In a highly risk-averse environment, the granting of conditional bail may be the only way in which to increase the percentage of persons given pre-trial release. The revised CPL provides greater detail regarding the posting of bail, including the recommendation that the authorities should consider the financial situation of the person to be released when setting the amount. However, there remain strong disincentives to agreeing to become a guarantor; not only is the guarantor required to deposit the bail, but they must also supervise and report infractions of any of the conditions under which pre-trial release is approved. Where the guarantor is deemed to have failed to comply with these obligations they face being fined or even a criminal prosecution (CPL 2012, Articles 68–70).

There have also been efforts to strengthen the role of the procuratorate's office within the *kanshousuo*. Seen as a critical component of measures to improve the protection of detainees' human rights, the procuratorate duty office in the *kanshousuo* is, however, understaffed and overworked. For *kanshousuo* holding up to 1,000 detainees there are likely to be just two procuratorate staff with responsibility for overseeing the conditions of the detention facility as well as handling individual complaints and monitoring detention time limits, serious incidents and hospitalisation (Dan 2012). Long used to paying scant attention to the needs of detainees, staff have received little professional training and are poorly prepared for their expanded responsibilities. Procedures too are underdeveloped and while the procuratorate staff in the *kanshousuo* may recommend release, the final decision rests with the case-handling department. Nevertheless, pilot projects which have sought to introduce simple decision-making tools to assist the procuratorate saw significant increases in the numbers of detainees granted bail.

While the public may largely accept the widespread use of pre-trial detention, there has been anger at accounts of detainees in *kanshousuo* being held well beyond the legal time limits (McConville et al. 2011). Attempts to resolve this problem have brought to the surface a number of underlying issues. No institution has responsibility for ensuring that time limits have not been exceeded and there is no single authoritative custody record which contains all information relating to the case. As a case progresses from investigation by the police, to the procuratorate and then to the court, no institution can hold the others to account for respecting time limits. The legal time limits on pre-trial detention are confusing and open to abuse by the police as facts emerge and approval can be sought to start the investigation detention period anew (CPL 2012, Articles 154–58). It is striking that the problem of extended detention (*chaoqi jiya*) has been discussed for over a decade (see Nesossi 2008) and appears to remain insoluble. Recent pilot projects have seen the procuratorate try to introduce a single record (*yizhengtong*) on which all decisions and approvals relating to detention must be recorded. One electronic pilot prevented the entry of new data in computerised case files once a time limit had been breached, unless authorised by a superior officer. Despite the modest ambitions of these initiatives to ensure compliance with domestic legislation, it has thus far proved impossible for the police, procuratorate and court to agree on a provincial, let alone national, system for monitoring detention time limits. Until lawyers are routinely able to see all documents relating to their client's detention and bring them as evidence before the court, it is unlikely that this problem will ever be solved by administrative procedures alone.

Treatment in detention

The 'hide and seek' case revealed just how unsafe detainees can be in a *kanshousuo*. A review of what is known of the conditions in the *kanshousuo*, the daily regime, detainees' contact with the outside world and the approach to security, suggests a substantial gap with prevailing international standards of good practice (see for example HMIP 2012). The *kanshousuo* is administered by the Bureau for the Management of Prisons and Criminal Detention Centres of the MPS while prisons are under the control of the Ministry of Justice (MoJ). Both *kanshousuo* and prisons however, are supervised by the people's procuratorate. In addition to the CPL 2012, the *kanshousuo* is also regulated by the *State Council Regulations of the Criminal Detention Centres of the People's Republic of China* (*Kanshousuo Tiaoli*) 1990 (hereafter '*Regulations 1990*') and by a number of specific provisions governing different areas of work. These regulations include provisions for the administration of detention, education and work by detainees, minimum standards for food and the use of punishment and rewards.

There is not much published information about the conditions in *kanshousuo*. Accounts of former detainees indicate considerable variation across the country since *kanshousuo* are normally established at the county level and are administered by the equivalent level public security organ. With increasing numbers of foreigners being detained, more first-hand reports are becoming available (see for example the discussion thread entitled *Captivity in a Chinese Prison (Detention Center)* 29 May 2013; Danwei 23 October 2009). The *Methods for Implementation of the 1990 Regulations* 1991 (*Kanshousuo Tiaoli De Shishi Banfa*) specify that each detainee should have at least two square metres of space in the cells. Despite regulations limiting the numbers of detainees in each cell, there are numerous reports of overcrowding, with former detainees telling stories of being unable to turn over on their packed sleeping platforms, sleeping in rota and on all available floor space. Many *kanshousuo*, particularly in cities, are reported to far exceed their authorised capacity. Men and women are held separately and the law also requires, in compliance with international standards, the separate detention of juveniles. Nevertheless, accounts of former detainees describe juveniles being held together with adults, with one former prisoner describing how children in the cell were expected to help a shackled prisoner, awaiting execution, to eat. While 2008 regulations call for the segregation of different categories of prisoners in separate cells, including convicted and on remand, they also permit the centralisation of custody where there are few prisoners (*Methods for the Administration of Prisoners Retained within Detention Centres for the Execution of Sentences* (*Kanshousuo liusuo zhixing xingfa zuifan guanli banfa*) 2008, Article 43).

The daily routine in the *kanshousuo* can be extremely tedious, with hours spent sitting upright on the edge of the sleeping platform (Danwei 23 October 2009). There are many reports of detainees awaiting trial being required to work in contravention of international law, although the regulations provide for criminal suspects and defendants, as well as those sentenced to death, to be able to work on a voluntary basis. Some of the accounts of working conditions are grim and there are anecdotal reports of the transfer of detainees between *kanshousuo* in order to meet local demands for labour. While detainees may receive symbolic amounts in wages even senior officials acknowledge the opportunities for corruption among *kanshousuo* managers. Legal and moral education is given a high priority and is one of the criteria used to grade different *kanshousuo*. Education may include collective admonitory talks by superiors, individual talks and admonition of detainees' relatives. As a result, detainees are expected to report to the authorities any illegal activities they know of taking place inside and outside the detention centre. Education is seen as an investigation tool with 'education' conversations and meetings intended to uncover new facts of a case.

Detainees are called periodically to attend police interrogations. The legal framework for regulating the conduct of police interviews is rudimentary. The law requires the suspect to be interrogated (*xunwen*) within twenty-four hours of being detained and released if detention is not necessary (*buyingdang juliu*) (CPL 2012, Article 84). However, the *Regulations* 1990 are silent on how many times a suspect can be interviewed, when interviews may take place and how long for. Police regulations require that suspects are given food, drink and necessary rest time, but minimum standards are not specified (*Procedural Regulations on the Handling of Criminal Cases by Public Security Organs* 2012, Article 196). Many detainees report to their lawyers that they were interrogated for hours on end with little or no opportunity to rest and eat. In 2013 the Supreme People's Court called for an end to the 'use of freezing, hunger, drying, scorching, fatigue and other illegal methods to obtain a confession' (Al Jazeera 2013), but lawyers continue to report the use of fatigue interrogations (see for example, reports of the interrogation of lawyer Pu Zhiqiang, *South China Morning Post* 2014). Interview rooms often include chairs that restrain the interviewee's legs and arms; overhead lights that can be directed at the suspect and the walls and furniture are often padded. The interrogation process *may* be audio or visually recorded although it is mandatory where the crime may be punishable by death or life imprisonment (2013 CPL, Article 43); more recently there have been calls to require the videoing of all police interviews.

In a further attempt to reduce the opportunities for torture and other ill treatment, the CPL 2012 forbids interrogations taking place outside the *kanshousuo* once the suspect is detained there (Article 116); this measure does not invalidate interrogations that take place before a suspect is delivered to the *kanshousuo*. Moreover, in the absence of a single tamper-proof custody record it is difficult to see how the procuratorate will be able to monitor compliance. Lawyers currently have no right to see the complete detainee record folder (*dang'an*); in a recent call by lawyers for revisions to the *Regulations* 1990 they recommended opening up the files in a bid to reduce the risk of torture or ill treatment when the detainee is taken out of the *kanshousuo*, for example to attend the crime scene (Xinhua Net 18 March 2013).

The law requires that a detained person's family should be notified within twenty-four hours of their detention. However, this fundamental right for someone to be informed can be denied in circumstances where notification is not possible or where state security or terrorism offences are suspected and notification would impede the investigation (CPL 2012, Article 83). This is arguably a strengthening of the right for family members to be informed; the old law allowed the police to deny notification in circumstances that would hinder the investigation. However, the broad powers of the police to decide that a case constitutes a state security offence undermine the measure's protective provisions and there are reports that family members have not received notification in cases of the detention of activists (Yu 18 October 2013). Worryingly, the revised measures have dropped a specific provision that family members should be notified of the reasons for detention and the place of custody (CPL 1996, Article 64). Aside from the requirement that a family member should be notified, detainees are not allowed to have contact with family members.

The *Regulations* 1990 require minimum nutritional and hygiene standards in the provision of food for detainees, but complaints abound about poor quality. Family members and friends can deposit funds for detainees to enable them to buy extra food and other essential supplies, but the prices within the *kanshousuo* may exceed the outside market price by three or four times (Xinhua Net 18 March 2013). Medical care in many *kanshousuo* is reported to be rudimentary and clinics are poorly equipped with basic medicines; medical staff are not independent, but work under the police.

Order within cells has traditionally been the responsibility of cell trusties who have been given responsibility by the police guards to maintain discipline among detainees in return for favours or less work. A former detainee in Shenzhen Number 2 Detention Centre describes the way 'cell bullies' set the rules in the cell and maintained the daily routines (Chineseforums.com 2013). *Kanshousuo* police can use a range of non-lethal instruments of restraint including handcuffs, shackles, tear gas and truncheons. Regulations issued in 1995 prohibit the use of electric batons within the *kanshousuo* without exception. Shackles, including leg irons, are used for prisoners awaiting execution (UN *Report of Special Rapporteur* 10 March 2006) and can also be used on prisoners who have attempted suicide or self-harm; there are also reports that suggest they are being used as a form of punishment (see for example a report on the use of shackles in the Daxing district *kanshousuo*, Chinese Human Rights Defenders 8–15 January 2015). Handcuffs are widely used when detainees move around the centre and for meetings with lawyers. Solitary confinement may be used as a punishment.

Strengthening oversight

The proposal from the Yunnan authorities to involve ordinary citizens in the investigation of Li Qiaoming's death illustrates the use of 'third party investigations' as a new approach to cases where the public rejects the findings of the official investigation (*Global Times* 23 November 2009). Greater public accountability and transparency for *kanshousuo* is now accepted by scholars, and many officials, as essential; two months after Li Qiaoming's death, the SPP launched a five-month campaign to ensure proper management of detention centres (Li 25 May 2009). An earlier pilot project in Liaoyuan, Jilin province, had introduced the concept of people's supervisors. Appointed by the procuratorate and mostly drawn from among delegates to the Local People's Congress, the scheme was grounded in the supervisory functions of both the Procuratorate and Local People's Congress delegates. Inspired by the practice of independent custody visiting in Britain and informed by the provisions in the *Optional Protocol to the Convention Against Torture*, a pilot project demonstrated that, with suitable training, citizens could act as fairly effective external monitors interviewing detainees about their treatment in the *kanshousuo* and checking up on the conditions in detention, including food preparation, healthcare and accommodation. A local initiative, it failed to secure the approval of the MPS for more nationwide piloting. The experience, however, has been well documented and offers a cost effective model to introduce greater independence in the monitoring of *kanshousuo* (Chen 2012).

The MPS's response to the revelation of problems in *kanshousuo* was the launch of an openness initiative culminating in the organisation of Open Days in 2012 during which the doors of the *kanshousuo* were open to visits by the general public and the appointment of 'guest supervisors' (State Council Information Office 14 May 2013). Not all members of the public were welcome, however: an outraged petitioner described to her lawyer being forcibly excluded from participating in an Open Day at a *kanshousuo* where she had previously been detained (Private communication, November 2012). Foreign journalists were invited by public security officials to visit Beijing Numbers 1 and 2 Detention Centres following recent refurbishment. While journalists were prevented from talking with detainees, the stage-managed visit nevertheless attempted to convey the message of an institution aspiring to be caring and modern (Branigan 25 October 2012).

The most significant change to the monitoring of *kanshousuo* in recent years has been the strengthening of the role of the procuratorate. Although the procuratorate has long had an office within the *kanshousuo*, the functions of its duty staff have been minimal. Tasked by the Constitution 1982 (as amended) and the *Organic Law on the People's Procuratorate (Renmin Jianchayuan Zuzhi Fa)* 1979 (amended in 1983) with oversight of detention, the role of on-site procurators was poorly defined and they had gained a reputation of rubber stamping police decisions. Following the 'hide and seek' case, the SPP required lower-level offices to conduct inspection visits to *kanshousuo* and monitor their performance against a range of indicators. Initiatives to support increased professionalism, enhance complaints procedures and assert the procuratorate's supervisory functions have included the setting up of new offices at city level to oversee the work of the on-site procuratorial officials and more clearly define their responsibilities towards detainees.

Access to a lawyer

The CPL is the main source of law governing access to justice for a detainee in the *kanshousuo* and the 2012 amendment introduces some important revisions. Under the CPL 1996, a person facing criminal charges could not appoint a defender (*bianhuren*) until the case was transferred to the prosecution for investigation (Article 36). Earlier access to lawyers was provided under the *Lawyers Law* (*Lüshi Fa*) 1996 (as amended in 2007), but, because of the law's relatively lowly status, lawyers reported routine disregard of the law by the *kanshousuo* authorities. The CPL 2012 confirms the improved provisions of the *Lawyers Law* and a criminal detainee can now appoint a lawyer from the date on which he or she is first interrogated or subject to compulsory measures. Implementing regulations require the police in the *kanshousuo* to inform the detainee of this right and to forward requests promptly to the investigation department handling the case (*ban'an bumen*); they are then required to forward the request to the lawyer (*Procedural Regulations on the Handling of Criminal Cases by Public Security Organs* 2012). The CPL 2012 also allows a detained person's custodian or close relative to appoint a lawyer on their behalf (Article 33). During the investigation period a detainee may only appoint a lawyer as their defender and not other persons, such as friends or relatives, who may, nevertheless, represent the defendant at trial (Article 37).

Also in line with the *Lawyers Law* 1996 (as amended in 2007), the CPL 2012 confirms that lawyers that hold current practice licences may request (*yaoqiu*) to meet with their client in the *kanshousuo*. The *kanshousuo* authorities are required to arrange such a meeting 'promptly' and no later than within forty-eight hours (Article 37). Where the offence is alleged to involve endangering state security, terrorism or serious bribery, however, the lawyer must have permission to meet with his client from the investigating authority. Since the CPL 2012 came into effect lawyers have tried to monitor implementation of the provisions for accessing their clients (Congressional Executive Commission on China (CECC) 19 March 2015). While lawyers are reporting that access to their clients in routine cases is generally being granted, there continue to be reports of lawyers being delayed or denied access to their clients in politically sensitive cases as well as specific lawyers being informed that they are not allowed to represent their client (HRIC Bulletin 22 July 2013).

For the majority of detainees in a *kanshousuo*, the main problem is being in a position to appoint a lawyer. Most detainees and their families will not know any lawyers and large numbers are unable to afford lawyers' fees. While some high profile criminal lawyers can earn substantial fees from criminal cases implicating the wealthy and some 'rights-protecting' or *weiquan* lawyers may take cases pro bono, criminal law practice in China, overall, is not well developed. A demand by many *kanshousuo* authorities that there must be two lawyers present at any meeting with a detainee further adds to potential costs. The CPL 2012 attempts, partly, to address these problems through the expansion of legal aid. Previously, criminal legal aid had only been available at the trial stage and only for defendants facing the death penalty or in one of the then designated categories of vulnerable defendants: juveniles or the blind, deaf or mute. Under the 2012 amendment, legal aid is now also available to persons with a mental illness and anyone facing life imprisonment. Moreover, anyone unable to appoint a defender due to financial difficulties may apply for legal aid and should have a lawyer assigned if the conditions for legal aid are satisfied (CPL 2012, Article 34). With 100 million people still living below the poverty line of $1.25 a day, China's legal aid system faces huge challenges in providing legal assistance to the poor and vulnerable, for whom conflict with the law may lead to a permanent loss of livelihood.

Although the revised CPL 2012 provides for improved access to a lawyer, many detainees question whether appointing a lawyer will be of much use. Research in Hubei revealed that most detainees felt that a defence lawyer was of little value (Ye et al. 2014) and this may help to account for the low defence representation rate in China. The CPL 2012 establishes that during the investigation phase the defence lawyer may offer legal advice, make complaints or accusations on behalf of their client and apply for bail or other changes to the compulsory measures; the defence lawyer may also learn from the police the nature of the alleged offence and other relevant information, as well as proffer opinions (Article 36). Once the case has been sent for 'review and prosecution' (*shencha qisu*), the lawyer may also discuss the evidence with their client and access and copy filed case materials (Articles 37 and 38). The defence lawyer is allowed to interview and correspond with their client in detention and the law also states that the meeting between the defence lawyer and his client is not to be monitored (*bu bei jianting*) (Article 37). Lawyers are, however, unable to be present during police interrogations of their client.

Although the CPL 2012 provides detainees in *kanshousuo* with improved access to a lawyer, the lawyer's ability to take instructions from his client and challenge the case being made against him is hampered by delays and difficulties in meeting with his client, limitations on disclosure by the police and prosecution, and the lawyer's exclusion from police interviews. Many of the documents relating to the person's detention in the *kanshousuo* are also excluded from the case materials available to the lawyer, hindering any effort by the lawyer to challenge the legality of continued detention. The obstacles facing the defence lawyer challenging his client's detention and arrest are part of a bigger difficulty over the role of independent defence counsel within the Chinese criminal justice system. In the face of seemingly insurmountable challenges to the conduct of a fair trial, reformers have focused on expanding access to lawyers, particularly in the initial stages of detention.

Introducing duty lawyers

The MoJ has responsibility for the legal profession in China as well as legal aid; over the years it has helped to expand access to legal assistance, particularly in rural areas and for poorer sections of the population. In 2006 the Ministry initiated a pilot legal aid duty lawyer project in Xiuwu county (Jiaozuo, Henan province). With support from the United Nations Development Programme, the project originally intended to introduce the concept of duty counsel for detainees. The main outcome of the project was, however, the setting up of a duty lawyers' office at the county court which provided free legal advice to the public and assisted migrant workers to settle claims. Following on from this initiative, in 2010 the Ministry encouraged the establishment of new duty lawyer pilot projects in a number of provinces. The guidance explained that the duty lawyer system would provide free legal assistance to criminal suspects who had not appointed lawyers. Pilot sites were not given explicit instructions on how to implement the new initiatives and a range of practices emerged around the country.

In several Shenzhen districts, a duty lawyers' office has been set up at the entrance to the local *kanshousuo*. Local lawyers help to staff these offices, providing their services pro bono; they help visitors obtain information about detained family members, appoint lawyers and apply for legal aid. With its large migrant population, most of the people detained in Shenzhen are from out of town; as family members congregated outside the *kanshousuo* in search of information, 'black lawyers' (*hei lüshi*) were accused of cheating families with their offers to help. In an attempt to manage the perceived threats to public order and, perhaps, the professional interests of local qualified lawyers, duty lawyers' offices were established.

Three rural counties in Hubei were among the locations to be nominated by the MoJ as pilot sites. Working with the Public Interest and Development Law Institute (PIDLI) at Wuhan University School of Law, legal aid officials at the county and provincial level explored international standards and practice, including the duty solicitors' scheme in Hong Kong. Challenged to go further than the duty lawyer models elsewhere, the pilot sites determined to set up a scheme targeted at protecting the rights of detainees and located within the walls of the *kanshousuo*. Although nothing in Chinese law prohibited establishing such a scheme, similarly there was nothing in the law or regulations that provided for the presence of legal aid duty lawyers within the *kanshousuo*. Setting up such a scheme, therefore, required the support of the local public security bureau which had control over the *kanshousuo* (Kong and Ding 2013). Since there was no higher level order that the police should cooperate with the legal aid bureau, local leaders needed to deploy their political and social capital as well as policy-based arguments to reach an agreement on the role of duty lawyers and the siting of their office within the *kanshousuo*.

The new office was located next to the office of the duty procurator while discussions continued over what should be the role of the duty lawyer and under what circumstances the duty lawyer would be able to meet with detainees. The coming into force of the CPL 2012 and the *Provisions of the Supreme People's Court, Supreme People's Procuratorate, Ministry of Public Security and Ministry of Justice on Legal Aid in Criminal Action* (*Guanyu Xingshi Susong Falü Yuanzhu Gongzuo De Guiding*) 2013 established new requirements for the police to submit applications for legal aid within twenty-four hours to the legal aid office and to ensure that within three days the applicant's family or other representative is informed of the need to supply supportive documentation. Under these new regulations there was a role for duty lawyers to facilitate applications for legal aid by detainees. In the duty lawyer scheme pilot, the *kanshousuo* management also identified a role for duty lawyers in supporting its disciplinary work (*guanjiao*), as well as providing legal advice (Kong and Ding 2013).

One of the stumbling blocks in the pilot projects is the status of the duty lawyer under the new law. In the interpretation of the CPL 2012 advanced by the police, a duty lawyer could not act as defence counsel to the detainee since he or she had not been properly appointed. In order to meet with a detainee, lawyers are required by the CPL 2012 to produce three documents: a practising license, a law firm certificate and a letter of attorney or an official legal aid letter. Not yet having been appointed, duty lawyers cannot provide a letter of attorney, but the pilot duty lawyers' scheme furnished lawyers with legal aid letters which could be signed by detainees. Underpinning much of the discussion was an understanding that if the duty lawyer were acting in the capacity of defence counsel, communications with their client should be confidential, a privilege the police were reluctant to honour with respect to duty lawyers. In the absence of regulations or clearer guidelines, the police supported a view of the duty lawyer as a 'neutral' actor who could inform detainees of their rights and assist with applications for legal aid, but who could not act in the capacity of defence lawyer in order to avoid 'potential conflicts of interest' (Kong and Ding 2013, 46).

The duty lawyers' scheme is in its infancy in China and there is no settled understanding of the role of a duty lawyer. Discussions reveal the police distrust of lawyers and their reluctance to concede a bigger role to defence lawyers; they also illustrate the interests of management in ensuring order within the *kanshousuo*. To the scheme's advocates, the pilot project has, nevertheless, been an institutional breakthrough with the setting up of a duty lawyers' office within the *kanshousuo*, establishing a rota of duty lawyers and enabling detainees to make prompt applications for legal aid. Substantial challenges remain in managing the scheme – for example, ensuring sufficient numbers of lawyers are available to meet with detainees, as well as in expanding its scope to assist detainees apply for pre-trial release on bail. Against a backdrop of poverty and inequality, and increasing social conflicts, the legal aid lobby remains influential and budgets have expanded. Nevertheless the preference of local legal aid authorities to support civil cases rather than see the funds go to assist 'bad people' (Kong and Ding 2013, 47) may mean the resources for expansion of criminal legal aid are limited.

The parameters of the policy response

Shocking reports of violent deaths in detention prompted criminal justice reformers to advance a number of policy measures to improve protection of pre-trial detainees' rights. Informed by international human rights law, overseas practice and greater awareness of the reality in *kanshousuo*, reformist officials, often with the support of scholars, undertook a number of measures to strengthen oversight and gate-keeping decisions on detention, enhance access to lawyers and improve detention conditions. Perhaps the area in which there is the most visible change is the refurbishment of *kanshousuo* buildings and the construction of new detention centres. Surveillance cameras in cells have been widely introduced to monitor prisoner behaviour and deter the kind of prisoner-on-prisoner violence that led to Li Qiaoming's death. However, policy measures which would restrain police powers have encountered greater obstacles to implementation.

The most striking illustration of the difficulties criminal justice reformers face is the continued failure to replace the *Regulations* 1990 governing *kanshousuo* with legislation that provides greater protection of detainees' rights, including the transfer of powers to manage long-term pre-trial detention to an agency fully independent of the investigating authorities. Similarly, an initiative to introduce more independent oversight at the local level, through the introduction of 'people's supervisors', foundered, and police-managed Open Days became the main mechanism to boost public accountability.

Although the police have retained their overall control of pre-trial detention, reforms have boosted the supervisory role of the procuratorate through giving more prominence to the procuratorate officials based in *kanshousuo* and reforms, in the CPL 2012, which address decisions to approve arrest and grant bail. Reports of procuratorate requests that the police conduct further investigations indicate that the procuratorate are scrutinising police requests for approval of arrest and the decision to prosecute more closely. However, where the suspect remains in detention during this period, extended investigations risk increasing the time detainees spend incarcerated awaiting trial.

Police antipathy to the involvement of lawyers has largely marginalised the role of lawyers in criminal proceedings. Nevertheless, the CPL 2012 brought an expanded role for the legal profession and many lawyers have been quick to exercise their right to earlier access to their clients. Measures to expand the provision of criminal legal aid to the police investigation phase remain in their infancy and require the cooperation of the often suspicious, if not hostile, public security authorities.

The contours of the policy response demonstrate the pervasive influence of the police. Some reformers hope that a stronger procuratorate will succeed in limiting police authority over criminal procedures and may eventually contribute to a greater separation of powers. However, the fact that both institutions are subordinate to the Party's Political-Legal Committee suggest that where difficult decisions need to be made, political rather than judicial opinions will prevail. Efforts to strengthen procuratorate oversight of treatment in detention centres are also hampered by inadequate levels of staffing and training.

Thus far, reforms have not resulted in any paradigm shift in the conceptualisation of pre-trial detention or wider appreciation of what constitutes a fair trial. There is little discussion of the presumption of innocence: some legal scholars have started to discuss *weijue jiya* (Peng 2011), detention of the un-convicted, but the extensive use of pre-trial detention is not widely seen as problematic. In 2013, the Central Political-Legal Committee called for application of the principle *yizui congwu*, ('not punishing cases in doubt') where the evidence is insufficient, as part of provisions to prevent miscarriages of justice (an unofficial translation can be found at China Law Translate 2014). The welcome shift in official language to recognise that someone suspected of a crime may not be guilty has not yet been translated into the popular understanding of criminal justice and there is little debate about the policy implications of such ideas.

There is no right to silence during interrogation and, despite extensive lobbying, lawyers remain excluded from police interviews. The CPL 2012 bids investigators to inform the suspect that they should answer the questions truthfully and that there are provisions for leniency for 'honest confessions of a crime' (Article 118). While confession evidence is not sufficient to convict, there remains a strong presumption that without a confession the courts are also unlikely to convict (Lu and Miethe 2003). Confession is also the first step in successful rehabilitation. It is too early to judge whether policy strictures to prevent miscarriages of justice and greater official openness to the possibility of innocence will begin to change attitudes to the use of pre-trial detention. In a system that rewards convictions, every effort is made to prevent the retraction of confessions. Detention in a *kanshousuo*, where police can interrogate suspects as often as they wish, ensures that the criminal process retains control of both the body, and mind, of the suspect, guaranteeing not only that they are present at trial, but that they do not deny the confessions around which so much of the prosecution case is built.

Conclusion

Scandals have been an important driver of criminal justice reform in many countries. Responding to public outrage can provide an opportunity for governments to tackle entrenched interests and bad practice. The 'hide and seek' scandal helped to establish, within China, ideas about minimum standards of treatment in detention and detainees' right to safety. The overriding policy objective of the reforms introduced following the death of Li Qiaoming, however, seems to have been limited to preventing cases of unnatural deaths within the *kanshousuo*. Public anger was directed at the reports of deaths in police custody and the attempted official cover-up at the local level. The resulting increased surveillance within the *kanshousuo* and strengthened procuratorate oversight have not, however, challenged police or Party authority in the pre-trial process or contributed to empowering more independent institutions. Indeed, addressing public disquiet arguably boosts the central government's legitimacy (see Lewis' 2011 similar point in a discussion of the introduction of the exclusionary rule); the authorities have avoided a similar outcome to the Sun Zhigang case. Increased budgets have enabled the refurbishment of dilapidated facilities. Pre-trial detention centres now aspire to the image of a modern and caring institution with measures in place to prevent detainee on detainee violence or police torture.

The current political environment belies the optimism of many who believe in step-by-step reforms. Despite the rule of law rhetoric, China's recent 'turn against law', as Minzer (2011, 935) terms it, suggests that the authorities have lost confidence in the law to ensure social control, without the Party ceding too much influence to more independent actors. Substantial reforms are unlikely to occur without removing the *kanshousuo* from police control and introducing greater independent oversight of the necessity to detain pre-trial. In the current political climate and with the emphasis on maintaining social stability, reformers cannot easily voice criticism of the police. Yet, without greater restraint on police and Party influence over the use of detention, recent reforms are unlikely to substantially reduce the numbers of pre-trial detainees and eliminate the risk of future unnatural deaths in custody.

Writing amidst a crackdown on the Internet and the dissemination online of 'rumours', one must also ask whether future cases of 'hide and seek' would ever come to light. Indeed, one of the bloggers who was instrumental in bringing Li Qiaoming's case to public attention was later detained (Reuters 21 October 2013). Scandal has fuelled public discourse and the dynamic among public opinion, lawyers and legal scholars has contributed to greater rights awareness and stronger demands for these rights to be respected. Nevertheless, there has been no broader public challenge to the state's right to deprive persons of their liberty pre-trial. If *kanshousuo* are to truly respect human rights, reformers will need to challenge the very rationale of the institution. Perhaps, however, more widespread criticism of the current presumption of pre-trial detention will not take place until a wider range of liberties are more extensively 'recognised and valorised' (Ci 2014, 219) in China.

Notes

1 Through the work of *The Rights Practice*, the author has been privileged to participate in private meetings and discussions with Chinese officials, legal scholars and lawyers. Except where comments have been published, the authors of remarks reported here remain anonymous.
2 In Chapter 2, Ashworth explores a framework for evaluating pre–trial criminal justice in England in terms of the purpose of the process and the extent to which it respects the human rights of all individuals affected.
3 This is an amendment of the Criminal Procedure Law 1996, Article 213, in which prisoners with less than one year to serve were sent to *kanshousuo*.

References

Al Jazeera. 21 November 2013. 'China's Highest Court Calls for End to Torture of Accused Criminals.' Available at http://america.aljazeera.com/articles/2013/11/21/china-s-highest-courtcallsforendto tortureofaccusedcriminals.html (accessed 16 February 2016).
Ashworth, Andrew. 1998. *The Criminal Process: An Evaluative Study*. Oxford: Oxford University Press.
Balme, Stéphanie and Dowdle, Michael W., eds. 2009. *Building Constitutionalism in China*. New York: Palgrave Macmillan.
Branigan, Tania. 25 October 2012. 'China Shows Off "Sunshine Detention Centre" To Allay Torture Claims.' *The Guardian*. Available at http://www.theguardian.com/world/2012/oct/25/china-beijing-dentention-centre-tour (accessed 16 February 2016).
Cape, Ed, Namoradze, Zaza, Smith, Roger and Spronken, Taru. 2010. *Effective Criminal Defence in Europe*. Antwerp: Intersentia.
Chen Weidong, ed. 2012. *Kanshousuo De Tounming Yu Kaifang: Jiya Xunshi Shouce (Detention Centres' Transparency and Openness: A Manual for Detention Visiting)*. Beijing: Zhongguo falü chubanshe.
China Copyright and Media. October 2014. *Unofficial English Translation of CCP Central Committee 'Decision on Certain Major Issues in Comprehensively Promoting Governing the Country in Accordance with Law.'* Available at https://chinacopyrightandmedia.wordpress.com/2014/10/28/ccp-central-committee-decision-concerning-some-major-questions-in-comprehensively-moving-governing-the-country-according-to-the-law-forward/ (accessed 16 February 2016). Chinese original at http://www.gov.cn/xinwen/2014-10/28/content_2771714.htm (accessed 16 February 2016).
China Law Translate. 18 February 2014. *Unofficial English Translation of Central Political-Legal Commission (2013) no. 27 'Provisions on Achieving Prevention of Unjust, False and Wrongfully Decided Cases.'* Available at http://chinalawtranslate.com/central-political-legal-committee-on-preventing-wrongful-criminal-cases/?lang=en (accessed 16 February 2016).
China Daily. 27 February 2009. 'Inmate Beaten to Death in "Hide-and-Seek".' Available at http://www.chinadaily.com.cn/china/2009-02/27/content_7521806.htm (accessed 16 February 2016).
China Daily. 27 February 2010. 'Suspect Dies in Police Detention.' Available at http://www.chinadaily.com.cn/china/2010-02/27/content_9513085.htm (accessed 16 February 2016).
Chinese-forums.com. 'Captivity in a Chinese Prison (Detention Center).' Discussion thread started by Already Taken, 29 May 2013 12:35 PM. Available at http://www.chinese-forums.com/index.php?/topic/40973-captivity-in-a-chinese-prison-detention-center/ (accessed 6 February 2016).
Chinese Human Rights Defenders. 8–15 January 2015. 'Torture and Ill-treatment of Detainees and Political Charges Returning Under Xi.' *China Human Rights Briefing*. Available at http://chrdnet.com/2015/01/chrb-torture-ill-treatment-of-detainees-political-charges-returning-under-xi-18-152015/ (accessed 16 February 2016).
Ci Jiwei. 2014. *Moral China in the Age of Reform*. New York: Cambridge University Press.
Congressional Executive Commission on China (CECC). 19 March 2015. *2014 Annual Report; Criminal Justice*. Available at http://www.cecc.gov/sites/chinacommission.house.gov/files/documents/AR14Criminal%20Justice_final.pdf (accessed 16 February 2016).
Dan Wei. 2012. 'Lun Renmin Jianchayuan Jiansuo Jiancha Gongzuo Gaige' (A Discussion on Reforms to the Procuratorate Supervision of Detention). *Henan Shehui Kexue* (*Henan Sociology*) 12: 009
Danwei. 23 October 2009. 'A Foreigner's Life in a Beijing Jail.' Available at http://www.danwei.org/crime/a_foreigners_life_in_a_beijing.php (accessed 16 February 2016).
Dikötter, Frank. 2002. *Crime, Punishment and the Prison in Modern China*. London: C. Hurst & Co.
Fu Hualing. 2009. 'Access to Justice and Constitutionalism in China.' In *Building Constitutionalism in China*, edited by Stéphanie Balme and Michael Dowdle, 163–78. New York: Palgrave Macmillan.
Galligan, Denis. 1994. 'Regulating Pre-Trial Decisions.' In *A Reader on Criminal Justice*, edited by Nicola Lacey, 151–76. Oxford: Oxford University Press.
Global Times. 23 November 2009. 'Death of Innocence Creates Crisis of Credibility.' Available at http://www.globaltimes.cn/special/2009-11/487137.html (accessed 16 February 2016).
Hand, Keith J. 2006. 'Using Law for a Righteous Purpose: The Sun Zhigang Incident and Evolving Forms of Citizen Action in the People's Republic of China.' *Columbia Journal of Transnational Law* 45(1): 114–95.

Her Majesty's Inspectorate of Prisons (HMIP). 2012. 'Expectations: Criteria for Assessing the Treatment of Prisoners and Conditions of Prisons.' Version 4, 2012. Available at http://www.justice.gov.uk/about/hmi-prisons/inspection-and-appraisal-criteria (accessed 16 February 2016).

Kong Yan and Ding Peng. May 2013. 'Tuijin Kanshousuo Zhiban Lüshi Shidian: Tansuo Xingshi Falü Yuanzhu Xin Moshi' (Piloting Duty Lawyers in Detention Centres: Exploration of a New Model of Criminal Legal Aid.' *Xuexi Yuekan* (*Study Monthly*) 5: 46–7.

Lewis, Margaret K. 2011. 'Controlling Abuse to Maintain Control: The Exclusionary Rule in China.' *International Law and Politics* 43(3): 629–97.

Li Huizi. 25 May 2009. 'Investigative Report: How a Chinese detention center ticks.' *Xinhua*. Available at http://news.xinhuanet.com/english/2009-05/25/content_11432759.htm (accessed 16 February 2016).

Lu, Hong and Miethe, Terance D. 2003. 'Confessions and Criminal Case Disposition in China.' *Law and Society Review* 37(3): 549–78.

McConville, Mike and Choongh, Satnam Choongh, Wan, Pinky Choy Dick, Hong, Eric Chui Wing, Dobinson, Ian and Jones, Carol, eds. 2011. *Criminal Justice in China: An Empirical Enquiry*. Cheltenham: Edward Elgar.

Minzer, Carl. 2011. 'China's Turn Against Law.' *American Journal of Comparative Law* 59: 935–84.

Nesossi, Elisa. 2008. 'Reforming Criminal Justice in the People's Republic of China? The Black Hole of Pre-Trial Detention.' *Journal of Comparative Law* 3(2): 305–15.

Open Society Justice Initiative. 2012. *Improving Pretrial Justice: The Roles of Lawyers and Paralegals*. New York: Open Society Foundations.

Pakes, Francis. 2004. *Comparative Criminal Justice*. Devon UK: Willan Publishing.

Peerenboom, Randall. 2007. *China Modernizes: Threat to the West or Model for the Rest?* Oxford: Oxford University Press.

Peng Bo. 2011. 'Lun Weijue Jiyazhe De Quanli Baozhang' (Discussing the Human Rights' Protection of Pre-Trial Detainees). Working Paper. Shenzhen University.

Reuters. 25 February 2009. 'China "Hide-And-Seek" Death Case Irks Web Users.' Available at http://uk.reuters.com/article/2009/02/25/oukoe-uk-china-internet-idUKTRE51O1Z820090225 (accessed 16 February 2016).

Reuters. 21 October 2013. 'China Holds Two Bloggers as It Expands Crackdown on Rumors.' Available at http://www.reuters.com/article/2013/10/21/net-us-china-rumour-idUSBRE99G0C320131021 (accessed 16 February 2016).

Rodley, Nigel. 1999. *The Treatment of Prisoners Under International Law*. Oxford: Oxford University Press.

Sapio, Flora. 2010. *Sovereign Power and the Law in China*. Leiden and Boston: Brill.

South China Morning Post (SCMP). Agence France-Presse in Beijing. 20 December 2014. 'Chinese Rights Lawyer Tortured in Detention Centre, Wife Claims.' Available at http://www.scmp.com/news/china/article/1666466/chinese-rights-lawyer-tortured-detention-centre-wife-claims (accessed 16 February 2016).

State Council Information Office. 11 June 2012. 'National Human Rights Action Plan of China.' Available at http://www.china.org.cn/government/whitepaper/node_7156850.htm (accessed 16 February 2016).

State Council Information Office. 14 May 2013. 'Progress in China's Human Rights in 2012.' Available at http://news.xinhuanet.com/english/china/2013-05/14/c_132380706_2.htm (accessed 16 February 2016).

United Nations. 10 March 2006. *Report of the Special Rapporteur on Torture, Cruel, Inhuman and Degrading Treatment, Manfred Nowak. Mission to China*. Available at http://daccess-dds-ny.un.org/doc/UNDOC/GEN/G06/117/50/PDF/G0611750.pdf?OpenElement (accessed 16 February 2016).

United Nations. 5 August 2013. *National Report Submitted in Accordance with Paragraph 5 of the Annex to Human Rights Council Resolution 16/21: China*. A/HRC/WG.6/17/CHN/1.

United Nations. 9 August 2013. *Interim Report of The Special Rapporteur on Torture and Other Cruel, Inhuman or Degrading Treatment or Punishment*. United Nations General Assembly A/68/295.

Xinhua Net. 20 February 2009. 'China Netizens Join Probe into "Hide-and-Seek" Prison Death.' Available at http://news.xinhuanet.com/english/2009-02/20/content_10855443.htm (accessed 16 February 2016).

Xinhua Net. 18 March 2013. 'Lüshi Shangshu Jianyi Xiugai Kanshousuo Tiaoli: Jinzhi Qiangpo Fanren Laodong (Lawyers Petition for Amendment of the Detention Centre Regulations: Prohibit Offenders' Forced Labour).' Available at http://news.xinhuanet.com/legal/2013-03/18/c_124471564_2.htm (accessed 16 February 2016).

Xinhua Net. 28 December 2013. 'China Abolishes Reeducation Through Labor.' Available at http://news.xinhuanet.com/english/china/2013-12/28/c_133003042.htm (accessed 16 February 2016).

Ye Xiaoqin, Li Jian and Wang Shaobo. 2014. *Kanshousuo Jiancha Jiandu: Shizheng Yu Bijiao Yanjiu* (Procuratorate Supervision of Detention Centres: An Empirical and Comparative Study). Beijing: Zhongguo jiancha chubanshe.

Yu, Verna. 18 October 2013. 'Lawyer and Sister Fear Dissident Guo Feixiong Has Been Mistreated.' *South China Morning Post*. Available at http://www.scmp.com/news/china/article/1334000/lawyer-and-sister-fear-dissident-guo-feixiong-has-been-mistreated (accessed 16 February 2016).

Zhang Yan. 16 September 2010. 'New Law Mandates Prosecutors to Interview Suspects.' *China Daily*. Available at http://www.chinadaily.com.cn/china/2010-09/16/content_11309480.htm (accessed 16 February 2016).

Part III
An assessment of the field

8 Framing imprisonment studies in China
Ideology, law and politics

Elisa Nesossi and Susan Trevaskes

Introduction

In any justice system, decisions about the scope and punitive value of deprivation of liberty are intrinsically political, since the powers given to prisons to incarcerate individuals are directly linked to the power of the state and its institutions. Custodial punishment is justified as a way of protecting society from offenders, by isolating them from the community. In addition, in a number of modern systems of justice, the rehabilitation of offenders through labour or through education and training is also an acknowledged purpose of prison incarceration. Regardless of the political system in which prisons operate, the stated intentions of authorities ranging from protection to rehabilitation are communicated through certain discourses about punishment that relate to its intended societal good. Like other political systems, the Party-state in China sees it as its prerogative to define the scope and means for the effective realisation of its protective role over society, and to create sets of narratives about punishment to justify its choices. This means that institutions involved in the administration of justice negotiate their roles and responsibilities in the punishment arena around certain key concepts that rationalise political choices and, at least in theory, seek to circumscribe their roles and powers.

Since the beginning of the 1980s, the political imperative to fight crime has inclined the criminal justice system towards a deep reliance on Party-initiated policies that have been driving prison policy and reform in China. Since this time, political ideology has determined how penal institutions are talked about internally within the overall criminal justice system, publicly in the media, and in the scholarly literature. We find in this chapter that political discourse – politics manifest as Marxist–Leninist ideology, institutional politics and reformist policies – matters to how prisons are analysed in the Chinese literature, to the way in which prisons operate and how these operations are rationalised by institutional players. Therefore, the underlying assumption in this chapter is that political ideology has shaped both prison discourses and prison reform processes from the 1980s to today. While the role of political discourse in shaping penal studies is not exclusively a Chinese phenomenon, in the People's Republic of China (PRC), the direct influence of ideology on the institutional discourses and reformist approaches is made particularly apparent by the omnipresent role of the Chinese Communist Party (CCP) in state and social governance. To be sure, political ideology defines the perimeters within which the idea of punishment can be discussed in the literature and translated into practice, since it is the CCP that provides the normative vision of how a society should be arranged and governed.

In this chapter, we follow the trail of the discursive changes in the Chinese literature on prisons that have occurred for over more than three decades, by investigating shifts in the scope, methodology and topics addressed. We interrogate how the ideas pertaining to imprisonment have been analysed and conceptualised by the Chinese scholarship on law and justice to show

how different political discourses interact and shape its contours. The first part of the chapter examines the main themes that have emerged in post-Mao approaches on imprisonment. It contends that, at least since the early 1980s, the field in China has been shaped by specific choices of what can or cannot be studied and scrutinised, and is driven by the dictates of political ideology. It looks at the directions that the literature has taken in thirty-five years of legal reforms, identifying the main substantive areas of the scholarly discourse. Here, we examine the discursive shift from 'reform studies' (*gaizao xue*) to 'prison studies' (*jianyu xue*) that began to occur in the early to mid-1990s, signalling a change in ideological focus and paving the way for the imminent enactment of the PRC's first *Prison Law* (*Jianyu Fa*) in 1994. The analysis highlights the extent to which the change from the Marxist idea of thought reform to a penology discipline-based approach is reflective of the process of legalisation on academic debates and theoretical outlook. We also examine the geographical shift that began occurring in Chinese prison studies in the late 1990s. Where once the source of foreign inspiration came solely from Soviet Union-focused literature on reform through labour, with time Chinese scholars became much more open to influences from Europe, America and other western jurisdictions. This shift mirrored wider changes in China as to what was considered a politically acceptable reference point for comparative scholarly literature.

In China today, political discourse continues to be encapsulated in politico-legal slogans that profess to embody certain political agendas. In the criminal justice arena, a key example is the recent dominance of the policy called Balancing Leniency and Severity (*kuanyan xianji*). This policy-cum-slogan is articulated as the manifestation of the broader political program of Harmonious Society (*hexie shehui*). It has been promoted in criminal justice circles as the incarnation of Harmonious Society objectives and therefore has provided the institutional and discursive framework for implementing the political agendas of the Party in the Hu Jintao era (2002–2012) and beyond. In the second part of this chapter, we analyse how, since 2012 (and in the aftermath of the Eighth Amendment to the *Criminal Law* (*Xing Fa*) 1997), balancing leniency and severity has been imposed as a new theme in prison reforms. Since its emergence in 2006 in the context of the Harmonious Society political agenda, this policy has been discussed primarily in the area of court reforms in criminal sentencing of both minor and serious crime, but seldom in the context of prison reforms. As an exemplar of the current Chinese literature on prisons, this section examines how the discourse based on the Harmonious Society doctrine has been used to reconceptualise prisons' organisation and prisoner's execution of sentences in twenty-first century China. Our analysis demonstrates that the way prisons are debated and conceptualised today in China remain strictly linked to domestic political changes. This part of the chapter relies primarily on the reflections by three Chinese prison officers Tang Xule, Liu Weidong and Li Cheng published in 2013 in the national journal *Prison Review* (*Jianyu Pinglun*).

The Chinese scholarly debates: an overview

The 1980s: the revival of reform studies

Of all the various facilities of detention and deprivation of liberty in China, Chinese scholars have focused most of their attention on prison facilities. The most intuitive explanation for this continued interest is that imprisonment represents one of the key forms of criminal punishments in the PRC. Furthermore, Chinese scholars have not considered PRC prisons as politically sensitive an issue as other institutions of detention. Since 1983, prisons have been administered by the Ministry of Justice (MoJ), which has been traditionally less conservative and more open than its Ministry of Public Security (MPS) counterpart that controls most of the other detention facilities in China. This has allowed potentially sensitive concepts attached to punishment, such as human rights, for example, to enter the Chinese academic discourse in prison studies in a less controversial way. In addition, its relative accessibility, in comparison to other politically contentious forms of detention, has made it possible for Chinese scholars to gain an empirical understanding of the basics of prison organisation and institutional practices. Another likely reason is that prisons both in China and in other parts of the world also have a longer historical legacy than other detention facilities. This has meant that prison studies have had a longer scholarly tradition and a richer theoretical and empirical foundation, as well as an extensive comparative framework.

Another possible reason why the Chinese literature on deprivation of liberty has been dominated by prison studies is that the discourses driving the prison system have always been closely aligned to the political providence of Maoism and to the protection of the socialist regime. In the early years of the PRC, custodial punishment was a way of bringing to heel socialism's recalcitrants and neutralising their political or social dangerousness. Remoulding criminals into new citizens of socialism required a language of political rationalisation that was directly informed by Maoism, Marxism and Leninism. Thought reform was the central rationalising principle of prisons – at the time labelled as 'reform through labour' (*laodong gaizao*) institutions – after the establishment of the PRC in 1949.

Changes in political ideology outside the prison system played a crucial role in shaping movements inside the system even after the end of the Cultural Revolution in 1978. This allowed thought reform to remain the centralising discourse in the study of prisons and in the related scholarly literature even in the early post-Mao era (Dutton and Xu 1998). Academic discussions on reform and imprisonment continued to be imbued with ideas that had clear Marxist and Leninist connotations and that derived from the traditional Russian school on reform through labour. Hence, thought reform was interpreted in the scholarly field through the discourse of 'reform' and '(re-) education' (for example, *gaizao/jianyu jiaoyu xue*) and later, psychology (*xinli xue*).

In the early 1980s, the Party-state continued to use its prerogative to define the scope and means to fulfil its protective role over society by promoting socialist narratives of punishment. Chinese scholarly literature on prisons closely mirrored these approaches, framing analyses around key political concepts used by the Party-state to define the scope and role of prisons. These discourses were tightly controlled through the establishment of key educational facilities. Following the Eighth National Conference on Reform Through Labour (*di ba ci quanguo laogai gongzuo huiyi*, generally known as *di ba lao*), organised by the MPS, the MPS opted for the establishment of a national official school on reform through labour, a number of local training facilities, along with various training classes. This led to the emergence of a scholarly study of imprisonment, publications of related teaching materials and, in 1983, to the establishment of the 'Specialised Teaching Material Editorial Department on Reform Through Labour' (*laogai zhuanye jiaocai bianji bu*). This department established a writing and publishing plan for the coming years and created contacts with relevant scholars at several Chinese universities – the Chinese University of Politics and Law (*Zhongguo Zhengfa Daxue*), Peking University (*Beijing Daxue*), People's University (*Zhongguo Renmin Daxue*), the Northwestern Institute of Politics and Law (*Xibei Zhengfa Xueyuan*), East China University of Politics and Law (*Huadong Zhengfa Xueyuan*), the Chinese Academy of Social Sciences (*Zhongguo Shehui Kexueyuan*) – and with the Peking Library and experts working at central and local institutions. The agenda set by this specialised department not only included the production of edited volumes on topics related to imprisonment and reform, but also the translation of teaching material and other literature on reform through labour studies coming from Russia. In September 1983, the Chinese University of Politics and Law established a Masters degree in reform through labour studies in the context of its criminal law curriculum. Similar courses were established soon after at the People's University, Southwestern Institute of Politics and Law (*Xinan Zhengfa Xueyuan*) and at the Northwestern Institute of Politics and Law. In 1984, the Ministry of Education inserted a course on 'Reform through labour legal studies' (*Laodong Laogai Faxue*) into the 'National Legal Specialised Teaching Plan', and after that, various courses were established around the country with an increased academic interest on the subject. High-level planning and active institutional involvement led the research produced during these years to be quite technical in nature, offering a fairly standard, departmental analysis of issues that aligned closely with Party policy.

In general, the literature on reform through labour studies published during the 1980s was strongly influenced by research conducted in the 1950s and 1960s and by socialist theories about the processes of thought reform required for society to arrive at the end goal of communism. A socialist understanding of the malleability of human thinking informed ideas about the process of reforming prisoners' thoughts. Thus, two assumptions underpinned reform through labour: first, that individual thinking is highly malleable and open to persuasion; and, second, that reform could be achieved through a process of re-education whereby a person's thinking could be adjusted and remoulded to reflect a new socialist person. These assumptions were connected to the Marxist idea about the perfectibility of humankind and the Leninist idea concerning the transformation of humanity under socialism (Munro 1977a; 1977b). The function of reforming prisoners through labour was therefore conceptually part of the broader re-education process operating in society at large and linked to a perceived 'fosterage' role (Munro 1977a; 1977b) of the Party-state in affecting the socialist transformation of society. The assumption underpinning this process was that once reformed in thought, an individual would have a 'prompting to act' consistent with that new knowledge (Munro 1977a; 1977b).

In short, in both language and content, reform through labour had a strong political ideological base within Marxist–Leninist–Mao Zedong Thought. Indeed, the first theoretical works published at the beginning of the 1980s on reform studies were aimed at presenting Mao's thought on the origins and development of the discipline, as well as Maoist approaches to issues related to education, psychology and management of prisoners. Generally, they included topics such as basic theoretical approaches to reform through labour studies, the history of the institution, offenders' psychological reform and education, prison management, labour reform studies, economic management, political work, investigation in prisons and basic legal documentation.

The 1990s and beyond: prison studies

The years from early 1980s to around the mid-1990s can be defined as a transitional and experimentation era in the contemporary study of imprisonment in China. In anticipation of the enactment of the *Prison Law* in 1994, a new area coined as 'prison studies' started to gain prominence over reform through labour studies. Discourses on law and imprisonment were progressively inserted into what was originally a purely political approach to reform studies in the previous decades. This led scholars to develop a new set of theoretical and methodological parameters and experiment with newly acquired concepts, ideas and language, adequate to the task of a bona fide new penology.

During those years, the creation of research groups in the field, exchange activities with foreign countries (for example, Australia, Italy, Germany, France, USA, Canada, UK and

Japan) and a surge of publications gradually shifted concerns away from Marxist assumptions about reform to disciplinary based issues in the fields of penology, law and psychology. Publications on reform through labour studies became increasingly rare and studies began to focus on a broader variety of subjects, including 'reform through labour legal studies' (*laodong gaizao faxue*), psychology studies, management studies (*guanli xue*), education studies (*jiaoyu xue*), comparative prisons studies (*bijiao jianyu xue*) and studies on juvenile offenders and drug related crimes. On the whole, up to the mid-1990s, most of these publications were edited volumes (*jiti hezuo*) intended as teaching material (*jiaocai*).

The issuing of the PRC's first *Prison Law* marked a crucial shift in the discourse on prison studies. In the second half of the 1990s, publications began focusing on more specific subject areas, interpreted and articulated through the lens of penology rather than purely through Marxist terminology. The scope and methodology of studies expanded to include analysis of foreign prison systems, discussions on human rights in places of detention, the treatment of juvenile offenders and – in particular after the turn of the new century – debates on restorative justice and reintegration programs.

Subtle changes in discourse on reform preceded the 1994 enactment of the *Prison Law*. In 1991, leading prison scholar Xu Zhangrun published the first book on 'prison studies' in the post-Mao period. The work represented a clear example of 'transitional prison studies' (*guodu jianyu xue*), whereby the language used to define the experience of imprisonment was quite new, while the content still partly reflected perspectives from traditional reform studies. Later, in 1997, a book edited by Professor She Yu – one of the first scholars to publish and teach on the subject of penology – published by the People's Public Security University (*Renmin Gong'an Daxue*) entitled *Reform and Prison Studies with Chinese Characteristics* (*Zhongguo Tese Laogai Xue Yu Jianyu Xue*) considered prison studies as the most recent development of reform studies, that is, 'reforms studies with Chinese characteristics'. However, no particular methodological or theoretical perspective was offered to support such a distinction between the two.

The first critical reflection on methodology and theoretical perspectives on the new stream of prison studies came some time later, at the beginning of the new century when, in 2003, Professor Guo Ming – an eminent professor in criminal justice and prison studies – published a trendsetting monograph entitled *On the Re-Establishment of Scholarly Models and Language – New Perspectives in Prison Studies* (*Xuexu Zhuanxing Yu Huayu Zhong Gou – Zouxiang Jianyu Xue Yanjiu De Xin Shi Yu*). According to the author, this work marked the scholarly consolidation of prison studies, replete with its own language and new theoretical and methodological perspectives. We find this new discourse also gradually emerging in the analyses in the two specialised journals published by the MoJ around the turn of the new century: *Prison Review* published by Law Press China (*Falü Chubanshe*) and *Study on Crime and Reform* (*Fanzui Yu Gaizao Yanjiu*). Prison studies began to be linked even more closely with legal and socio-legal studies – in particular those related to criminal justice, criminal law, criminal procedures and human rights – rather than exclusively Marxist interpretations of criminality and prisoner reform. This change in approach was reflected in the language used to discuss offenders' rehabilitation and the idea of 'reforming' the criminal mind which became associated with the concept of *jiaozheng zhuyi*, which, translated as 'correctional-ism' or 'rectification-ism', merged themes and trends from both the Russian and the Anglo-American tradition of correctional studies.

Overall, after the enactment of the *Prison Law*, Chinese sources in the literature, including both legal and political official documents and analysis offered by Chinese legal scholars, were enriched considerably in scope and nuance. The *Library Catalogue on Chinese Prisons*, compiled in 2012 by the Chinese Prisons Working Association, and published by the Chinese University of Politics and Law in 2013, demonstrates the extent to which Chinese literature on imprisonment has developed since 1994 to cover increasingly expansive ground. The *Catalogue* classifies the current literature into five main categories:

- basic theoretical approaches (*jichu lilun*) to detention including prison studies literature and teaching material;
- theoretical approaches toward prison work and the related legislative material – laws and regulations (*falü guishang*);
- practical application (*shixian yingyong*) – compilations of laws, regulations, official documents and directives;
- chronicles (*shishi*) – history and chronicles of Chinese and local prisons, prisons' brief overviews and yearbooks; and
- literary and artistic (*wenxue yishu*) works including legends and memoirs from prisons, poems, narratives, fiction, films and other artistic representations.[1]

Compare the categories above to the 1980s and early 1990s literature and it becomes clear that not only has the scholarly field expanded in theme, but that it has shifted in focus from 'red discourse' to a more institutional-based 'expert discourse' framed around law and regulations.

Looking outside Chinese borders: in search of models and ideas

Since the beginning of the twentieth century, foreign prisons have gradually become an important source of inspiration for Chinese scholars and reformers. Indeed, the move from reform through labour to disciplinary-based issues drawing on criminology, law and psychology was influenced not only by the diminishing importance of Marxist theory but also by the increasing importance of related Western studies within China. Chinese prison scholars first looked to Japan, then Russia, Europe, America, and, finally, to 'the whole world as a teacher' (Zhang 2001). Since the 1980s, significant changes in the Chinese literature on the study of foreign prisons began to occur in light of increasing access to translations of foreign authors, exchanges between Chinese and foreign academic institutions, cooperation projects, and attendance by Chinese scholars and officials at international conferences.

During the 1980s, comparative literature on prisons was based either on translations of foreign books or on very rudimentary descriptive work. The choice of material to translate was often informed by China's institutional and 'diplomatic politics'. Thus, the first kind of foreign literature that was translated into Chinese was Russian teaching material on reform through labour.[2] The first book on comparative perspectives published in 1982 jointly by the Chinese University of Politics and Law and the People's University *Reference Legal Study Material for Reform through Labour* (*Laodong Gaizao Faxue Cankao Ziliao*), collected data mainly on Russia and Japan. Other comparative collections were published during the late 1980s, with a significant increase after 1994. In the late 1990s, China started to participate regularly in international and regional conferences on corrections, with the result of related publications and an increased number of comparative articles published in Chinese specialised journals (more than 100 between 1994 and 2003, for example). A course on foreigner prison systems was also established at colleges of Politics and Law around the country. On the whole, the approach taken by comparative studies has been that of observing the principles that inspired reforms in foreign systems and assessing whether and how these could be adapted to Chinese circumstances. At the beginning of the twenty-first century, protecting prisoners' human rights started to be discussed in relation to the reforms of the *Criminal Procedure Law (Xingshi Susong Fa)* 1996 (CPL) and the expected ratification of the *International Covenant on Civil and Political Rights* (signed by the PRC in 1998).

Approaching prisons through the lens of 'balancing leniency and severity': an example from the prison literature

The de-Marxificaton of prison studies in the late 1990s and early 2000s did not spell the death knell for ideologically-based studies on prisons in China. Conceptual approaches to the topic of imprisonment continued to be informed by ideologies and political agendas. In the decade of the 2000s, the guiding ideology was not Marxism but the Party's Harmonious Society doctrine. One of the clearest examples of this is the Harmonious Society-related discourse called 'balancing leniency and severity' and its introduction into the study of prisons in the second decade of the new century.

'Balancing Leniency and Severity' was touted as China's leading criminal justice policy in the mid-2000s and remains so today. This new 'balancing' discourse evolved from Maoist dialectics embedded in a policy first called 'Combining Suppression and Leniency' (*zhenya yu kuanda xiangjiehe*) developed after the first six months of the Suppression of Counter-revolutionaries Campaign in the early 1950s (Li 2014). This rhetorical severity-leniency dialectical mechanism first came into use after Mao had realised that in exhorting Party officials to 'kill many' people, the campaign to suppress had gone into overdrive, leading to the indiscriminate execution of many hundreds of thousands of individuals (up to 720,000 in the first year or so of the Campaign). Mao implored officials to 'kill fewer' (*shaosha*) by suspending the death sentences of the majority while executing a minority through a Maoist invention called *sihuan* (the suspended death sentence) in which an offender's death sentence would be commuted to a life sentence after two years in prison (Trevaskes 2012). Renamed 'Combining Punishment with Leniency' (*chengban yu kuanda xiang jiehe*) in the late 1950s, the policy referred to the idea of punishing the most serious criminals and sparing accomplices from harsh punishment, leniency for those who confessed and severity for those who refused to admit guilt, and rewarding criminals who performed meritorious acts (Dai 2010).

'Combining Punishment and Leniency' survived into the post-Mao era and it was given prime place in Article 1 of the first *Criminal Law* issued in 1979. However, the various 'Strike Hard' (*yanda*) campaigns that had characterised criminal justice policy since the early 1980s overshadowed the main principles inscribed in 'Combining Punishment and Leniency' and favoured the development of a highly punitive culture that lasted at least until the end of 2003 (Trevaskes 2010). In 2005, the idea of balancing leniency and severity started to re-emerge with the Party's Politico-Legal Committee re-adapting it to its needs in key areas of justice administration. Later, in 2006, it was announced officially that a national policy called 'Balancing Leniency and Severity' had become China's new 'foundational' (*jiben*) criminal justice policy in the context of building a Harmonious Society. In court and prosecution practices, the main gist of this policy was to ensure that a range of minor offences could be decriminalised or treated with lighter penalties, while only a relatively narrower range of serious criminal offences could receive severe punishment.

After the adoption of the Eighth Amendment to the *Criminal Law* in 2012, Balancing Leniency and Severity began to serve as a new discursive framework to help cement new Party-state policy towards prison organisation and treatment of prisoners. This new lexicon – introduced into the prison system and the prison literature in the form of 'policy', rather than law – has created a context for institutional action, enabling authorities to rationalise political choices about how to treat different prisoners in different ways. The key tenet of the 'balancing' policy as it applies to prisons is that prisoners should not be treated as one single category. They should be treated relative to the degree of risk that they pose to fellow prisoners. With this simple principle in mind, scholars and practitioners in recent years have begun to re-rationalise the organisation of prisons based on the imperative of maintaining a 'balanced' and relativist approach. This new discourse contains underlying principles that can help to disgorge long-standing punitive mindsets from prison management practices. In adapting a 'balancing' or 'tempering' principle as espoused in the policy of Balancing Leniency and Severity, scholars these days are essentially promoting a relativist-based (*xiangdui zhuyi*) approach to correctional work, which they see as a positive development. It is relativist in that it encourages prison authorities to make decisions about individual prisoners that relate to their discrete circumstances rather than to treat all offenders in a similar way. Up until recently, an absolutist-based (*juedui zhuyi*) principle was the dominant way of classifying prisoners, an approach which essentially entailed treating everyone in a similar way. Scholars nowadays see the balancing policy as a way of rationalising rearrangements to the operational landscape of prisons, to balance the heavy security that needs to be provided for a small minority of violent offenders, with scope and facilities for 'rehabilitation' of the vast majority of prisoners. This essentially entails lowering security requirements for most prisoners (as a manifestation of 'leniency' principle) but at the same time maintaining strict security policies for the minority of violent or dangerous prisoners or high-security risk situations inside prisons (Tang et al. 2013).

Debating 'security' and 'rehabilitation'

In China, when a new discursive framework enters the area of both prison studies and administration, existing frameworks are readjusted to support new priorities both conceptually and in practice. This has meant that since 2012 over two dozen scholarly journal articles have addressed the issue of how the policy of Balancing Leniency and Severity might apply to prisons. In the context of this chapter, however, we describe in detail a single article published in *Prison Review* in 2013 by three prison officials Tang Xule, Liu Weidong and Li Cheng.[3] Their study is paradigmatic because it is the first of its kind that engages with the practical implications of transposing the criminal justice discourses of balancing leniency and severity on to existing penal discourse. It reflects on the complexities involved in infusing new policy into old penal wine skins in prisons and highlights 'security' and 'rehabilitation', 'criminal reconciliation' and classification of prisons and prisoners as three areas in which balancing leniency and severity is likely to have a key impact. The authors' main concern relates to the systematic errors that can potentially emerge when discourses shift and prisons re-rationalise and reorder their practices to fit these discursive changes.

For many years, two main discourses, 'security' and 'rehabilitation', have driven prison organisation and procedure. Tang et al. (2013) maintain that one of the main potential problems with the implementation of the policy of Balancing Leniency and Severity is that it remains unclear how 'security' and 'rehabilitation' should be folded into the new discourse. The authors see the security principle of prison organisation as having an intimate connection to 'severity' and the 'leniency' aspect bearing close relationship with the old concept of 'rehabilitation'. 'Security' refers to securitising spaces to protect the majority of non-violent prisoners from the minority of violent offenders. 'Rehabilitation' is an objective that aims to reform the individual but also, albeit indirectly, bring benefits to prison management. That is, it rationalises various educational and other programs that keep prisoners sufficiently busy as a way of avoiding outbreaks of violence or isolated incidents that often result from inactivity and boredom.

Superimposing Balancing Leniency and Severity on existing principles such as rehabilitation and security creates a potential dilemma for prisons: how should prisons approach the crucial issue of selecting the context in which 'severity' should apply and the context in which 'leniency' should be implemented? In other words, when is the 'security' framework of prison organisation appropriate and in which context is the rehabilitation ethos more appropriate? According to Tang et al. (2013), the main concern is less about the policy bringing too much leniency into prisons and more about it compromising the 'severity' or 'security' end of the spectrum. Indeed, they argue that any declining punitive function has the potential to weaken the security measures against dangerous prisoners; this can lead to a change in prison culture that adopts an 'anything goes' approach.

Tang et al. (2013) warn against any implementation of the policy that might lead to indiscriminately imposing greater leniency across the spectrum without first working through the possible consequences of such a shift. In this, they see echoes of the new policy of Balancing Leniency and Severity in a humanitarian theory of punishment that gained traction in the 1990s and that was largely about placing emphasis on prisoner welfare. At the time, it was hoped that the introduction of a variety of rehabilitative treatments would enable inmates to shift their behavioural patterns, with the ultimate goal being to reintegrate them into society when their sentence expired. For the few institutions that could afford to do so, humanitarian theories translated into giving prisoners greater access to facilities such as heating, reading rooms, libraries and entertainment rooms. The principle of humanitarian punishment, however, was simply not a viable option in many rural prisons that could not afford even the basics. Forcing the introduction of a new policy in less developed areas meant that the gap between actual expenditures and the allocated funds remained extremely wide, making it impracticable.

Prisons and prisoners' classification

The issue of prisons' security classification also offers an example of the dilemmas that prison management can face when reforming the system to fit a new discursive framework. In this context, Tang et al. (2013) explain that while until recently prisons in the PRC have all been medium-security facilities, there is currently a push by senior policy-makers to segregate high-risk prisoners from the main prison population. This will involve either building new maximum-security wings in existing prisons or new prisons that are discrete maximum-security facilities.[4] This has also implications for how high-security inmates should be treated and whether they should receive education and rehabilitation.

On the whole, the policy of Balancing Leniency and Severity promotes the principle of disaggregation to replace the longstanding 'aggregated concept' (*jihe gainian*) of prisoner management whereby prisoners, regardless of their sentences or crimes, were treated in a similar manner. Enacting the policy of Balancing Leniency and Severity in prisons can therefore translate into a new organisational framework whereby prisons are reorganised into different gradations of 'severity', thus integrating 'severity' with 'security' and relative leniency with 'rehabilitation' by categorising prisoners into three main categories: high, medium and low risk. According to the authors, this also means promoting a relativist approach to correctional work and encouraging prison authorities to make decisions about individual prisoners that relate to their individual circumstances. A 'balanced' relativist security approach – as opposed to the 'absolutism-based' principle of the past, entailing treating all the prisoners similarly – they argue, should serve as a way of rearranging the operational landscape of prisons and of avoiding the longstanding punitive mindset whereby 'security' overrides 'rehabilitation'.

The 'rehabilitation-first thinking' essentially entails lowering security requirements for most prisoners (as a manifestation of the 'leniency' principle) but at the same time, maintaining strict security policies for the minority of violent or dangerous prisoners or high-security risk situations inside prisons. Tang et al. (2013) also envisage potential for the 'severity' end of the balancing leniency and severity principle to be manifest in the development of a management system that not only establishes new maximum-security prisons, but also opens up the possibility of developing new semi-open prisons (*bankai jianyu*) at the other end of punishment spectrum. As they explain, provisions in the CPL 2012 have the potential to bring about change to the configurations of prisons, in that they provide that prisoners whose sentences exceed three months, but are below one year, should serve their sentences in (low security wings of) prisons. While these legal reforms ostensibly shift these prisoners out of (police-run) detention centres, they also lead to massive overcrowding in prisons. In this context, semi-open prisons may be able to relieve the majority of prisons of this new resource burden that resulted from the 2012 reform of the CPL.

Conclusion

The Westernisation of the legal and justice system in China was rebranded into a Marxist mould after 1949 and Marxism–Leninism–Mao Zedong Thought closely guided state development. It is not surprising, therefore, that socialist discourses have so strongly guided the scholarly literature in this area. Throughout this study we have observed the impact of the Party-state's prerogative to define the scope and means for the effective realisation of its protective role in society and to create its own narratives to justify its choices in relation to imprisonment. Chinese scholars also make choices about how they conceptually interrogate the issue of punishment but these choices and approaches are informed by the limitations of political ideology imposed on the penal system and on academia in general. As in other areas in the field of law and social sciences, the Chinese scholarly literature on prisons in the immediate post-Mao period was limited, relatively technical in nature and highly descriptive. In the early 1980s, any critical analysis was highly discouraged; indeed, its aim was to justify the need for punishment based on socialist principles rather than promoting a new political mindset. As observed in this chapter, new discourses started to emerge just before the issuing of the *Prison Law* 1994 and the PRC's interaction with foreign countries. Since the mid-1990s, through academic literature, boundaries have been pushed and new ideas brought forward to the general public.

While we have observed shifts in the discourse from Marxist-based reform of the individual to penological approaches that are more at home in modern Western penality, we do not claim that political ideology has been abandoned. What we witness, rather, has been an increasing diversification and refinement of the techniques used to correct offenders and discourses that rationalise punishment. We find this is the case with the above discussion of Balancing Leniency and Severity. Broad political agendas (in this case, the Harmonious Society agenda from which the policy was born in 2005) continue to shape prison discourse and prison reform processes, defining the perimeters within which the idea of punishment can be discussed in the literature

The analysis of Tang et al. (2013) reveals that academic assessments are still constrained by the complex dynamics characterising institutional politics and its discursive approaches. The majority of scholars investigating issues related to imprisonment are either attached to academic public security institutions or work units responsible for law-making or law enforcement, or to prison institutions themselves. While self-censorship is still practised, institutionally-based scholars can serve a useful purpose in bridging the theory-practice divide and subtly promoting change from within the system. This also means that these discourses act concomitantly to serve a higher political purpose (for instance, to develop a Harmonious Society agenda) and to serve a mundane purpose of improving the organising principles of prison life.

Following the discursive trail over the last three decades, we have investigated changes and continuities in the scope, methodology and key discourses addressed by the scholarly literature in China since the early 1980s. In particular, we have looked at how the various rationales of imprisonment are interpreted in line with changing political priorities related to social control and social management in China over recent decades.

It is important to capture both the ruptures and continuities with the past since they are indicative of wider changes in the administration of the criminal justice. Acknowledging the key role played by political discourse is revealing of more subtle movements in Chinese approaches, both of politics in general and, more narrowly, the politics of punishment. Therefore, rather than dismissing the intrinsically political nature of the literature on prisons in China, we have acknowledged the crucial and inevitable link that we see existing between criminal justice discourse and the formats and institutions of punishment that this discourse serves, in ways that reflect the wider trajectory of political power in China.

Notes

1 In addition, the *Catalogue* includes compendia for people's police, educational material for prisoners and detainees and other booklets compiled for specific practical purposes.
2 The translation was done by the Ministry of Justice Reform Specialised Teaching Material Publishing Department in 1983.
3 All three work at a large prison in Jiangsu province called Lianyungang. The prison has over 2,000 inmates and is one of China's largest prison facilities spanning an area of 75 square kilometres. Tang is the Deputy Party Committee Secretary of the prison and Liu and Li work in the prison's legal education section, which delivers both propaganda and legal education to prisoners. For an outline of the prison see: http://www.jsjy.gov.cn/
4 The authors argue that building new stand-alone maximum-security prisons, in theory at least, is preferable in terms of optimal allocation of resources and is easier to manage in terms of prisoners' risk control. But, as they point out, the principle of 'rehabilitation' upon which prison work and education is based, holds that rehabilitation is a dynamic process. If the process of rehabilitation (through education and labour) actually works in a positive way to change prisoner behaviour, then placing prisoners in maximum security limits their opportunities for rehabilitation. If prisoners need to be split across various gradations of prisons (that is, split between low risk and maximum-security prisons), the cost is much greater when a prisoner is deemed safe enough to be transferred to a less secure facility. On the other hand, building maximum-security wings within prisons can enable prisoners to be detained separately inside the one facility, making the management of prisoners more economical. They deem this configuration more suitable to the current reality of prisons. In addition, they recommend that there should be at least one or two maximum-security prisons in each province and in addition, maximum-security wings should also be established inside medium-security and minimum-security prisons to make up for the lack of discrete maximum-security prisons.

References

Chinese Prisons Working Association. 2013. *Zhongguo Jianyulei Tushu Zongmulu (1950–2012)* (*Catalogue on Works Concerning Chinese Prisons*). Beijing: Zhongguo zhengfa daxue chubanshe.
Chinese University of Politics and Law and People's University eds. 1982. *Laodong Gaizao Faxue Cankao Ziliao (Reference Legal Study Material for Reform through Labour)*. Beijing: Beijing zhengfa xueyuan xingfa jiaoyan she, Zhongguo renmin daxue xingfa jiaoyan she.
Dai Yuzhong. 2010. 'The Pursuit of Criminal Justice.' In *China's Journey Toward the Rule of Law: Legal Reform, 1978–2008*, edited by Cai Dingjian and Wang Chenguang, 155–97. Leiden: Brill.

Dutton, Michael and Xu Zhangrun. 1998. 'Facing Difference: Relations, Change and the Prison Sector in Contemporary China.' In *Comparing Prison Systems: Toward a Comparative and International Penology*, edited by Robert P. Weiss and Nigel South, 289–336. Amsterdam: Gordon and Breach Publishers.

Guo Ming. 2003. *Xuexu Zhuanxing Yu Huayu Zhong Gou – Zouxiang Jianyu Xue Yanjiu De Xin Shi Yu* (On the Re-Establishment of Scholarly Models and Language – New Perspectives in Prison Studies). Beijing: Zhongguo fangzhen chubanshe.

Li Lu. 2014. 'Zhenya Yu Kuanda Xiangjiehe Xingshi Zhengce Fansi (Reflections on the Criminal Justice Policy of Combining Suppression and Leniency).' *Renmin Luntan* (People's Forum) 10. Available at http://paper.people.com.cn/rmlt/html/2014-04/11/content_1427879.htm (accessed 16 February 2016).

Munro, Donald J. 1977a. 'Belief Control: The Psychological and Ethical Foundations.' In *Deviance and Social Control in Chinese Society*, edited by Amy Auberacher Sidney Wilson, Leonard Greenblatt and Richard Whittingham Wilson, 14–36. New York and London: Praeger Publishers.

Munro, Donald J. 1977b. *The Concept of Man in Contemporary China*. Ann Arbor: University of Michigan Press.

She Yu. 1997. *Zhongguo Tese Laogai Xue Yu Jianyu Xue* (Reform and Prison Studies with Chinese Characteristics). Beijing: Zhongguo gong'an daxue chubanshe.

Tang Xule, Liu Weidong and Cheng Li. 2013. 'Kuanyan Xiang Ji Zhengce Yu Jianyu Xingxing Gaige (The Policy of Balancing Leniency and Severity and Prison Reform).' *Jianyu Pinglun* (Prison Review) 5: 307–20.

Trevaskes, Susan. 2010. *Policing Serious Crime in China: From Strike Hard to Kill Fewer*. Abingdon: Routledge.

Trevaskes, Susan. 2012. *The Death Penalty in Contemporary China*. New York: Palgrave Macmillan.

Xu Zhangrun. 1991. *Jianyuxue* (Prison Studies). Beijing: Zhongguo renmin gong'an daxue chubanshe.

Zhang Jing. 2001. *Zhongguo Jianyu Zhidu Cong Chuangtong Zouxiang Xiandai* (The Chinese Prison System Moving from Tradition to Modernity). Beijing: Haihu chuabanshe.

9 Western analyses of deprivation of liberty in China

Flora Sapio

Introduction

One of the first studies ever produced on China's correctional system in the twentieth century, if not the first, was authored in 1950 under the auspices of the Human Resources Research Institute. Known as the HRRI, the Research Institute was a think tank of the US Air Force Headquarters, an institution that used to publish a series entitled *Studies in Chinese Communism*. One of the volumes in this series, by Henry Wei, contained a description of the People's Republic of China's (PRC) correctional system. The goal of this and other studies sponsored by the HRII was to explore 'the psychological and sociological vulnerabilities of the Chinese Communist Regime' (Wei 1955, vii). While the newly established Chinese government may indeed have felt vulnerable – in 1950 large areas of Southern China were not yet fully controlled by the People's Liberation Army – it is interesting to notice how those who explained the goal and rationale of research on China's prisons thought of China's vulnerability as being somehow related to disclosing information about the country's correctional institutions. After all, Henry Wei's (1955) research was largely descriptive, and while his ideas were expressed using the style, language and vocabulary popular in the 1950s, he refrained from articulating any explicit moral judgment about China. Wei's (1955) work, *Courts and Police in Communist China*, was paradigmatic, as it set the main themes of discussion in Western literature on Chinese prisons in the 1980s and beyond. This chapter provides a bird's-eye view of these themes, comparing them to those that have been popularised by the Western media. In the absence of detailed information on how prisons operate in China, Western scholarly analyses have relied on descriptive rather than analytical approaches. Up until James Seymour's (2005) publication *Sizing up China's Prisons*, scholarship had largely struggled to conduct analyses of China's prisons.[1] While information about prisons may be provided by those who have had direct experience of deprivation of liberty, the difficulty of accessing their testimonies is significant. Even in the absence of such difficulty, it can be imagined how the majority of those who have witnessed the reality of deprivation of liberty would hesitate to provide their testimonies, if only out of their desire not to relive emotionally painful experiences. Such a paucity of information, as well as the limited number of scholarly analyses, has affected the media's ability to provide a nuanced picture of China's correctional systems, and the significant gaps that still exist in our knowledge of China's corrections result in difficulty for scholars to shed light on the grey areas that exist in them. These grey areas thus continue to exist. Their existence can either lead to attempts to explore them, or prompt reliance on existing tropes.

Early analyses of corrections in China emerged immediately after World War II, at the height of McCarthyism and the Cold War, and were thus preoccupied with China's justice system. The memories of Nazi extermination camps and Soviet gulags were still all too vivid in the minds of authors and their public to allow for any discussion of prisons and re-education through labour (RETL) institutions that avoided relying on the tropes of the 'Camp' or the 'Gulag'. The most recent literature on deprivation of freedom has started to question this orientation, and has searched for different points of view from which to tackle the difficult issue of corrections in China. But the many grey areas and blind spots in our epistemologies and heuristics seem to be connatural with the object we are attempting to analyse. A closely similar set of limitations existed during what I will term the 'first wave' of analyses of China's corrections. Works authored towards the end of the nineteenth century are historically and authorially unrelated to the literature that has been produced since the 1950s. But perhaps locating empirical data on Chinese prisons today is as much a demanding task today as it was in 1800. While technology has significantly facilitated the work of researchers and analysts in the most diverse fields, constraints in time and in access to data pose limitations which, if transposed into the contemporary context, bear distant similarities to the difficulties experienced by those who researched China's prisons during the nineteenth century.

Sinologists Ernest Alabaster and Jean Escarra developed a body of available knowledge and contemporary analyses of Chinese prisons. While examining how their ideas were transmitted to the next generation of China scholars is beyond the scope of this chapter, a mention of their scholarship is in order to understand what knowledge existed prior to our discovery of China's prison camps in the 1950s, and how contemporary writers have produced significant advances in such knowledge.

Alabaster, Escarra and the Commission on Extraterritoriality

Between 1844 and 1943, Western nation-states extended the reach of their legal systems beyond their national borders in an effort to claim jurisdiction over their nationals who resided in China. China's lack of law, so claimed Thomas Millard (1931, 116), an American journalist and advisor to the Chinese Republic, could 'guarantee' neither 'security to foreign investments' nor 'safety and justice to foreigners'. In his report *The End of Extraterritoriality in China*, Millard (1931) adopted an analytical approach whereby – having placed the imperial and republican legal codes side by side with European equivalents – he proceeded to outline the differences that existed among them. One of the most striking differences was the lack, at least in imperial China, of custodial punishments. In China, prisons existed merely to detain those awaiting trial or execution. The imperial legal system had long been relying on a different set of sanctions, which included corporal punishment, exile and capital punishment (for a classical account see Bodde and Morris 1967).

Ernest Alabaster (1899), a barrister and a Sinologist, and Jean Escarra (1961), a French legal scholar and a consultant of the Republican government, noticed the same differences. They furthermore asserted that imperial gaols were overcrowded and unhygienic, an environment which they described as 'loathsome and horrible dens of iniquity and filth' (Alabaster 1899, 73) and a living hell of torture and abnormal deaths (Escarra 1961, 334). The Commission on Extraterritoriality (1926), a body tasked to analyse the Republican legal system, developed recommendations on the establishment of a sound legal system and on the abolition of extraterritorial privileges enjoyed by Western states; they came to very similar conclusions. At the time when Alabaster, Escarra, the Commission on Extraterritoriality and Thomas Millard were pioneers in the study of Chinese law, Spain, Britain and the United States of America had created extraterritorial concentration camps. Thousands of Cubans (Benton 1908), Boers (Devitt 1941), Zulus and Filipinos were confined in these camps. The enjoyment of extraterritorial privileges was an ordinary component of Western legal systems, and China's practices were by no means an exception. Analyses of Chinese prisons endeavoured to understand whether the country's legal system was 'mature' enough to be granted full autonomy, or whether the Chinese Republic still needed to receive tutelage and advice from Western nation-states. Analyses of deprivation of liberty were useful, in that they allowed Western nation-states to gather the information needed to make those decisions they deemed the most appropriate. Given that the fields of comparative law and sinology were still quite young, early authors relied on relatively simple methodologies. Besides narrating abuses as they occurred in Chinese prisons, they compiled lists of Chinese modern prisons and analysed legal reform in China. This data was used to measure China's performance in reforming its criminal justice system, and to make appropriate suggestions. Decades later, stories about places of detention would be narrated by former inmates,[2] while monitoring China's compliance with its obligations under international law became a competence shared between intergovernmental organisations, non-governmental organisations and Western academics. Correctional policy analysis became a task of Chinese government agencies, research foundations and academics. While no deep and enduring connections perhaps exist between studies of detention authored by Millard, Alabaster, Escarra and analyses produced since the 1950s, a vague analogy is evident between these bodies of knowledge. Analyses published in the late eighteenth century as well as those produced since the 1950s were authored by lawyers, who were often also China studies scholars. Their analyses were not significantly influenced by approaches developed in Western criminology and penology; neither did these analyses seek to open an intellectual and scholarly dialogue with Chinese criminology and penology. In the 1950s, Chinese criminology and penology were still in their infancy, and furthermore existing books and articles were meant for consultation by a narrow circle of specialists, rather than by the general public. Beginning such a dialogue in the 1950s would have been not so much unthinkable as unfeasible. Chinese criminology and penology began developing in the 1980s, a time when a greater number of scholarly works became available. An understanding of Chinese prisons based also on this literature would perhaps have allowed for analyses more sensitive to China's context, reducing a certain politicisation of the Western discourse on prisons.

Vague analogies aside, the study of detention in China has in part been shaped by the legacy of studies published in the 1950s. Today there are still divisions among debates on corrections in China; these take place in the field of sinology, and in Western and Chinese criminological and penological literature. Next, I explore how this divide has contributed to shaping the study of detention in China in peculiar ways.

Contemporary scholarly literature on Chinese prisons

The very first analyses of Chinese prisons emerged during the Cold War and reflected the concerns of those times. The nature and scope of information which resulted from these analyses were furthermore affected by the climate of ideological closure that still prevailed in the PRC, and Chinese sources on prisons were not accessible to Western researchers. The legacy of studies produced before the 1980s is, to some extent, still visible in the separation of sinology from mainstream penology and criminology. This is evident in the limited set of themes addressed by sinology, and in the difficulty sinology has in contributing its views to a reform debate that still remains largely domestic, and relatively difficult to access. Even today the study of deprivation of liberty in the PRC is largely studied by sinologists and lawyers trained in Chinese law. Such a division of labour between mainstream criminology and 'sino-criminology' results both from the difficulty in accessing sources that remain for the most part either unavailable or untranslated and from the design of college education curricula. Therefore, it is hardly unavoidable.

Analyses produced by sinologists and lawyers are published either in sectorial journals or in law reviews that focus on the Pacific Region, and address an audience different from Western and Chinese penologists and criminologists. On the other hand, mainstream criminology has for the most part neglected the study of China. From 1978 until 2015, only nine articles on China appeared on top criminology journals. Three were published in the *British Journal of Criminology* (Biddulph and Xie 2011; Dikötter 2002a; Epstein and Wong 1996); five in *The Prison Journal* (Bracey 1988; Jiang et al. 2014; Liu and Chui 2014; Miller 1982; Shaw 1998) and just one in the *International Criminal Justice Review* (Anderson 1996). The *Correction Management Quarterly*, the *New England Journal on Criminal and Civil Confinement*, the *International Review of Criminal Policy* and *the International Criminal Law Review* published no articles on China. During the same period of time, interdisciplinary journals published only ten articles on China. The *International Journal of Law and Psychiatry* has, compared to other journals, devoted sustained attention to mental health legislation, publishing four articles on psychiatric hospitals (*ankang*) (Hu et al 2011; Pearson 1992, 1996; Shao et al. 2010) and one on the *Mental Health Law* 2012 (Ding 2014). The *International Journal of the American Academy of Psychiatry* and the *Law and Social Science and Medicine* published one article (Munro 2002; see also the responses to Munro's article in the same issue) and three articles on public health issues in administrative detention (Gil et al 1996; Merli et al 2015; Tucker et al. 2010).The disconnect in publication avenues is matched by a disconnect between the themes analysed by penology and criminology on one hand, and China studies on the other. Besides the debate on privatisation, recent mainstream discourse focuses on themes of prison performance, and alternatives to imprisonment such as non-custodial sentencing, restorative justice and community based correction programs. Another important theme is the welfare of inmates and correctional officers. This latter topic has been analysed from a variety of perspectives and not just a consideration of mental health, but also factors that may contribute to inmates and officers enjoying a higher quality of life. These factors have varied from HIV/AIDS prevention and treatment programs to inmate misconduct; from prison violence and prison gangs to correction officers' burnout. Some of the more classical penological themes evident are legal reform, penal philosophies, recidivism, juvenile justice and offenders' reintegration. The Chinese language literature on detention has been evolving along the same or closely similar themes, while Western studies of detention in China have been going down a widely different road.

Rather than being focused on single themes, as Western mainstream penological and criminological literature demonstrates, Western studies of detention in China have analysed single measures limiting personal freedom and concentrated attention on RETL. The reason for such an emphasis is both intellectual and pragmatic. First, from a merely heuristic point of view, RETL, as a now-abolished measure, had the ability to capture researchers' attentions in ways in which imprisonment could not. As is well-known, RETL had legal grounding, although admittedly inadequate and inconsistent with the procedural guarantees that China's criminal procedure legislation afforded to criminal suspects. Compared to criminal detention and imprisonment, RETL could be perceived as an anomalous and exotic institution. Such a perception was powerful enough to attract a significant amount of intellectual energy from Western scholars. A second, and favoured, theme of Western scholarship has been the study of Chinese prisons. While detention powers other than RETL and imprisonment existed, Western scholarship only began paying sustained and systematic attention to them in the 2000s.

As conventional as it may seem, a periodisation of this body of literature that adopts the 1980s as a key watershed is necessary, as it was around 1980s that Chinese research on detention was reborn, thus enabling Western scholars to access a wider amount of information on prisons than before. The pre-1978 literature on RETL camps was mostly scattered among descriptive studies of Chinese criminal law (for example, Bathia and Tan 1974; Leng 1977; Wei 1955) and provided a simple and sometimes sketchy picture of the system. The lack of separation between RETL institutions and reform through labour camps was a key feature of the correctional system as it existed until the eve of the Dengist reforms. Therefore, virtually each one of the analyses published between 1950 and 1978 described these institutions together. As explained earlier in this chapter, the purely descriptive approach of the pre-1978 literature was the only possible choice at a time of extreme ideological closure. The increasing availability of information about the camps and life in the camps (for example, Leng 1981; Bracey 1988) could have contributed to the emergence of a new trend. Instead, two different scholarly orientations became visible after 1978. One of them, which for ease of reference I will call the 'mainstream' orientation, analysed and discussed RETL with reference to norms in international procedural law, with the result that RETL was judged as an anomalous institution. Within this conceptual framework, the mainstream orientation provided a nuanced picture of RETL. Despite its unconstitutional and unlawful nature, RETL was considered a necessary component of what was at least in name a socialist state (Mühlahn 2009). Western discussions on the feasibility and potential consequences of abolishing RETL (Fu 2009; Hung 2003) were thus informed by a much more solid grasp of the stated goals of the RETL system (Clarke and Feinerman 1995; Fu 2005a), of its changes over time (Bejesky 2004; Biddulph 2007; Fu 2005b), and of its structural problems (Tanner 1994, 1999). A different, and perhaps a minority, instead considered RETL as a controversial yet given component of China's criminal justice, rather than a juridical monstrosity. As a result of a heated domestic debate (in China) about the abolition of RETL, many took a step back from viewing RETL as an anomaly (an approach followed by this chapter). Such an approach has allowed an analysis of RETL within the broader contexts of Chinese politics and society, unearthing the several tensions that marked the very birth of RETL (Smith 2013a; see also Smith 2012, 2013b, 2013c), and proving how a vocal and articulated public opinion played a key role in contesting its existence (Rosenzweig 2013). Over time, discussion of RETL came to overshadow what used to be the favoured theme of prison in early Western scholarship.

The lack of separation between RETL institutions and reform through labour camps, a condition that persisted until 1978, led to analysing these institutions together (Seymour and Anderson 1999). Analyses of prisons in China followed, at least until 1980, in the same trend as analyses of RETL. After the 1980s, while discourse on RETL became embedded in the field of law, studies of prisons embarked on an entirely different trajectory, and were solidly rooted in historiography (Bodde 1969; Dikötter 1997, 2002a, 2002b, 2003, 2005; Griffin 1974). Exceptions were those authors that used the prison to shed light on the unfolding of dynamics of modernity and social control in China (Dutton and Xu 1998; see also Dutton and Xu 2005). Aside from these approaches, legal analyses focused on the themes of convict labour (see Wu and Goodrich 2014 for a recent discussion of RETL from this perspective) and organ transplants. Both themes have tight connections to the foreign trade policy of Western and African states alike (Cowen 1993; Yan and Sautman 2012). Their dual and perhaps aporetic connection to the immediate, utilitarian concerns of trade and the deontological imperatives of rights' protection seems to have somehow precluded other possible analyses of imprisonment. Very few studies of sentencing exist, but they have examined distinct categories of criminal defendants (Epstein and Wong 1996). The prison system today includes 681 correctional institutions, which are staffed by about 300,000 officers, and host 1,700,000 prisoners (Sifabu Guanliju 2014). The most recent comprehensive analysis by Seymour dates to 2005; however, he provided a snapshot of the prison system as it was in the late 1990s. As a result, little is known about the legal and structural reforms that have taken place in the meantime. Generally speaking, and with all the exceptions already mentioned, as the PRC *Prison Law* was passed in 1994, Chinese prisons seemed to attract less and less attention among legal scholars. Forms of corrections and deprivation of freedom is not limited to RETL institutions and prisons, but apart from these, we still know very little about what else exists. The revival of compulsory drug rehabilitation and the reform of shelter and education (Biddulph 2007; Biddulph and Xie 2011), pre-trial detention (Nesossi 2008, 2012), compulsory psychiatric treatment (Munro 2006), as well as certain forms of investigative detention were introduced to the Western public only a few years ago by authors who then shifted their research to other areas of the criminal justice system. The study of institutions such as shelter and deportation and shelter and examination (Wong 1996, 1997) ceased with their alleged abolition, despite ample proof of their continued existence under different guises. A similar trend seemed to exist with respect to community corrections. The interest of scholarship shown in RETL has yet to be matched by an equal – or at least a comparable – interest in community corrections (*shequ jiaoyu*). While community corrections has been reformed following the abolition of RETL, it is still severely under-researched. Other measures limiting or depriving personal freedom are yet to be explored. Besides the most obvious instances of covert arrest and residential surveillance, the reality of Japanese internment camps (Leck 2006), and Unit 731 have been only tangentially touched upon.

The media

Even before we embark on a course of studies on China or on Chinese law, we first learn about the existence of detention in China through newspaper and Internet media. It is through their narratives of detention in China that we come to understand what exists in China's correctional system. After all, we can only think about or do research on those institutions and practices which we know to exist. Very few persons in the West become aware of corrections in China through Chinese sources. Those who do may stumble upon publications which, as the 1992 White Paper on criminal reform (Information Office of the State Council 1992), presented an idealised and perhaps unpersuasive picture of the prison system. While the Chinese media tends to portray the prison system under a favourable light, the Western media has tackled the gaps and grey areas in our knowledge of China's correctional system by relying on a set of tropes about 'concentration camps'. Despite the absence of a detailed understanding of how prisons and RETL institutions operate in China, already in 1992 Jean-luc Domenach tried to articulate the reasons why Chinese prisons and RETL institutions differed from Nazi concentration camps and Soviet Gulags. Dutton and Xu (1998) later observed how neither prisons nor RETL institutions were replicas of extermination camps or gulags (see also Dutton and Xu 2005), a point further proven by historical analyses of prisons (Dikötter 2002b). The influence these works have had in the field of China studies was not matched by their impact on the mass media. While sinology has abandoned its earlier analogies between Chinese correctional institutions and Nazi or Soviet concentration camps, the media's rhetorical tropes and arguments seem to have changed relatively little over time. In post-war Europe and America, the making of such analogies was the most natural emotional response to any kind of exposure to knowledge about corrections characterised by excessive limitation of personal freedom. As imperfect as it may be, our knowledge about corrections has in the meantime been augmented, yet not all media outlets have drawn upon it.

As late as 2012, in a series entitled *Slavery: A 21st Century Evil*, Al Jazeera, a news source otherwise known for its accurate reporting, presented a confusing image of corrections in China. As it is well-known, prisons and RETL institutions are entirely distinct facilities – their separation having occurred in the early 1980s. The term '*laogai*', or reform through labour camp, is a colloquialism that used to be *en vogue* until the 1980s, and was then abandoned. In a report suggestively entitled *Prison Slaves*, however, Al Jazeera conflated all correctional institutions – that is, those holding persons responsible of crimes against the state, as well as persons found guilty of crimes such as murder, rape, and robbery, not to mention drug-dependent persons – under the label of '*laogai*':

> China has the biggest penal colony in the world – a top secret network of more than 1,000 slave labour prisons and camps known collectively as 'The Laogai'. And the use of the inmates of these prisons – in what some experts call 'state sponsored slavery'– has been credited with contributing to the country's economic boom. (Al Jazeera, 25 March 2012)

Most of the websites relaunching the story (Levin 27 December 2012) made ample references to 'gulags', with the stated goal to persuade Western consumers that they should avoid purchasing Chinese products. The same argument in favour of a Western boycott of Chinese goods was made at least a decade earlier by the International Society for Human Rights (ISHR), an NGO founded in West Germany in the 1970s:

> It is practically impossible to identify any product originating in the PRC which can be guaranteed free from the taint of labour camps. Until the circumstances alter, ISHR advises consumers wishing to avoid forced labour produce not to buy any product emanating from the PRC. (ISHR, undated)

The International Society for Human Rights also suggested a boycott of Chinese products. In the 1990s, the issue of trade and human rights 'played well on a gut level with the US press and the American public' in the domestic debate on the PRC's MFN status (Cowen 1993, 191). Even though it was motivated by trade concerns, the analogy between correctional institutions in China and concentration camps invoked the themes of liberty, and of human nature and their negation. The most immediate effect of this was capturing readers' emotions into a Battle-of-Armageddon-like dichotomy between Good and Evil. As an anonymous Taiwanese group explained in a pamphlet published in 1978 'we can neither live in a society that is half free and half enslaved, nor we can exist in a world that half respects human rights and half neglects them' (The Continent Press 1978, 3).

The tropes employed by the Western media seem to have been inspired by NGOs' advocacy reports rather than by existing academic analyses, as well as by the thought-reform literature (Lifton 1956, 1957a, 1963; Schein 1956). The motive of gulags was echoed in publications by the World Anti-Communist League (1997) until the late 1990s, exactly as it had happened in the late 1970s, when above-mentioned anonymous Taiwan-based group referred to mainland Chinese correctional institutions as gulags (The Continent Press 1978). The thought reform literature, particularly the research conducted by Lifton in the 1950s on mind control techniques, seems to have inspired the rhetoric of 'brainwashing', that is sometimes used by the press with reference to RETL institutions. 'The Chinese Communists', wrote Lifton (1957b, 626) 'have developed a peculiar brand of soul surgery . . . the process of thought reform'. In 2013, the International Business Times mentioned how RETL detainees were being moved to 'brainwashing centers', as RETL institutions were being turned into drug rehabilitation facilities (FlorCruz 17 December 2013).

The reason of such an enduring and sustained attention towards RETL is simple. The mass media narrative relies on the premise that any institution, particularly correctional institutions, enjoys moral and political legitimacy only if it conforms to the system of political morality underpinning substantive and procedural international law. Differently stated, legitimacy descends from a country's adoption of the values of democracy, a market economy and human rights, understood and interpreted as these values are in liberal and democratic systems. Such views in political morality gained their moral traction in the wake of World War II. China's political system has adopted the same set of values attributing, however, a different and 'socialist' connotation to them. This fact – that is, the existence of a different system of political morality – has become the main focus of international criticism. Also, it has oriented analyses of deprivation of freedom towards all those legal institutions which were procedurally problematic. RETL was not the only focus, as many other forms of deprivation of freedom existed, such as *shuanggui*, the detention of internal migrants under shelter and deportation (*shourong qiansong*), drug rehabilitation (see Biddulph in Chapter 2 of this volume), and the detention of prostitutes under shelter and education (*shourong jiaoyu*) to name only four of them. Among these various forms of detention, RETL had the broadest scope of targets, and it was therefore natural for Western critique to focus on it.

As the media's critique of RETL was made on procedural grounds, it contained within itself the potential for its own demise. The media's main criticism was not the physical network of RETL facilities or the behaviours for which RETL could be used, but that public security officials, rather than the judiciary, were given the power to impose RETL. The procedural critique had the effects of transfiguring RETL into a *legal form*, which was illegitimate as it did not comply with international public law norms. The concrete, bricks-and-mortar walls of RETL institutions, the actions performed by individuals who were sanctioned with RETL, the dormitories, the canteens and the factories – all these elements were abstracted and doubled into a legal construct. This meant that the legal construct could be brought into compliance with relevant international norms, yet such reforms and changes could easily remain confined to the formal plane, never seriously affecting what may or may not have been going on behind the closed gates of RETL institutions. The means to monitor legal reform and its implementation existed, yet monitoring had the goal of assessing conformity between domestic and international *legal forms*, rather than between legal forms and *reality*. The moment when detention powers would be bestowed upon the judge, or RETL would be abolished, this critique would lose its reason to be, regardless of how grim the realities of RETL may have been or the forms of detention that would replace RETL might turn out to be. Sensing how this critique, as tempting as it may have been, could obscure the roots of the domestic controversy over RETL, as well as the reform of this institution, Biddulph (2007) analysed the problems caused by RETL by listening to the views and arguments articulated by those who, in China, designed, operated and were reforming the system. RETL had never been a static institution, as the media had represented it. Also, the domestic debate on its abolition meant that there existed a political will to consider the elimination of RETL as a possibility. Such a possibility became real in December 2013, as the National People's Congress repealed all domestic legislation on RETL (*Decision of the Standing Committee of the National People's Congress Repealing Legal Provisions Relevant To Re-Education Through Labour* 28 December 2013). In the absence of a sustained and shared conversation between academics and the media, the abolition of RETL was likely to cause the entire media narrative on corrections in China to lose much of its rhetorical bite.

As we know from the works of Michael Dutton, Børge Bakken, Sarah Biddulph, Randall Peerenboom (2004), Elisa Nesossi, Joshua Rosenzweig and others, in the PRC the power to limit personal freedom belongs to courts, public security organs and other administrative agencies (such as health organs),[3] party discipline and supervision organs, and railway and naval officers. Through the *Criminal Law* (*Xing Fa*) 1979 (as amended in 2011), courts can impose the punishments of control and surveillance (*guanzhi*) (Article 33(1)), criminal detention (*juyi*) (Article 33(2)), imprisonment (Articles 33(3), 33(4)) and deportation (Article 35). However, public security organs enjoy the power to decide and enforce a range of twelve administrative measures which involve a limitation or a deprivation of personal freedom.[4] If the media had to replace the theme of RETL with something capable of stirring equally powerful emotions in the public, their choice could in principle have fallen on community corrections (*shequ jiaoyu*), the measure that would substitute RETL, or on a variety of forms of deprivation of liberty. Instead, it fell on so-called 'black jails' (*hei jianyu*).

The Anyuanding case, 'black jails' and prison privatisation

The term 'black sites' was introduced into popular parlance in 2005, when the press uncovered the existence of a system of covert detention centres operated by the CIA in various countries (Priest 2 November 2005). This label was quickly picked up by the press and used to designate deportation to the place of residence – a police power targeted to those who organised assemblies, marches and demonstrations outside of their place of residence (*Law on Assemblies, Processions and Demonstrations* 1989, Article 33). Use of this power had become more frequent as petitioners expressed their discontent by organising small-scale assemblies and demonstrations in Beijing and in other major cities. The rationale of this police power had to be placed within the broader contexts of stability maintenance (*weiwen*) and social management (*shehui guanli*), which among others mandated the diffusion of social tensions, and a tighter control on public protests (Sapio 2013). As explained elsewhere (Sapio 2013), deportation to a place of residence was a problematic power; uncertainty existed as to whether it belonged to public security officials serving at the place where demonstrations were being held, or to officials at the protestors' place of residence. The solution to this legal procedural problem was to dispatch teams of public security officials to major cities in an effort to intercept and retrieve protesters. Such a solution was procedurally legal, yet it entailed significant costs in terms of time, funds and deployment of personnel. A more economically efficient arrangement was contracting the handing over of petitioners to private security companies. But private security officers do not possess detention powers, and besides such an arrangement could introduce a host of perverse incentives. The immediate deportation of petitioners who travelled to Beijing from distant provinces was not always possible – they had to be detained prior to their departure. Given that public security companies would be paid on the basis of the number of days of a protestor's detention, a clear economic incentive existed to hold protesters for as long as possible, minimising the costs of their food and 'accommodation' by holding them in shabby facilities and refusing to feed them. Companies quickly exploited this incentive; for instance, the notorious Bejing Anyuanding (*Beijing Anyuanding Bao'an Gongsi*) pocketed generous payments from the police to detain petitioners. The Anyuanding scandal saw the company's chairman and general manager detained under suspicion of illegal detention (*feifa jujing*) (Xinhua Net 25 September 2010). The media narrative framed the case as merely involving the illegality of 'black jails' – an expression picked up even by the mainland press (*China Daily* 27 September 2010), and the enforced disappearance of petitioners. Raising the problem of 'black jails' was a morally commendable act, yet much more was at stake in the Anyuanding case. The prevailing narrative worked to obscure how the detention of petitioners, beyond the arbitrariness of such act, was not causally linked to the changes in RETL but rather to dynamics resulting from policies related to stability maintenance and social management. Besides, there were more disturbing implications to this case. Private security companies have strong institutional and leadership links to public security organs (Sapio 2010). On one hand, the case was a classic affair of corruption in which public funds were channelled through private companies to benefit those with strong connections to officials. On the other, Anyuanding set a dangerous precedent by creating one of the very first private jails. What landed Zhang Jun and Zhang Jie, Anyuanding's chairman and general managers, in a publicly run remand jail (*kanshousuo*) was perhaps the simple fact that neither the Political–Legal Committee, nor the Ministry of Justice, nor the Ministry of Public Security have yet considered contracting prisons and other detention facilities to the private sector as a viable option. Even so, there were clear signs that authorities had begun considering such an option. Long before the Anyuanding case, a no less prestigious institution than the Chinese Academy of Social Science had sponsored research on prison privatisation (Wang 2007). In addition to this, scholars had started creating arguments in favour of prison privatisation. The rhetoric of human rights protection had been invoked to hold that privatising prisons and other detention facilities, such as the ones set up by Anyuanding, might improve inmates' living conditions, and contribute to advancing the enjoyment of their human rights (Renminwang 1 February 2005). In the West, the debate on prison privatisation has been periodically fuelled by cases as the one that saw the jailing of 2,000 Pennsylvania children in exchange for bribes (Monbiot 3 March 2009). Aside from debates on prisons, official corruption, inmates' escape, recidivism and sexual assaults in prisons (Dolnick 16 June 2012), the privatisation debate is a key theme in Western mainstream correctional studies. The Western media's discussion of China has, however, avoided any references to the nascent trend towards prison privatisation in China. All of this while Chinese scholarship began calling for the introduction of market mechanisms in what – under the rhetoric of 'social management innovation' (*shehui guanli chuangxin*) – has been termed the 'governance of crime' (*fanzui zhili*) (Wang 2012). Despite initial bouts of indignation among the public, the theme of 'black jails' has failed to achieve the same sustained, widespread and enduring attention RETL attracted. The motif of 'black jails' has further contributed to the displacing of attention away from ongoing debates on prison privatisation, and from community corrections. Legal reform in the PRC relies on models inspired by the legislation and the practices of Western countries. If, in the West, abuses that occur in detention can be causally linked to the profit-maximisation activities of private prisons, it is possible that privatising Chinese detention facilities may produce very similar outcomes. The Western media, however, was unable to point out such a risk. Had the Anyuanding case been framed differently, the themes of rights abuses and prison privatisation could have been discussed in a less confrontational way. After all, many of us first learn about detention in China through the Western media. Therefore, providing a more nuanced view of the repatriation of petitioners could have contributed, no matter how indirectly, to the renewal and progress of a notoriously challenging field of study. Perhaps bringing such a contribution to China studies is not a stated goal of the media narrative on detention in China. Yet such a narrative has represented, and still represents, an important epistemic baggage of China studies.

Concluding thoughts

The geostrategic imperatives of the Cold War and more recent foreign policy considerations have not been the only factors that contributed to shaping analyses of deprivation of freedom in China into what they are today. Equally important has been the sheer unavailability of information about the correctional system and administrative detention powers. This unavailability stems from the fact that issues related to corrections and administrative detention used to be discussed internally, and that relevant publications were for internal circulation only (*neibu*). Access to information and data about the correctional system, not to mention access to correctional facilities, has been granted to domestic researchers only, and then not always. Closely connected to reform programs, domestic research agendas do sometimes draw on Western scholarship. However, sometimes Western debates on issues as privatisation, drug treatment and misdemeanours do not receive the attention they deserve. Western models are indeed studied, but the inherent flaws and shortcomings of Western models perhaps do not always receive the amount of attention that they deserve. Limited in their scope and breadth, Western analyses simply cannot approach themes as prison violence and officers' burnout, or suggest possible ways to maintain the limited amounts of agency and autonomy convicts can enjoy (Jacobs 2013). The drawing of a neat line between international and domestic research is further illustrated by the lack of works co-authored by Western and PRC–based scholars. Unlike other areas of legal research, in which there is significant co-authorship, in this sub-field co-authorship is an exception rather than the norm (Chen and Spronken 2012). Also, they take place within legal cooperation programs sponsored by supranational institutions (for example, the European Union). Despite these limitations, a flourishing of academic publications in Chinese on corrections provides an opportunity to bridge some of these differences. A first and important step in this sense would be analysing contemporary philosophies of punishment, as well as the systemic drivers behind reforms of the correctional system. Some of these are emulation campaigns and performance indicators (Minzner 2011). Slogans and catchwords, and campaigns and indicators were introduced or revamped following the quasi-privatisation of police work (Dutton 2005). The use of quasi-market mechanisms and incentives in police work, something which has also impacted corrections, poses first and foremost the problem of how the performance of contractors should be monitored. Performance indicators are the mechanism of choice because no other feasible alternative exists. While these and other monitoring mechanisms are a most immediate cause of abuses and misuses of law, the first-order cause is a result of the contractualisation of police work itself, its causes and its unfolding over time. This is a much-neglected area of research, and a very promising one. Contractualisation had to be accommodated in a socialist system; it thus impacted on philosophies of punishment, on the very construction of detention facilities, on the creation or reform of regulatory framework, and finally on correctional practices. It induced deep, radical changes, the consequences of which we have only just begun to explore (Fu 2005a). This much-neglected theme of research can be the prism through which certain themes, for example, patterns of sentencing, community corrections, juvenile justice, recidivism, HIV/AIDS prevention and the electronic monitoring of certain prospective offenders, could be observed. The relative neutrality of this approach would perhaps enable a bridging of some of the differences that still separate Western correctional studies in China from the fields of criminology, penology and from analyses conducted in the PRC.

Notes

1 Seymour (2005) analyses the prison system as it existed in the late 1990s.
2 There are a number of non-fictional accounts of life in reform and re-education through labour camps (see for example, Brother Yun 2009; Chen and Larourelle 2009; Dai 2005; Fazzini 2009; Harbert 1973; Kang 2007; Lee 1993; Liao 2013; Jiang 2012; Soepa 2008; Sommer 1992; Stockwell 1953, 1954; Tubten 2008; Wei and Torgenson 1998; Wu 1992; Wu and Vecasey 1996;

Wu and Wakeman 1993; Xiao 2010; Zhang 1995). In addition, literary works have been an object of aesthetic and literary analyses (Williams and Wu 2004, 2006; Wu and Livescu 2011).
3 Powers enjoyed by public health organs are medical observation (*yixue guancha*), the closest equivalent to quarantine, and isolation for treatment (*geli zhiliao*). Their targets are actual or suspected carriers of infectious diseases: Article 39(1), *Law on the Prevention and Treatment of Infectious Diseases* (*Zhuanranbing Fangzhi Fa*), issued on 21 February 1989, as amended on 28 August 2004, effective from 1 December 2004.
4 These are: public security summons (*zhi'an chuanhuan*) (*Security Administrative Punishment Law* (*Zhi'an Guanli Chufa Fa*) 2006 (as amended in 2012), Article 82); stop-and-question (*panwen jiancha*) (*Police Law* (*Renmin Jingcha Fa*) 1995, Article 9); compulsory drug rehabilitation (*qiangzhi geli jiedu*) (*Drug Prohibition Law* (*Jindu Fa*) 2007, Article 38); community rehabilitation (*shequ jiedu*) (*Drug Prohibition Law* 2007, Article 33); commitment to health-recovery centers (*liuzhongxing jiuye*) (*Drug Prohibition Law* 2007, Article 49); shelter and education (*shourong jiaoyu*) (*Measures for Detention for Education of Prostitutes and Clients of Prostitutes* (*Maiyin Piaochang Renyuan Shourong Jiaoyu Banfa*) 1993 (as amended in 2011, Article 7); shelter and reform of juveniles (*shourong jiaoyang*) (*Criminal Law* 1979 (as amended), Article 17 and *Law on the Prevention of Juvenile Crime* 1999, Article 38); compulsory medical treatment (*qiangzhi yiliao*), (*Criminal Law* 1979 (as amended), Article 18); restriction (*yueshu*) (*Security Administrative Punishment Law* 2006 (as amended in 2012), Article 15); forcible removal (*qiangzhi daili xianchang*) (*Law on Assemblies, Processions and Demonstrations* (*Jihui Youxing Shiwei Fa*) 1989, Article 27 and *Police Law* 1995, Article 8; *Security Administrative Punishment Law* 2006 (as amended in 2012), Article 24); forcible dispersion (*qiangzhi qusan*) (*Law on Assemblies, Processions and Demonstrations* 1989, Articles 27 and 33 and *Law on the Exit and Entry Administration* (*Chujing Rujing Guanli Fa*) 2012, Article 60); limitation of the scope of activity (*xiangzhi huodong fangwei*) (*Law on the Exit and Entry Administration* 2012, Articles 20, 61 and 62 and *Police Law* 1995, Article 48).

References

Al Jazeera. 25 March 2012. 'Prison Slaves. China Is the World's Factory, but Does a Dark Secret Lurk Behind this Apparent Success Story?' Available at http://www.aljazeera.com/programmes/slavery-a21stcenturyevil/2011/10/20111101091153782814.html (accessed 16 February 2016).

Alabaster, Ernest. 1899. *Notes and Commentaries on Chinese Criminal Law, and Cognate Topics. With Special Relation to Ruling Cases. Together with a Brief Excursus on The Law of Property, Chiefly Founded on the Writings of the Late Sir Chaloner Alabaster*. London: Luzac & Co.

Anderson, Allen F. 1996. 'A Perspective on China's New Prison Law.' *International Criminal Justice Review* 6: 79–88.

Bathia, H. S. and Tan Chung. 1974. *The Legal and Political System in China (Pre-1949)*. New Delhi: Deep and Deep Publishing.

Bejesky, Robert. 2004. 'Falun Gong and Re-Education Through Labor: Traditional Rehabilitation for the "Misdirected" to Protect Societal Stability within China's Evolving Criminal Justice System.' *Columbia Journal of Asian Law* 17(2): 147–89.

Benton, Elbert Jay. 1908. *International Law and Diplomacy of the Spanish-American War*. Baltimore: John Hopkins Press.

Biddulph, Sarah. 2007. *Legal Reform and Administrative Detention Powers in China*. Cambridge, UK: Cambridge University Press.

Biddulph, Sarah and Xie Chuanyu. 2011. 'Regulating Drug Dependency in China: The 2008 PRC Drug Rehabilitation Law.' *The British Journal of Criminology* 51(6): 978–96.

Bodde, Derk. 1969. 'Prison Life in Eighteenth Century Peking.' *Journal of the American Oriental Society* 89(2): 311–33.

Bodde, Derk and Morris, Clarence. 1967. *Law in Imperial China. Exemplified by 190 Ch'ing Dynasty Cases*. Cambridge, MA: Cambridge University Press.

Bracey, Dorothy H. 1988. 'Like a Doctor to a Patient, Like a Parent to a Child. Corrections in the People's Republic of China.' *The Prison Journal* 68(1): 24–33.

Brother Yun. 2009. *The Heavenly Man: The Remarkable True Story of Chinese Christian Brother Yun*. Peabody, MA: Hendrickson Publishers Marketing.

Chen Weidong and Spronken, Taru. 2012. *Three Approaches to Combating Torture in China*. Maastricht: Intersentia.
Chen Ziming and Larourelle, J. 2009. 'Bearing Witness to Suffering with the Pen of Freedom.' *China Rights Forum* 2: 20–7.
China Daily. 27 September 2010. 'Black Jails Investigated for Illegally Holding Petitioners.' Available at http://www.chinadaily.com.cn/china/2010-09/27/content_11351127.htm (accessed 16 February 2016).
Clarke, Donald C. and Feinerman, James. 1995. 'Antagonistic Contradictions: Criminal Law and Human Rights in China.' *The China Quarterly* 141: 135–54.
Commission on Extraterritoriality. 1926. *Report of the Commission on Extra-territoriality in China*. London: H.M. Stationery Office.
Cowen, Jonathan. 1993. 'One Nation's "Gulag" Is Another Nation's "Factory within A Fence": Prison-Labor in the People's Republic of China.' *UCLA Pacific Basin Law Journals* 12: 190–236.
Dai Qing. 2005. *Tian'anmen Follies. Prison Memoirs and Other Writings*. Norwalk: Fastbridge.
Devitt, Napier. 1941. *The Concentration Camps in South Africa During the Anglo-Boer War of 1889–1902*. Pietermaritzburg: Shuter and Shooter.
Dikötter, Frank. 1997. 'Crime and Punishment in Post-Liberation China: The Prisoners of a Beijing Gaol in the 1950s.' *The China Quarterly* 149: 147–59.
Dikötter, Frank. 2002a. 'The Promise of Repentance: The Prison in Modern China.' *The British Journal of Criminology* 42(2): 240–49.
Dikötter, Frank. 2002b. *Crime, Punishment and the Prison in Modern China*. Hong Kong: Hong Kong University Press.
Dikötter, Frank. 2003. 'The Emergence of Labour Camps in Shandong Province, 1942–1950.' *The China Quarterly* 175: 803–17.
Dikötter, Frank. 2005. 'Penology and Reformation in Modern China.' In *Crime, Punishment and Policing in China*, edited by Børge Bakken, 29–64. Lanham: Rowman and Littlefield.
Ding Chunyang. 2014. 'Involuntary Detention and the Treatment of the Mentally Ill: China's 2012 Mental Health Law.' *International Journal of Law and Psychiatry*, 37(6): 581–88.
Dolnick, Sam. 16 June 2012. 'As Escapees Stream Out, A Penal Business Thrives.' *The New York Times*. Available at http://www.nytimes.com/2012/06/17/nyregion/in-new-jersey-halfway-houses-escapees-stream-out-as-a-penal-business-thrives.html?_r=2 (accessed 16 February 2016).
Domenach, Jean-luc. 1992. *Chine, L'archipel Oublie*. Paris: Fayard.
Dutton, Michael. 2005. 'Toward a Government of the Contract: Policing in the Era of Reform.' In *Crime, Punishment and Policing in China*, edited by Børge Bakken, 189–234. Lanham: Rowman and Littlefield.
Dutton, Michael and Xu Zhangrun. 1998. 'Facing Difference: Relations, Change and the Prison Sector in Contemporary China.' In *Comparing Prison Systems. Towards a Comparative and International Penology*, edited by Robert P. Weiss and Nigel South, 289–336. Amsterdam: Gordon and Breach.
Dutton, Michael and Xu Zhangrun. 2005. 'A question of Difference: The Theory and Practice of the Chinese Prison.' In *Crime, Punishment and Policing in China*, edited by Børge Bakken, 103–140. Lanham: Rowman and Littlefield.
Escarra, Jean. 1961. *Chinese Law, Translated from the French by Gertrude R. Browne*. Seattle: University of Washington Press.
Epstein, Edward J. and Simon Hing-Yan Wong. 1996. 'The Concept of "Dangerousness" in the People's Republic of China and Its Impact on the Treatment of Prisoners.' *British Journal of Criminology* 36(4): 472–500.
Fazzini, Gerolamo. 2009. *The Red Book of Chinese Martyrs. Testimonies and Autobiographical Accounts*. San Francisco: Ignatius Press.
FlorCruz, Michelle. 17 December 2013. 'Amnesty International Warns China's Labor Camps are Revived as "Black Jails" and "Brainwashing Centers".' *International Business Times*. Available at http://www.ibtimes.com/amnesty-international-warns-chinas-labor-camps-are-revived-black-jails-brainwashing-centers-1512582 (accessed 16 February 2016).
Fu Hualing. 2005a. 'Punishing for Profit. Profitability and Rehabilitation in a *Laojiao* Institution.' In *Engaging the Law in China. State, Society, and Possibilities for Justice*, edited by Neij J. Diamant, Stanley Lubman and Kevin J. O'Brien, 213–29. Stanford: Stanford University Press.

Fu Hualing. 2005b. 'Re-Education Through Labor in Historical Perspective.' *The China Quarterly* 184: 811–31.

Fu Hualing. 2009. 'Dissolving *Laojiao*.' *China Rights Forum* 1: 54–8.

Gil, Vincent E., Wang, Marco S., Lin, Guo Matthew and Wu, Zongjian Oliver. 1996. 'Prostitutes, Prostitution and STD/HIV Transmission in Mainland China.' *Social Science and Medicine* 42(1): 141–52.

Griffin, Patricia E. 1974. 'Prison Management in the Kiangsi and Yenan Periods.' *The China Quarterly* 58: 310–31.

Harbert, Mary Anne. 1973. *Captivity. How I Survived 44 Months as a Prisoner of the Red Chinese*. New York: Delacarte Press.

Hu Junmin, Yang Min, Huang Xiaoqi and Coid, Jeremy. 2011. 'Forensic Psychiatry in China.' *International Journal of Law and Psychiatry* 34(1): 7–12.

Hung, Veron Meiying. 2003. 'Improving Human Rights in China: Should Re-Education Through Labour Be Abolished?' *Columbia Journal of Transnational Law* 1: 303–26.

Information Office of the State Council. 1992. *Criminal Reform in China*. Beijing.

International Society for Human Rights. (No Date). 'About Us.' Available at http://www.ishr.org/about-us/faqs/ (accessed 16 February 2016).

Jacobs, Jonathan. 2013. 'Agency, Character, and Criminal Sanction: Implications of their Interaction.' Paper Presented at the CUHK Faculty of Law, Centre for Rights and Justice, June 18–20. Available at http://www.law.cuhk.edu.hk/en/research/crj/events/20130621-jjacobs-presentation.php (accessed 16 February 2016).

Jiang Shanhe, Xiang Deping, Qi Cheng, Huang Chengxiang, Zhang Dawei, Zhao, Anna and Yang Shengyong. 2014. 'Community Corrections in China: Development and Challenges.' *The Prison Journal* 94: 75–96.

Jiang, Qisheng. 2012. *My Life in Prison: Memoirs of a Chinese Political Dissident*. Lanham: Rowman and Littlefield.

Kang Zhengguo. 2007. *Confessions. An Innocent Life in Communist China*. New York and London: W.W. Norton Company.

Leck, Greg. 2006. *Captives of Empire. The Japanese Internment of Allied Civilians in China 1941–1945*. Bangor, PA: Shandy Press.

Lee, Gregory B. 1993. *I Am a Prisoner in Exile: Wen Yiduo in the United States*. Chicago: Centre for East Asian Studies, University of Chicago.

Leng, Shao-chuan. 1977. 'The Role of Law in the People's Republic of China as Reflecting Mao Tse-Tung's Influence.' *The Journal of Criminal Law and Criminology* 68(3): 356–73.

Leng, Shao-chuan. 1981. 'Criminal Justice in Post-Mao China: Some Preliminary Observations.' *The China Quarterly* 87: 440–69.

Levin, Dan. 27 December 2012. 'Are your Christmas Gifts Made in the Chinese Gulag?' *The Daily Beast*. Available at http://www.thedailybeast.com/articles/2012/12/27/are-your-christmas-gifts-made-in-the-chinese-gulag.html (accessed 16 February 2016).

Liao Yiwu. 2013. *For a Song and a Hundred Songs: A Poet's Journey Through a Chinese Prison*. New York: Houghton Mifflin Harcourt Publishing.

Lifton, Robert Jay. 1956. 'Thought Reform of Western Civilians in Chinese Communist Prisons.' *Psychiatry* 19: 173–95.

Lifton, Robert Jay. 1957a. 'Thought Reform of Chinese Intellectuals: A Psychiatric Evaluation.' *Journal of Social Issues* 3: 5–20.

Lifton, Robert Jay. 1957b. 'Chinese Communist "Thought Reform": Confession and Re-Education of Western Civilians.' *Bulletin of the New York Academy of Medicine*, 33(9): 626–44.

Lifton, Robert Jay. 1963. *Though-Reform and the Psychology of Totalism: A Study of 'Brainwashing' in China*. New York: Norton & Co.

Liu Liu and Chui Wing Hong. 2014. 'Social Support and Chinese Female Offenders' Prison Adjustment.' *The Prison Journal* 94: 30–51.

Merli, Maria Giovanna, Moody, James, Smith, Jeffrey, Li Jing, Weir, Sharon S. and Chen Xiangsheng. 2015. 'Challenges to Recruiting Population Representative Samples of Female Sex Workers in China Using Respondent Driven Sampling.' *Social Science and Medicine* 125: 1–214.
Millard, Thomas F. 1931. *The End of Extraterritoriality in China*. Shanghai: ABC Press.
Miller, Eugene. 1982. 'Prison Industries in the People's Republic of China.' *The Prison Journal* 62(2): 52–7.
Minzner, Carl. 2011. 'China's Turn against Law.' *The American Journal of Comparative Law* 59: 935–84.
Monbiot, George. 3 March 2009. 'This Revolting Trade in Human Lives Is an Incentive to Lock People Up.' *The Guardian*. Available at http://www.theguardian.com/commentisfree/2009/mar/03/prison-population-titan-jails (accessed 16 February 2016).
Mühlahn, Klaus. 2009. *Criminal Justice in China*. Harvard: Harvard University Press.
Munro, Robin. 2002. 'Political Psychiatry in Post-Mao China and Its Origins in the Cultural Revolution.' *Journal of the American Academy of Psychiatry and the Law* 30(1): 97–106.
Munro, Robin. 2006. *China's Psychiatric Inquisition. Dissent, Psychiatry and the Law in Post-1949 China*. London: Wildy, Simmonds and Hill.
Nesossi, Elisa. 2008. 'Reforming Criminal Justice in the People's Republic of China. The Black Hole of Pre-Trial Detention.' *Journal of Comparative Law* 3(2): 305–15.
Nesossi, Elisa. 2012. *China's Pre-Trial Justice: Criminal Justice, Human Rights and Legal Reforms in Contemporary China*. London: Wildy, Simmonds and Hill.
Pearson, Veronica. 1992. 'Law, Rights and Psychiatry in the People's Republic of China.' *International Journal of Law and Psychiatry* 15(4): 409–23.
Pearson, Veronica. 1996. 'The Chinese Equation in Mental Health Policy and Practice: Order Plus Control Equal Stability.' *International Journal of Law and Psychiatry* 19(3–4): 437–58.
Peerenboom, Randall. 2004. 'Out of the Pan and into the Fire: Well-intentioned but Misguided Recommendations to Eliminate All Forms of Administrative Detention in China.' *Northwestern University Law Review*, 98(3): 991–1104.
Priest, Dana. 2 November 2005. 'CIA Holds Terror Supects in Secret Prisons.' *The Washington Post*. Available at http://www.washingtonpost.com/wp-dyn/content/article/2005/11/01/AR2005110101644.html (accessed 16 February 2016).
Renminwang. 1 February 2005. 'Tanfang Ling Qiufan Shouchong Ruojing De Siying Jianyu (Visiting Convicts Who Are Pampered in Britain's Scary Private Prison).' Available at http://www.people.com.cn/GB/junshi/42964/3159982.html (accessed 16 February 2016).
Rosenzweig, Joshua. 2013. 'Public Opinion and Chinese Criminal Justice Reform.' *Paper Presented at the Eighth European China Law Studies Association Annual Conference*, 19–20 September.
Sapio, Flora. 2010. *Sovereign Power and the Law in China*. Boston and Leiden: Brill.
Sapio, Flora. 2013. 'Legal Erosion and the Policing of Petitions.' In *Comparative Perspectives on Criminal Justice in China*, edited by Mike McConville and Eva Pils, 345–69. Cheltenham: Edward Elgar.
Schein, Edward H. 1956. 'The Chinese Indoctrination Program for Prisoners of War: A Study of Attempted "Brainwashing".' *Psychiatry* 19: 149–72.
Seymour, James. 2005. 'Sizing up China's Prisons.' In *Crime, Punishment and Policing in China*, edited by Børge Bakken, 141–67. Lanham: Rowman and Littlefield.
Seymour, James D. and Anderson, Richard. 1999. *New Ghosts, Old Ghosts. Prison and Labor Reform Camps in China*. Armonk: M. E. Sharpe.
Shao Yang, Xie Bin, Del Vecchio, Mary Jo and Good, Byron L. 2010. 'Current Legislation on Admission of Mentally Ill Patients in China.' *International Journal of Law and Psychiatry* 33(1): 52–7.
Shaw, Victor N. 1998. 'Productive Labor and Thought Reform in Chinese Corrections: A Historical and Comparative Analysis.' *The Prison Journal* 78(2): 186–211.
Sifabu Guanliju. 25 March 2014. 'Zhongguo Jianyu Zuifan Jiaoyu Gaizao Fazhan Gaikuang (The Status of Convicts' Criminal Reform in China's Prisons).' Available at http://www.moj.gov.cn/jyglj/content/2014-03/25/content_5393650.htm (accessed 16 February 2016).

Smith, Aminda M. 2012. 'Remoulding Minds in Postsocialist China: Maoist Reeducation and Twenty-First-Century Subjects.' *Postcolonial Studies* 15(4): 453–66.

Smith, Aminda M. 2013a. 'The Dilemma of Thought Reform. Beijing Reformatories and the Origins of Reeducation through Labor, 1949–1957.' *Modern China* 39(2): 203–34.

Smith, Aminda M. 2013b. 'Thought Reform and the Unreformable: Reeducation Centers and the Rhetoric of Opposition in the Early People's Republic of China.' *The Journal of Asian Studies* 72(4): 937–58.

Smith, Aminda M. 2013c. *Thought Reform and China's Dangerous Classes: Reeducation, Resistance, and the People*. Lanham: Rowman and Littlefield.

Soepa, Tenpa. 2008. *20 Years of My Life in China's Death Camp*. Bloomington: Author House.

Sommer, Robin Langley. 1992. *Nien Chieng: Prisoner in China*. Woodbridge, Conn: Blackbirch Press Books.

Stockwell, Francis Olin. 1953. *With God in Red China. The Story of Two Years in Chinese Communist Prisons*. New York: Harper.

Stockwell, Francis Olin. 1954. *Meditations from a Prison Cell: Devotional Talks from a Chinese Communist Prison*. Nashville: The Upper Room.

Tanner, Harold M. 1994. 'China's "Gulag" Reconsidered: Labor Reform in the 1980s and 1990s.' *China Information* 9(1): 40–71.

Tanner, Harold M. 1999. *Strike Hard! Anti-Crime Campaigns and Chinese Criminal Justice, 1979–1985*. Ithaca: Cornell University Press.

The Continent Press. 1978. *Peiping Abuses Human Rights*. Hong Kong: Continent Press.

Tubten, Khetsun. 2008. *Memories of Life in Lhasa under Chinese Rule*. New York: Columbia University Press.

Tucker, Joseph, Ren Xin and Sapio, Flora. 2010. 'Incarcerated Sex Workers and HIV Prevention in China: Social Suffering and Social Justice Countermeasures.' *Social Science and Medicine* 70(1): 1–9.

Wang Mingliang. 2012. 'Fanzui Zhili Guocheng Zhong De Shichang Jizhi (The Market Mechanism in the Process of the Governance of Crime).' *Renmin Gong'an Daxue Xuebao* (Journal of the People's Public Security University) 6: 132–42.

Wang Yanhui. 2007. 'Meiguo Jianyu Siyouhuade Shijian Fenxi (A Synchronic Analysis of Prison Liberalization in America).' *Meiguo Yanjiu* (Research on America) 3: 70–85.

Wei, Henry. 1955. *Courts and Police in Communist China to 1952*. Lackland Air Force Base, Texas: Air Force Personnel and Training Research Centre.

Wei Jinsheng and Torgenson, Kristina M. 1998. *The Courage to Stand Alone. Letters from Prison and Other Writings*. New York and London: Penguin.

Williams, Philip and Wu, Yenna. 2004. *The Great Wall of Confinement. The Chinese Prison Camp through Contemporary Fiction and Reportage*. Berkeley, Los Angeles and London: University of California Press.

Williams, Philip and Wu, Yenna. 2006. *Remolding and Resistance Among Writers of the Chinese Prison Camp. Disciplined and Published*. London: Routledge.

Wong, Kam C. 1996. 'Police Powers and Control in the People's Republic of China: The History of Shoushen.' *Columbia Journal of Asian Law* 10: 367–90.

Wong, Kam C. 1997. *Sheltering for Examination (Shoushen) in the PRC: Law, Policy and Practices*. Baltimore: University of Maryland School of Law.

World Anti-Communist League. 1997. *Documented Evidence How the Chinese Communists Impinge on Human Rights*. Republic of China (Unknown Binding).

Wu, Harry and Goodrich, Cole. 2014. 'A Jail by Any Other Name: Labor Camp Abolition in the Context of Arbitrary Detention in China.' *Human Rights Brief* 21: 2–69.

Wu, Harry and Vecasey, George. 1996. *Troublemaker. One Man's Crusade Against China's Cruelty*. New York: Times Books.

Wu, Hongda Harry. 1992. *Laogai. The Chinese Gulag*. Boulder: Westview Press.

Wu, Hongda Harry and Wakeman, Carolyn. 1993. *Bitter Winds: A Memoir of My Years in China's Gulag*. New York: John Wiley and Sons.
Wu, Yenna and Livescu, Simona. 2011. *Human rights, Suffering and Aesthetics in Political Prison Literature*. Plymouth: Lexington Books.
Xiao Xiaoda. 2010. *The Visiting Suit. Stories from My Prison Life*. Two Dollar Radio Movement.
Xinhua Net 25 September 2010. 'Andingyuan Bao'an Gongsi Bei Bejing Jingfan Li'an Zhencha (Beijing Police Investigates Andingyuan Private Security Company).' Available at http://news.xinhuanet.com/video/2010-09/25/c_12603891.htm (accessed 16 February 2016).
Yan Hairong and Sautman, Barry. 2012. 'Chasing Ghosts: Rumours and Representations of the Export of Chinese Convict Labour to Developing Countries.' *The China Quarterly* 210: 398–418.
Zhang Xianliang. 1995. *Grass Soup*. London: Warburg.

10 Opportunities and challenges for legislative and institutional reform of detention in China

Elisa Nesossi, Sarah Biddulph, Flora Sapio and Susan Trevaskes

What is reform?

Throughout this volume, we have used the word 'reform' to refer to the changes to legislation governing deprivation of liberty in contemporary China, as well as to the institutions responsible for enforcing such legislation. As many other words do, 'reform' carries two distinct connotations, which depend on the ideological and cultural context of the speaker. For most Western scholars who are active in the field of China studies, the word 'reform' conjures up the idea of a teleological march from Marxism to liberal modernity. This connotation is absent from the word 'gaige', the Chinese original for 'reform' which lacks such a directional element. Because of this, 'reform' is a term that all those who write or speak in China about detention often want to use cautiously, as it belongs to two distinct universes of meaning at the same time.

The chapters in this book explore and critically evaluate a number of significant positive developments in both discourse in the field of scholarship and practice in the areas of detention and imprisonment that have either occurred over the last decade or are currently under way. But equally they attest to the problems inherent in marking a change as a 'reform' (at least in various and sometimes incompatible senses this term has been used by Western scholars and the media). In fact, what we have called reform may be better understood and described as variations or fluctuations over time.

Actors and factors in reform

A key theme that runs throughout this book is that change within the justice system and in the practice of and rationale behind deprivation of liberty is a particularly complex process. This change can be better understood only if placed in context. This collection seeks to do that by interrogating the rationale behind specific reformist projects, as well as their short and long-term social, legal and political effects. The broader political, social and legal ramifications of changes in systems of detention sometimes become visible both in debates prior to and following reforms, which make it possible for the voice of public opinion to be heard. At other times, these broader ramifications can be 'divined' through a careful analysis of elite discourse on reform. Once enacted as law, the consequences of amending a legislative document can be seen in the practical impact it has on the apparatus of social governance and the justice system at large. The creation or dismantling of an institution, however, does not only produce the concrete consequences normally associated with the closing down or the opening up of new detention facilities. It might have broader systemic effects that require further amendments to existing substantive and procedural legislation. Changes in the justice system can also signal more subtle changes in ideology or, conversely, act as a catalyst for ideological change.

The close nexus between law and politics that characterises the Chinese justice system has been often and rightly criticised in scholarship and the media as placing the individual at disadvantage vis-à-vis the institutions of the Party-state. While acknowledging the well-founded nature of this criticism, at the same time we wish to offer another possible reading of what the outcomes of such a fusion between law and politics might be. As changes in legislation and in detention institutions require reconciliation of a complex web of institutional interests and ideological positions, the close inter-relationship between Party and state means that an array of political and legal actors, situated at both the central and local levels, are involved (and so implicated) in the dynamics of change.

The chapters in this book illustrate the many sources of impetus for change, and the sometimes shifting coalitions that form to advocate for a particular set of reforms. They document developments that emerge out of political opportunities at the central institutional level, as well as out of those that result from local level initiatives. Developments are not the sole province of either the Party or the state, and so we must also take into account each of these two faces of the Chinese Party-state when evaluating factors that drive or hold back change. Accordingly, this volume both examines the role of state agencies and acknowledges the key role of the Chinese Communist Party (CCP) in shaping both debates and the reform agenda. Alterations to the ways in which citizens can be deprived of their liberty are highly revealing of the extent to which the CCP is willing to bend its approach to justice administration to initiate or else accommodate changes in societal values and international calls for the protection of human rights.

At the same time the majority of the studies collected here also acknowledge that in China today discourses on reform are shaped by numerous other factors that develop outside of the Party-state's initiative. This means that while reforms are responsive to political imperatives set by Party authorities in Beijing, the needs and interests of the institutional powers in the justice system and, increasingly, the pressures exercised by individual citizens through civil society organisations and the media, are also forces to be reckoned with.

Challenges and opportunities

The studies collected in the present volume suggest that the reformist path that has been followed so far has brought about a number of the key opportunities and challenges. Authors discuss some of the wider social, legal and political processes that influence the nature of contemporary Chinese penal policy. In so doing, they have identified pressures that shape ideas about punishment and the administration of criminal and administrative justice that may pull in different directions with different degrees of intensity. Of central importance is continuing adherence to a philosophy of punishment which is highly utilitarian in its orientation. Aside from the sometimes conflicting imperatives of rehabilitation versus retribution, detention has the most immediate goal of maintaining social stability, as well as control over individual citizens and, indirectly, society as a whole. And so, despite rapid changes in social and economic conditions in China, change within the justice system does not always seem to obey that logic. While a number of places of detention and imprisonment are undergoing significant and relatively rapid changes in their design, functions, organisation and legislation, others have been left untouched.

The paradox of coexistence of opportunities and challenges is that they are not inevitably connected to actual change in detention or the lack thereof. Opportunities may exist where an institution has been left untouched, while the occurrence of extraordinarily rapid changes within an institution may present challenges that their reformers never foresaw, and vice versa.

In the sections below, we explore the elements identified in the chapters of this book that we think operate to produce both opportunities and challenges for reform in the area of detention. They are: shifting institutional coalitions around questions of reform; Party-state interactions with civil society and media; the role of scandals in reform; and changing ideas, values and sensibilities. Political authorities and political will are significant factors in initiating any penal reform. However, we also see how, in China today, factors other than political motivations and opportunities may also contribute to or trigger change. Even though we can see that increased civil society dynamism and media activism may facilitate the development and popularisation of new ideas and sensibilities, it is also clear that deep conceptual shifts are possible only if supported by those in power, as they are the ones who have the final say in legal and institution-making processes. Governmental needs and interests are far from being homogeneous and often diverge both institutionally and geographically. Thus, legislative and institutional reforms in the area of detention and imprisonment – as in many other areas of the justice system that are strictly related to the maintenance of social order – are just the tip of an iceberg. They are built upon complex social and political dynamics which form a crucial component of any investigation into the broader themes in law, politics and sociology in China.

Political will and institutional compromise

The chapters in this book build their analysis more or less explicitly around the fact that China is a country where law and politics are intermingled. In areas of justice administration that touch the core of the relationship between the state and individual citizens, the hand of the Party in state administration is clearly visible. Drastic changes or subtle reformist turns happen only if sanctioned by Party authorities, and only when the time is considered politically ripe. The activist disposition of the Party-state (Trevaskes et al. 2014) extends to both higher and lower level political levels. Thus, politics involves negotiation between CCP authorities in Beijing and at the local levels, state agencies and key figures within ministries and justice departments responsible for the administration of public order. Understandably, it is difficult for reforms to be approved if there are important unresolved issues between agencies, or where reforms hamper their powers and interests.

The abolition of the system of re–education through labour (RETL) at the end of 2013 is one clear example of the complexity of political interactions in the justice arena. This form of detention had been the subject of vigorous debate and criticism among scholars, justice officials, legal practitioners and NGOs in China, and internationally for decades. In early 2013 RETL was designed by the Central Political–Legal Committee as one of the four priority areas for reform in the politico-legal system (see Biddulph, Chapter 2 in this volume). At the end of that year, it ceased to exist. Suddenly, finally, the public security agencies had lost one of their most flexible and abused tools for dealing with rapidly changing social order problems.

However, the abolition of RETL had also a number of positive political effects. For one, the abolition of RETL was greeted with almost unanimous public and official approval, both domestically and internationally. It enabled the Xi Jinping leadership to mark the beginning of a renewed approach toward justice and social stability. It both signalled a retreat from the politics of law and order of Zhou Yongkang's stability maintenance program and underlined his political demise.

A series of institutional changes instituted since 2008 also meant that the social order impact of the closure of RETL was minimised. The Ministry of Public Security (MPS), in almost full control of the complex system of administrative detention, had over a number of years put in place a series of alternative institutional mechanisms to ensure that its power over the administration of public order would not be undermined by the eventual reform or abolition of RETL. Thus, as Biddulph explains, at the time RETL was dismantled, many detainees had already been transferred into other institutions like drug detoxification centres, detention centres for prostitutes, or into the criminal justice system.

Other reforms to legislation regulating institutions and powers of detention may also be interpreted according to the same utilitarian logic of political advantage and institutional compromise. Various chapters in this book address this issue. The limited and problematic reforms to the system of residential surveillance in the process of amending the *Criminal Procedure Law* 1996, for example, were connected to the Party-state's obsession with social and political stability. Notwithstanding the numerous requests for its abolition, residential surveillance was retained in the 2012 version of the law for its demonstrable utility as a law enforcement mechanism (see Rosenzweig, Chapter 5 in this volume). By maintaining it in both its 'ordinary' and 'exceptional' forms, public security authorities could continue to maximise their ability to detain alleged trouble-makers incommunicado without onerous limits imposed by the legislation. Indeed, the compromise implicit in the legislation may be seen as legalising previously unauthorised practices by the public security authorities.

When official commentators claim that 'the time for reform is not yet ripe', very often they are implying that internal institutional debates are not settled and new power-sharing arrangements have not yet been clearly defined or agreed. As both Cheng and Nesossi (Chapter 6) and Macbean (Chapter 7) discuss, pre-trial detention offers a key example in this respect. The institutional battle over these reforms again involves the key interests of public security authorities. The MPS maintains its monopoly over criminal pre-trial detention, with its firm control both over criminal pre-trial proceedings and pre-trial detention institutions. From its perspective, any suggestion that procedures of arrest and detention may be separated may be interpreted as a challenge to its authority. Besides, the MPS does not see any advantage in either separating such procedure, or in giving up its control of pre-trial detention centres. Consequently, institutional and legislative reforms have, for a long time, been considered to be a prerogative of public security authorities. As public security authorities have the most significant and direct concerns in any reform of the system they administer, it has been in their interest to keep discussions about reform away from public scrutiny.

A similar link between reforms and institutional interest has been identified in the process of creating new laws. In Chapter 4, Guo delves into the *Mental Health Law* 2012 to reveal the extent to which the document is the result of a process of negotiation amongst the institutions involved in the treatment of the mentally ill and in the governance of mental health institutions. Thus, drafting the *Mental Health Law* 2012 largely involved internal debates among the MPS, the Ministry of Justice, and authorities involved in health management.

From scandal to reforms

Party and institutional politics retain their central position in the process of reform, but, in contemporary China, politics can no longer be insulated from public and media scrutiny. At different moments in the reform era, the Chinese media and the Internet have become key sites in exposing cases of egregious abuse by justice officials. As highlighted in Chapter 1 in this volume, since the early 2000s publicity surrounding a number of deaths in custody and wrongful detention both raised public awareness of problems concerning deprivation of liberty and galvanised public dissatisfaction with the institutional status quo.

The landmark case that brought problems with administrative detention into the spotlight was the death of Sun Zhigang in a centre for custody and repatriation. In March 2003, the young fashion designer was beaten to death while in custody in the city of Guangzhou. Official attempts to cover up the event, denunciations by the media of an obsolete and brutal system used indiscriminately to deprive citizens of their liberty and the feeling of empowerment brought by the then recently enacted *Legislation Law* 2000 paved the way for the issue of detention under *shourong qiansong* to be brought into the public discourse on justice reforms. Three young law graduates – Xu Zhiyong, Teng Biao and Yu Jiang – wrote to the National People's Congress (NPC) to demand the abolition of custody and repatriation. The time was no doubt politically ripe and the system was abolished (Hand 2006).

Allegations of mistreatment and cases where criminal suspects were either 'forgotten' in places of detention or subject to abuse by other inmates or detention guards similarly opened up debates about the various faults and failures inherent in China's complex systems of detention. Growing official sensitivity to public exposure of abuses and unnatural deaths in detention centres contributed to an increased official appetite for legal reform. In 2008, strengthening the supervision of police stations and detention centres, and improving their legislative framework were listed among the priorities of criminal justice reforms. In January 2009, the MPS was made responsible for amending the *Regulations on Criminal Detention Centres* 1990 and, as discussed in Cheng and Nesossi's Chapter 6 and Macbean's Chapter 7, a few months later the debate on reform reached its apex. However, even these modest reforms of pre-trial criminal detention were soon overshadowed by scandals. This time the media reported that a young man, Li Qiaoming, had died in the Jinning detention centre in Yunnan Province playing a game of 'hide and seek'. Once again, attempts to cover up the circumstances of Li's death by the authorities with a completely unbelievable story as well as the terrible circumstances of his death generated widespread public indignation. At the official level, the immediate response was fault-finding, but in the longer term this incident provoked serious more systematic reflections on possibilities for reforms of pre-trial detention institutions administered by the MPS.

In 2012, the case of Tang Hui helped cement public consensus around the need to reform the long-criticised system of RETL. Driven by a mother's insistence on seeing justice done to those responsible for the rape and forced prostitution of her eleven-year-old daughter, Tang Hui responded to the indifference of local law enforcement agents by petitioning for the intervention of provincial and central officials (Rosenzweig 2014). After a protracted trial process in which two defendants were eventually sentenced to death (though these death sentences were subsequently overturned on review by the Supreme People's Court), police responded to Tang's ongoing efforts to hold individual officers accountable for alleged acts of dereliction or malfeasance by sending her to RETL for eighteen months. When news of Tang's detention became public, a surge of public opinion put pressure on provincial authorities to announce a thorough investigation and to quickly release her on 'humanitarian' grounds.

Other scandals within China most probably have helped channel public attention toward other problematic mechanisms for detention, including administrative measures like RETL and other extra-legal measures such as 'black jails' or extra-legal forms of 'residential surveillance'. Following a number of denunciations by international organisations and NGOs, in 2010 the Chinese authorities admitted to the existence of 'black jails' which were mainly used to detain petitioners, and at the same time acknowledged the need to solve this problem.

As Macbean's chapter concludes, scandals have acted as powerful catalysts for recent reforms. Chinese law scholar Fu Hualing has described this as a 'from scandal-to-reform' pattern of reform (Fu 2009, 164). It is important to acknowledge though that such cases were most probably 'sentinel events', exemplifying a series of longstanding and widespread problems in the system of administration of justice in the PRC that the media was then allowed to discuss openly. Enabling such public discussion has an additional institutional benefit of strengthening the hand of those who have an interest in promoting reform. While some observers might have seen such grim reports of deaths in custody as confirmation of their fears concerning repeated violence within these places, for reform-minded scholars and officials, these cases also represented a useful opportunity to move their proposals for legal and institutional reforms into the spotlight to be heard and debated. Scandals triggering public debate offer opportunities for initiating processes to revise systems that may have been in place for years. Cases exposed in the media also provide an opportunity for authorities to gauge changes in public attitude and tolerance levels of those in civil society who can no longer abide abusive behaviours within places of detention, thus stimulating a public outcry and calls for legislative change.

Ideas, values and sensibilities

Our account above of the impact of institutional interest and scandals on attitudes towards detention points to the existence of three distinct constituencies: political power holders and their representative institutions, civil society and the media. From that discussion we can also point to at least three overlapping, but possibly divergent, sets of conceptual approaches to the deprivation of liberty that in turn influence the development of new ideas, values and sensibilities. The first are political ideas about maintenance of social order and crime control which underpin the general orientation of policy and official decision-making about detention. In this volume two sets of political ideas in the form of policies emerge as central. One is 'stability maintenance'; the other is the criminal justice policy of 'Balancing Leniency and Severity'.

The second set of conceptual approaches concerns the issue of the legal and fundamental human rights of individual prisoners and detainees. The third relates to broader social values that have arisen out of economic development, new cultural and social interactions and non-official political discourses. Social views and sensibilities about criminality, punishment and exclusion more generally have evolved alongside changes in social values. Each of these three approaches has been developed in the chapters of this book. We summarise some of the ideas that have emerged in these three areas below.

First, top-level political ideology has been decisive in defining the terms in which criminal justice is discussed and in setting the parameters for criminal justice reforms. As Nesossi and Trevaskes explain in Chapter 8, political ideology has long defined the parameters within which the idea of punishment is articulated in the literature and translated into practice. In the post-Mao era, the continuing use of Marxist discourse of reforming the individual has had a significant impact on both the approaches to and institutions of punishment. Another discursive trope originating in the Mao era is 'balancing leniency and severity'. This form of rhetoric has shaped the way that institutional practices are described and debated both in prison literature and by practitioners in prisons.

The policy of 'Balancing Leniency and Severity' (attached to Hu Jintao's harmonious society policy) was proclaimed by Party and judicial authorities alike to be China's new foundational criminal justice policy. In court and prosecution practices, its main gist is to ensure that a range of minor offences can be decriminalised or subjected to lighter penalties, while a relatively narrower range of serious criminal offences can be treated with severe punishment (Trevaskes 2010). Clearly this policy was intended to focus on the trial process involving conviction and sentencing decisions. Nevertheless, as growing emphasis came to be placed on the harmonious society agenda, by extension the policy of 'balancing leniency and severity' also increasingly came to influence the rhetoric and practice of prison organisation. Since 2012, it has enabled authorities to justify and advocate for political choices which displace old prison discourse and enhance new ideas about prison organisation. After the Eighth Amendment to the *Criminal Law* in 2012, which highlighted the importance of 'balancing leniency and severity', prison authorities began to adapt 'balance' to recast longstanding prison discourses related to prison organisation and prison life. Terms such as 'security', 'rehabilitation' and 'criminal reconciliation', as well as the ways prisons and prisoners are classified nowadays is couched in the language of balancing leniency and severity. Changing the context and so the meanings ascribed to the language spoken by political-legal agencies creates the possibility that practice may become more respectful of the substantive and procedural rights of individuals.

The substantive and procedural rights of individuals provide the second set of ideas that underpin the analysis of a number of chapters in this volume. In the area of prison reform, the introduction of rights-related discourse in the mid to late 1990s gave reformist-minded scholars and practitioners a new vocabulary with which to argue about the failures of longstanding prison discourse and policy. While some scholars fully embraced rights discourse, others like Zhang Shaoyan took advantage of the increasingly rights-related debates on prisons in the 1990s to argue for a thorough rethinking of the entire concept of reform through labour (*laogai*). Zhang, one of the most outspoken scholars who questioned not only the concept of *laogai* but also explicitly denounced its political nature in the late 1990s, offered one of the first examples of an approach critical of the Maoist idea that prison and punishment were designed to reform (as opposed to punish) the individual. In a seminal article, Zhang (in Chu et al. 2002) argued:

> When we talk about reform we talk about reforming an individual's thinking since behaviour is dependent upon thought. This means that only by reforming their thoughts, can we modify their behaviour. I see a problem here: can we really reform somebody's thought patterns? Anybody can change, but can this be considered a reformation [of thinking]? I believe that this is not the case. A person can change, but [changing one's thinking is] not the same as coerced reform. This is because one's thoughts are free, and can only ever be free. In this case, how can we coercively reform their thoughts? This is impossible. Secondly, if we do assume that somebody's thoughts can be reformed, do we also assume that the reformer has the power to do so? Reform in China has quite powerful ideological and political connotations; it does not simply mean that you change into a well-behaved person. It signifies [a deeper] change in thought and reform. And, I believe it is crucial to reflect about whether we actually have the capacity to reform a person's thinking.

Rights discourse is not the sole province of individual scholars and practitioners. The Chinese government itself and its agencies have been increasingly inclined to utilise rights discourse in the international arena. As Macbean (Chapter 7) has noted in her study, at the official level China has made several undertakings to respect international law regarding the treatment of persons deprived of their liberty. China's second National Human Rights Action Plan (2012–2015) makes specific promises to improve the protection of detainees' rights including to prevent unnecessary detention, to supervise detention time limits and to improve oversight and investigations into deaths in custody. In its report for the *Universal Periodic Review by the UN Human Rights Council* in 2013, China outlined a number of measures it had taken to strengthen safeguards of detainees' rights, including the promulgation of regulations on detention centres (*juliusuo tiaoli*). As in other areas of justice administration, such official commitments, though not reliably translated into practice, at least to some extent help to change the baseline in domestic scholarly narratives and in the official language used to discuss deprivation of liberty.

Concepts of individual and legal human rights sit in tension with the current modes of crime fighting and control of public order. The discourse on rights of detainees is an example of this tension. The numerous debates surrounding the revision of the *Criminal Procedure Law* 1996 have brought to light illegal practices like torture in pre-trial detention centres operated by the public security authorities that were both common and routinely condoned. Debates over the system of residential surveillance have equally questioned the meaning of the term 'coercive measures' during pre-trial proceedings, by highlighting how easily these measures may be manipulated for punitive purposes by the public security authorities in clear breach of the rights of the criminal suspects. Over the last decade and particularly in recent years, numerous Chinese scholarly debates about administrative detention have been framed in terms of legality and respect for constitutional and individual rights of detainees. We saw this particularly in Cheng and Nesossi's chapter discussing the drafting of the new Detention Law.

Reports by the media about abuses in places of detention build on a base of increasing public dissatisfaction with Party-state institutions and may also help to increase rights consciousness within certain segments in society. The reporting of abuse may also be indicative of increasing sensitivity to more inclusive ideas of social justice and individual rights. These reports create expectations among the general public that individuals should be treated equally before the law and not be left at the mercy of arbitrary and abusive conduct by the authorities. Scandals have fuelled critical public discourse on the power of the police and lawyers and legal scholars have contributed to greater rights awareness and stronger demands for these rights to be respected. However, increasing rights awareness in Chinese society, to date, has not resulted in widespread public calls to limit the state's power to deprive persons of their liberty. There are also real limits to the capacity of these sensibilities to affect enforcement practice.

Indeed, the increasing rights consciousness in many sectors of Chinese society has not translated into a deepening sympathy for all people, especially those caught up in the justice system. As this volume illustrates, general feelings of dissatisfaction and disillusionment toward state-run detention institutions has not lessened the stigma of people labelled criminals. For instance, Macbean, and Cheng and Nesossi lament the general popular disengagement with the rights of prisoners and detainees. Guo's chapter shows that this lack of sympathy extends to the treatment of the mentally ill, with continuing lack of attention and concern for their rights. Li explains in his chapter how social stigmatisation and rejection of offenders have generated an environment where 'community programs are functionally misunderstood and locally repulsed.' Offenders, sex workers and the mentally ill are perceived by members of the community to be potential threats to social order and morality as well as a potential drain on community resources.

Conclusion: looking behind the cosmetic

The chapters in this collection highlight the need to view legal and institutional change as the outcome of a complex set of political dynamics and *structural transformation*. The broader framework of the Party's utilitarian approach toward detention and imprisonment as part of its quest for public order, social stability and power control impedes any form of linear progression from Maoism towards modernity. We see that reforms influenced by economic development and new social dynamics continue to be impacted by a refusal of authorities to relinquish the ideology of the Maoist era. Therefore governance priorities and the development of approaches toward crime and criminality that hark back to the Maoist times coexist in tension with newer ideas about justice and individual rights held by the elites and many at the grassroots level.

The abolition of RETL is a prime example of the need to broaden our perspective to see the wider political, institutional and social picture. RETL's abolition needs to be interpreted in light of its historical antecedents and its relationship with other forms of administrative detention. It has to be read in the context of new forms of crime that have emerged with economic development and new approaches toward public order. Its abolition also raises numerous questions for the future, concerning for example, the establishment of viable substitute punishments, and the advantages and risks of such alternatives. As Li has highlighted in his chapter, the difficulty of imposing community corrections penalties on minor offenders also points to broader features of China's contemporary socio-economic landscape. In particular, institutional conflict with the *hukou* system, the shortage of community resources and local resistance undermine both its implementation and its capacity to realise the objectives of education and persuasion.

The lack of reform to law and practice in pre-trial detention and imprisonment is equally problematic. This lack of movement could prove that the *status quo* is considered by authorities to be satisfactory or that an available alternative to the problems posed by these institutional and legislative settings has not been identified yet.

On the whole, deprivation of liberty in China today still remains a powerful tool in the hand of the authorities to exercise control over society, to influence the direction of politics and to maintain Party rule. As long as the public security organs maintain the discretionary power to detain people, and as long as reformers are prevented from expressing their criticisms of the police even in the most muted tones, claims about 'reform' need to be interrogated in a critical manner. At the very least, this means that scholars and observers of the Chinese system of detention should be careful to distinguish cosmetic changes from genuine reform. Identifying opportunities for future reforms requires sensitivity to the past, a detailed understanding of each form of detention and how change in any one form of detention impacts on the rest of the penal system, and a degree of optimism that more humanist approaches to detention may one day prevail.

References

Chu Huaizhi, Chen Xingliang, Zhang Shaoyan. 2002. *Lixing Yu Zhixu: Zhongguo Laodong Jiaoyang Zhidu Yanjiu*. Beijing: Falü chubanshe.

Fu Hualing. 2009. 'Access to Justice and Constitutionalism in China.' In *Building Constitutionalism in China*, edited by Stéphanie Balme and Michael Dowdle, 163–78. New York: Palgrave Macmillan.

Hand, Keith. 2006. 'Using Law for a Righteous Purpose: The Sun Zhigang Incident and Evolving Forms of Citizen Action in the People's Republic of China.' *Columbia Journal of Transnational Law* 45: 114–95.

Rosenzweig, Joshua. 17 March 2014. 'Public Opinion, Criminal Justice, and Incipient Popular Liberalism in China.' *The China Story Journal*. Available at https://www.thechinastory.org/contributor/joshua-rosenzweig/ (accessed 16 February 2016).

Trevaskes, Susan. 2010. 'The Shifting Sands of Punishment in China in the Era of Harmonious Society.' *Law and Policy* 32(3): 322–61.

Trevaskes, Susan, Elisa Nesossi, Flora Sapio and Sarah Biddulph, eds. 2014. *The Politics of Law and Stability in China*. Cheltenham: Edward Elgar.

Index

Administrative Compulsion Law (*Xingzheng Qiangshi Fa*: 2011) 27, 33
administrative detention 1, 4, 14, 43–4, 57n3; history of abolition of powers 23–6; recidivism 45; reforms 7, 8–10, 45–6; and social order 45, 50, 51, 52; *see also* community corrections; RETL abolition
Administrative Procedure Law (APL) (*Xingzheng Susong Fa*: 1989) 82
Administrative Punishments Law (*Singzheng Chufa Fa* 1996; 2009) 27
Ai Weiwei 89
Al Jazeera 119, 151
Alabaster, Ernest 146, 147
Anderson, Allen F. 45
anti-Party behaviour 5
anti-social behaviour 5
Anyuanding case 153–4
APL *see Administrative Procedure Law*
arrest 4, 117

bail *see* taking a guarantee and awaiting trial (*qubao houshen*)
Bakken, Børge 153
Balancing Leniency and Severity 5, 134, 139–40, 167–8; classification of prisons and prisoners 141–2; 'security' and 'rehabilitation' 140–1
Biddulph, Sarah 45, 152, 153, 165
'Big RETL' 33–5, 39
'black jails' 153–4, 166
British Journal of Criminology 148
Bund Picture 55
Bureau for the Management of Prison and Criminal Detention Centres 11, 12, 95, 99, 103, 118

C&R (custody and repatriation) *see* detention for repatriation
CCP *see* Chinese Communist Party
Central Discipline Inspection Committee 115
Central Political-Legal Committee 12, 28, 84, 125, 139, 154, 164
Chen Dan 75n17

Chen Jianxin 83
Chen Weidong 85–6
Cheng Lei 102
China Centre for Disease Control and Prevention 63
Chinese Academy of Social Science 154
Chinese Communist Party (CCP) 1, 2, 3–4, 6, 133, 163, 164
Chinese Constitution (1982) 115, 121
Chinese University on Politics and Law 135, 136, 138
Chu Huaizhi *et al.* 168
Chu Kuizhi 49
coercive drug rehabilitation *see* compulsory quarantine for drug rehabilitation (CQDR)
coercive summons 4
Combining Punishment and Leniency 139
Combining Suppression and Leniency 139
Commission on Extraterritoriality (1926) 146
Committee for the Elimination of Counter-Revolutionaries 96, 108n9
Committee on Economic, Social and Cultural Rights 27
community corrections 14, 36, 38, 44, 46, 150; conflict with *hukou* system 51–3; inapplicability in rural society 53–4; institutional deficiencies and limits 51; legal impediments 46–50; practical obstacles 46; social rejection and discrimination 54–6; conclusion 56
community drug treatment 44, 47, 48, 49, 50
community rehabilitation 29–31, 44, 45–6, 47
comparative studies 138–9
compulsory quarantine for drug rehabilitation (CQDR) 10, 30, 45–6, 56n2
confinement in custody, defined 97
Confucianism 54
The Continent Press 151
'correctional-ism' (*jiaozheng zhuyi*) 137
corruption (*shanggui*) 34, 35
CPL *see Criminal Procedure Law*
CQDR *see* compulsory quarantine for drug rehabilitation

crime: defined 49; expanding scope of 35–6
criminal characterisation 49
criminal conduct 49
Criminal Detention Centres Law (draft) 103–7
Criminal Detention Centres Working System (*Kanshousuo Gongzuo Tiaoli*: 1979) 98
Criminal Detention Law 12
criminal justice system: deprivation of liberty 1, 4–5; reforms 35, 37; *see also* Hard Strike (*yanda*) policy
Criminal Law (*Xing Fa* 1979) 4, 23, 31, 32, 34, 49, 139; amendments 35, 36, 50, 139, 153
Criminal Law (*Xing Fa* 1997) 64
Criminal Procedure Law (CPL) (*Xingshi Susong Fa*: 1979, 1996, 2012) 23, 36–7, 139, 169; community correction 36, 48–9; deprivation of liberty 4, 6, 7, 11, 13; detention for investigation 24, 26, 37, 38, 115, 116; mental health 62, 64, 65–6, 67, 68, 69, 73; pre-trial detention centres 101–2, 103, 108n16, 121, 122; residential surveillance 15, 79–80, 81, 82, 84–5, 86–8, 165
criminal quantity 49–50
Cui Min 81
Cultural Revolution 63, 80
custody and repatriation (C&R) *see* detention for repatriation

Dan Wei 117
deaths in custody 12, 96, 100, 101, 113, 124, 166; *see also* 'hide and seek' scandal
Decision concerning Some Major Questions in Comprehensively Promoting Governing the Country According to Law (2014) 113–14
Decisions on the Armed Protection of Prisons, Reform through Labour Team and Detention Centres (1950) 97
Deng Xiaoping 52
deportation to the place of residence 153
deprivation of liberty 1–2, 115, 170; *see also* mental health institutions
deprivation of liberty reforms: administrative and criminal systems 4–5; historical perspective 2–4; institutional reforms 12; legislative reforms 11–12; reforming administrative detention 7, 8–10, 45–6; reforming pre-trial detention centres 10–11; reforming prisons 12–13, 134; trajectories of reforms 5–7
detention: for compulsory rehabilitation of drug dependent people 4, 5, 8–10; defined 17n2, 97; of sex workers and clients 4; *see also* pre-trial detention centres
detention for education 1–2, 34, 44
detention for investigation 23–4, 26, 37, 38, 39n2, 115, 116
detention for repatriation 8, 17n3, 24–5, 26, 38, 166

Dikötter, Frank 114, 150
Ding Peng 124
Directive on Thorough Elimination of Hidden Counter-Revolutionaries (1955) 32
dissenters 63, 64, 74n5
Domenach, Jean-luc 150
drug dependency: community drug treatment 44, 47, 48, 49, 50; community rehabilitation 29–31, 44, 45–6, 47; detention for rehabilitation 4, 5, 8–10; recovering health in the community 30, 47; social rejection 54–6
Drug Detoxification Regulation (*Jingdu Tiaoli*: 2011) 47, 48, 50
Drug Prohibition Law (*Jindu Fa*: 2007) 29–30, 38
Drug Prohibition Law (*Jindu Fa*: 2008) 10, 30, 45–6, 47, 50, 51
Drug Prohibition Regulations (*Jindu Tiaoli*: 2011) 10
Du, James 108n8
Dutton, Michael 108n9, 150, 153
duty lawyers 123–4

education 54; detention for education 1–2, 34, 44; in pre-trial detention centres 119; *see also* re-education through labour (RETL)
Escarra, Jean 146, 147

Falungong 5
FlorCruz, Michelle 152
fraud 5
Fu Hualing 166

Gil, Vincent E. 45
globalisation of justice 113–14; pre-trial detention and human rights 114–15
Guo Ming 137

Hand, Keith 25
Hard Strike (*yanda*) policy 5, 12, 28, 56, 98, 139
Harmonious Society (*hexie shehui*) 45, 134, 139
He Depu 88–9
'hide and seek' scandal 15–16, 96, 100–1, 112, 126, 166; death of Li Qiaoming 112–13, 120, 166; globalisation of justice 113–15; *see also* pre-trial detention centres
Hong Qiusheng 81
household registration (*hukou* system) 51–3
Hu Jintao 7, 25, 134
Huang Haibo 34, 39
hukou system 51–3
Human Resources Research Institute (HRRI) 145
human rights 38–9, 84, 151, 168–9; and administrative detention 43, 45; conviction of lawyers, activists 36; pre-trial detention 6, 96, 99, 101–2, 103, 104, 106, 107, 112, 113, 114–15, 116; and prison privatisation 154; under residential surveillance 88–9, 90–1

ICCPR *see* International Covenant on Civil and Political Rights
illegal conduct 49
imprisonment, defined 17n2; *see also* imprisonment studies in China; prison studies; prisons
imprisonment studies in China 16, 133–4; 1980s: revival of reform studies 134–6; 1990s onward: prison studies 136–8; Balancing Leniency and Severity 5, 134, 139–40, 167–8: (classification of prisons and prisoners 141–2, 143n4; 'security' and 'rehabilitation' 140–1); comparative studies 138–9; political ideology 133–4; conclusion 142–3
institutional reforms 12
Instructions for the Transferring of Prisons, Detention Centres and Reform through Labour Team to the Ministry of Public Security (1950) 97
International Business Times 151–2
international civil society groups 6–7, 45
International Covenant on Civil and Political Rights (ICCPR; 1976) 38, 84, 114, 115, 116, 139
International Criminal Justic Review 148
International Journal of Law and Psychiatry 148
International Journal of the American Academy of Psychiatry 148
International Society for Human Rights (ISHR) 151
investigation *see* detention for investigation

Jia Jianying 89
Jiang Zemin 84
justice 1–2, 38–9, 113–15

kanshousuo see pre-trial detention centres
Kong Yan 124

labour *see* re-education through labour (RETL); reform through labour
Law and Social Science and Medicine 148
Law on Correcting Illegal Behaviours (*Weifa Xingwei Qiaozheng Fa*) 43, 56n1
Law on the Correction of Misdemeanours 29, 31
Law on the Protection of Minors (*Weichengnian Ren Baohu Fa*: 2006) 34
Lawyers Law (*Lüshi Fa*: 1996; 2007) 11, 121
legal aid 69, 106, 114, 122, 123–4
Legislation Law (*Lifa Fa*: 2000) 26, 27, 33, 103, 109n17, 166
legislative reforms 11–12
Leninism 135, 136
Levin, Dan 151
Li Cheng 134, 140–2, 143n3
Li Pengcheng 54
Li Qiaoming 100, 112–13, 120, 126, 166

Li Tiantian 89
Li Yinhe 55
Library Catalogue on Chinese Prisons 137–8, 143n1
Lifton, Robert Jay 151
Liu Renwen 33
Liu Shihui 89
Liu Weidong 134, 140–2, 143n3
Liu Xinhui 55
Lu Feng 83

Ma Jinghua 83
Ma Li 55
Macartney, Jane 74n5
McConville, Mike *et al.* 116
Maoism 12, 63, 135, 136, 139, 145, 169–70
Marxism 135, 136, 137
Measure of the Implementation of Community Corrections 46–7, 48
the media 150–3, 154
mental health institutions 14–15, 148; deprivation of liberty against one's will 62, 74n5; dissenters 63, 64, 74n5; historical development 62–3; psychiatric service system 65, 74n6; conclusions 73
Mental Health Law (MHL) (*Jingshen Weisheng Fa*: 2012) 34, 62, 64, 73, 148, 165; absence of judicial review 72; involuntary hospitalisation 70–1; principle of voluntariness for diagnoses and exceptions 71; principle of voluntariness for hospitalisation and dangerousness exception 71–2
mental health legislation 62, 63–4, 73, 148; *see also* Mental Health Law
mental illness: family responsibility 63, 64, 68, 69, 70, 71, 75n17; prevalence 63; recent legal reforms 63–4; stigma 73, 75n19; *see also* mental health institutions; *Mental Health Law*; mental health legislation; mental illness: compulsory treatment
mental illness: compulsory treatment: codification 64; commitment hearing: judicial review 68, 74n11–12; criteria 65–6, 74n7; initiation of procedure 66–7; legal framework 65; release to community 68–9, 74n13; rights protection 69–70; supervision by procuratorate 70, 74n14, 75n15–16; temporary restrictive measures for protection 67–8, 74n8
Methods for the Administration of Prisoners Retained within Detention Centres for the Execution of Sentences (2008) 118
Methods of Implementation of the Regulations on Criminal Detention Centres (1991) 11, 118
Methods of Implementation of the Regulations on Pre-Trial Detention Centres (1991) 98, 108n14
MHL *see Mental Health Law*

Millard, Thomas F. 146, 147
Ministry of Justice (MoJ) 3, 11, 12, 98, 118, 123, 134–5, 137, 154
Ministry of Public Security (MPS) 3, 108n3, 154; *Criminal Procedure Law* 24; institutional reforms 12; pre-arrest 116; pre-trial detention centres 93, 98, 100–1, 101–2, 103–4, 120–1; reform through labour 135–6; *Regulations* (1990) 11–12, 95, 96, 98, 103, 118, 119–20, 166; residential surveillance 82–3, 86, 87–8; RETL cases 5, 29, 164–5; *see also* Bureau for the Management of Prison and Criminal Detention Centres; MPS Rules (2013)
minor offences 49, 50
minors committing offences 34
Minzer, Carl 126
MoJ *see* Ministry of Justice
Mou Yuchuan 28
MPS *see* Ministry of Public Security
MPS Rules (2013) 65, 67, 68, 74n9–10
Munro, Robin 63

National Human Rights Action Plan (2012–2015) 116, 168
National People's Congress (NPC) 14, 25, 46, 64, 84, 96, 109n17, 112, 152, 166
Nesossi, Elisa 153
New York Times 27
Ng, Vivien 62, 73n1
non-custodial punishments *see* community corrections
Northwestern Institute on Politics and Law 135, 136

opportunities and challenges 163–4; ideas, values and sensibilities 167–9; political will and institutional compromise 164–5; from scandal to reforms 165–7; conclusion 167–9
Optional Protocol to the Convention Against Torture (2006) 115, 120
Organic Law on the People's Procuratorate (1979; 1983) 121

Pakes, Francis 115
Peerenboom, Randall 113, 153
Peng Dongyu 86
People's Police Law (*Renmin Jingcha Fa*: 1995) 33, 64
People's University 135, 136, 138
petty theft 5
PIDLI (Public Interest and Development Law Institute), Wuhan 123
pocket offences 35–6
police 115–16; *see also* public security organs
police interrogations 119
Police Law (*Jingcha Fa*: 1995) 11

police-operated detention 1–2, 7, 8–9, 10, 11, 99, 116
political ideology 2, 133–4, 167
population mobility 52–3
pre-arrest detention 4
pre-arrest detention centres (*juliusuo*) 103, 116
pre-trial coercive measures 4
pre-trial detention centres (*kanshousuo*) 6–7, 10–11, 15, 95–6, 98, 108n1, 115–16, 165; before 1990 12, 96–8; 1990–2009 3, 98–9; 2009–2014 99: ('hide and seek' effect 100–1; 2012 revision of Criminal Procedure Law 101–2); access to lawyer 121–2; decisions to detain 117–18; duty lawyers 123–4; human rights 6, 96, 99, 101–2, 103, 104, 106, 107, 112, 113, 114–15, 116; MPS or MOJ? regulations or law? 102–3: (draft of Pre-trial Detention Centre Law 103–7); procuratorate 117–18, 121; strengthening oversight 120–1; treatment in detention 118–20; parameters of policy response 124–5; conclusions 107, 126; *see also* 'hide and seek' scandal
Prison Journal 148
Prison Law (1994; 2012) 13, 103, 136, 137, 150
Prison Review 137, 140
prison studies 136–8, 147–50
Prison Studies (*Jianyu Pinglun*) 134
prisons 3, 12, 96, 98, 108n7, 118; historical perspective 2–3; imprisonment defined 17n2; privatisation 154; reforms 12–13, 134; *see also* imprisonment studies in China; prison studies
private security companies 153–4
Pu Zhiqiang 119
Public Interest and Development Law Institute (PIDLI), Wuhan 123
public order detention 4, 44; *see also* re-education through labour (RETL); RETL abolition
public order offenders 7, 32–3, 43, 47, 50, 52–3, 55–6
public security organs 2, 23, 32, 47, 153, 154, 156n4

Qi Linde 54–5
Qing dynasty (1644–1912) 62, 63, 96

recovering health in the community 30, 47
re-education through labour (RETL) 2, 3–5, 7, 8–9, 155–6n2; Western critique 148, 149–50, 151–2; *see also* RETL abolition
Reference Legal Study Material for Reform through Labour (*Laodong Gaizao Faxue Cankao Ziliao*) 138
reform 1; actors and factors 162–3; definitions 162; *see also* opportunities and challenges
reform through labour 3, 135–6, 137, 149, 155–6n2

Regulations for Reform Through Labour (*Laodong Gaizao Tiaoli*: 1954) 97, 108n11
Regulations on Arrest and Detention (*Daibu Juliu Tiaoli*: 1954) 80, 97, 108n11
Regulations on Criminal Detention Centres (1990) 11–12, 95, 96, 98, 103, 118, 119–20, 166
Regulations on Public Security Organs Handling Re-Education Through Labour Cases 32
rehabilitation 140–1; *see also* drug dependency
religious beliefs and practices 5
repatriation *see* detention for repatriation
repeat and nuisance petitioning 5, 7, 28, 29
residential surveillance 4, 7, 15, 79–80, 166; adaptation and practice 83; 'designated area' 80, 81, 82; 'designated residence' 82, 86, 87–9, 90, 91; 'disguised detention' 81, 82; 'domicile' 82, 87; early intentions and articulations 80; human rights 88–9, 90–1; 'non-residential' surveillance 86–8; problematic enforcement practices 80–2; reforming residential surveillance 82–3, 165; further reform 83–4; and 'secret arrest' debate 84, 85–6; the experience 88–9; concluding thoughts 89–91
RETL *see* re-education through labour
RETL abolition 7, 14, 25, 26, 149, 164–5, 166, 170; impact on public order 26, 27: (changing perceptions of effectiveness 28; limiting numbers of people 28; transferring drug dependent people 29–31); policy or social changes 26, 27, 31–2: (alternative administrative powers 32–3; areas of flexibility in criminal justice system 37; 'Big RETL' 33–5, 39; conduct no longer punished/unintended consequences 37; criminal justice reforms 35; criminal procedure reforms 36–7; expanding non-custodial punishments 36; expanding scope of crimes 35–6); pressure for reform 26–7; implications 38–9
right to liberty 115; *see also* deprivation of liberty; deprivation of liberty reforms
Rojek, Dean G. 55
Rosenzweig, Joshua 85, 153
rule of law 1, 45
rural migrants 23, 24–5, 52, 53*t*, 55, 83
rural society 53–4

Sapio, Flora 153
'secret arrest' 84, 85–6
security 140–1
Security Administrative Punishments Law (SAPL) (*Zhi'an Guanli Chufa Fa*: 2006; 2012) 8, 31, 32–3, 50
Series in Chinese Communism 145
sex trade 4, 8, 29, 33–4, 39, 52, 55–6
Seymour, James 145, 150
She Yu 137

Shen Jiaben 3
social order 2, 17; and administrative detention 45, 50, 51, 52; and mental illness 63; *see also* re-education through labour; RETL abolition
social rejection: of drug users 54–6; of mental illness 73, 75n19; of prostitution 55; of public order offenders 55–6
social stability 100, 101; *see also* stability maintenance (*weiwen*) program
Song Yinghui 7
South China Morning Post 119
Southern Metropolis Daily 28, 86
Southwestern Institute of Politics and Law 136
SPC Interpretations (2013) 65, 66, 68, 69–70
SPP Regulations (2013) 65, 67, 70, 86, 87–8
stability maintenance (*weiwen*) program 7, 153, 164, 167
state power 2
Statute of the Chinese Soviet Republic Provisions Governing Punishment (1934) 97
structural transformation 169
Study on Crime and Reform (*Fanzui Yu Gaizao Yanjiu*) 137
Sun Yuhua 90
Sun Zhigang 8, 25, 113, 165–6
supervised residence *see* residential surveillance
Supreme People's Court (SPC) 81, 82; *see also* SPC Interpretations (2013)
Supreme People's Procuratorate (SPP) 12, 116; pre-trial detention centres 98, 100; *see also* SPP Regulations (2013)

taking a guarantee and awaiting trial (*qubao houshen*) 4, 49, 95, 108n5, 116, 117
Tang Hui 7, 18n9, 26–7, 166
Tang Xule 134, 140–2, 143n3
Teng Biao 166
thought reform 135, 151; *see also* reform through labour
Tian Gen 54
torture: extraction of confessions 12, 24, 99, 101, 105, 119; international prohibition 7, 114, 115, 116, 120; in pre-trial detention centres 115; prevention mechanisms 102, 105; in residential surveillance 86, 91
Trevaskes, Susan 28

United Nations: *Convention Against Torture* (1984) 114, 116; Special Rapporteur on Torture and other Cruel, Inhuman or Degrading Treatment or Punishment 7; Working Group on Arbitrary Detention 7; *see also Optional Protocol to the Convention Against Torture* (2006)
Universal Periodic Review by the UN Human Rights Council (2013) 168
urbanisation 53

vagrants and beggars 5, 24–5

Wang Lihui 54
Wang Mingliang 154
Wang Mingwen 86
Wang Yahui 113
Wang Yongle 49
Wei, Henry 145
Wen Jiabao 25
Western analyses of deprivation of liberty in China 16, 138, 145–6; Alabaster, Escarra and Commission on Extraterritoriality 146–7; Anyuanding case 153–4; 'black jails' 153–4, 166; Chinese prisons 147–50; the media 150–3, 154; concluding thoughts 154–5
Whitwell, Tom 74n5
Wong Kam 108n13
World Anti-Communist League 151
World Health Organization 71, 72, 74n14

Xi Jinping 7, 164
Xie Xiaodan 28
Xu Lindong 74n5
Xu Yongjun 116
Xu Zhangrun 137, 150
Xu Zhiyong 166

Yan Mu 86
Yang Lin 54
Ye Zhusheng 86
Yu Jiang 166
Yuan Zheng 55

Zhang Jie 154
Zhang Jing 138
Zhang Jun 154
Zhang Shaoyan 168
Zhang Sujun 36
Zhang Yan 116
Zhao Chunguang 101–2
Zhou Yongkang 7, 100, 164
Zuo Weimin 87–8, 91